I CAN GO HOME AGAIN

ARTHUR G. POWELL

I CAN
GO
HOME
AGAIN

Chapel Hill
THE UNIVERSITY OF NORTH CAROLINA PRESS

B l

June 26. 1944

E

5. 702 / R t

975.8t

P882

For
ANNIE

CONTENTS

I CAN GO HOME AGAIN

The Piney Woods of Southwest Georgia

NOT LONG AGO, ON A BRIGHT, SUNSHINY MORNING IN EARLY summer, a young law partner of mine and I were returning by automobile to Atlanta from Panama City, Florida, the busy port on Saint Andrews Bay. We had crossed the Chattahoochee River into that part of extreme southwest Georgia where the States Georgia, Florida, and Alabama corner; we had just left Blakely and were on State Highway No. 1.

To the right and to the left, as far as eye could see, stretched farm after farm. Fields of cotton, corn, and peanuts were lush with the promise of abundant harvests in the early autumn. The country consisted of gently rolling low hills. The soil was of fertile loam over a red clay subsoil, and the small black pebbles in the soil indicated the presence of the potash which would make for a maximum fruitage. To the westward the hillocks finally lost themselves in the larger hills through which the Chattahoochee pierces its way to the sea. To the eastward the fields became flat, or nearly so, as they approached the swamps and hammocks of the creeks that make their way toward Flint River, fringing the fields at their farthest reaches.

In the pastures cows grazed, and pigs grunted and rooted the ground. Roosters crowed and hens cackled in the barnyards. The farmhouses were neat and well kept. On the brow of a hill stood a modern brick schoolhouse. Here and there the steeple of a newly painted church rose above the grove of a country churchyard. An air of newness debarred the scene from the grace of ancient culture; yet it was a sight to delight the soul of any man.

My young companion said to me, "I believe this is the most beautiful farming country I have ever seen. Don't you think it beautiful?"

It was impossible for him to know the pleasure I took in that scene. About seventy years ago—in the fall of 1873, to be exact —I was born in Blakely, the town we had just passed. When I first knew the country through which we had been riding since early morning, all the way from St. Andrews to the place we then were and even for miles beyond, it was a veritable backwoods; and I had seen it rise from primitive conditions to a state of prosperity and culture.

We were in the Colomokee District. To the front and to the left of us was Colomokee Creek, on the banks of which, a few miles away, were the Indian mounds where we used to go on picnics when I was a boy and hunt for arrowheads and pieces of Indian pottery.

In Early County, of which Blakely is the county seat, the creeks that run into the Chattahoochee have beautiful Indian names—Colomokee, Caheelee, Sowhatchee. Why the creeks that flow into the Flint River do not have such names I do not know. They are called Mill Creek, Spring Creek, Dry Creek, Blue Creek, and names of that kind. Someone played a mean trick on the Flint River. The Indians called it the Thronateeska, and some white man named it Flint.

"Pow!" We did not need the corroboration of the shimmying automobile to know what that sound was. We had a puncture. As we stopped the car, we were in front of a gasoline filling station run in connection with a small country store. On the other side of the road was an attractive farm cottage with flowers in the yard and a vine at the corner of the porch. An alert young man, handsome in his overalls, was sitting in front of the store. Instantly he came to our assistance and set himself to helping us. He introduced himself as John Hall, and later, in response to my inquiries, told me that he had moved to the Colomokee district from the Rock Hill district in the lower part of the county when he had married a daughter of Frank Wil-

ended, and for reasons I can't remember, I decided to take a trip around the world. But my money lasted only as far as New Orleans. On the way back to New York, the boat I was on rammed and sank a freighter in a fog off Cape Hatteras. One of the survivors we picked up was a pretty girl named Edna Harris. When I handed her one of the five life-preservers I was wearing, it started a beautiful friendship. Before we docked, I made a date to see her in New York.

The first night I took her out, we walked up Broadway. Though I was crowding twenty at the time, I had never been on the Big Street at night. But Edna knew her way around. She steered me to Wolpin's, one of those underground delicatessens where celebrities gathered to eat the life-giving pastrami and quaff great beakers of celery tonic.

"That's Fred Fischer," she said, pointing to a man with an outsized head. "He wrote 'Dardanella.' And that's Walter Donaldson, the writer of 'Mammy.'"

"What kind of money do they make?" I asked.

"No telling," said Edna. "Couple of thousand a week, maybe."

"How long has this been going on?" I said to myself.

From then on, I did most of my eating at Wolpin's, and after a while got to know most of the songwriters. In those days I was a simple-hearted little bloke. My ambitions were to make a million dollars and marry Mary Pickford. I believed what everybody believed in 1922—that U. S. Steel would hit 500, that nice girls didn't kiss the first time you took them out, and that Heaven was not for Democrats.

One night at Wolpin's I asked Harry Ruby, the composer, "Has anybody ever thought of rhyming 'June' with 'macaroon'?"

The entire delicatessen applauded and Harry shook

my hand. A waiter handed me a pencil and a clean menu and said, "Mr. Rose, you're in business."

Six cups of coffee later, I dotted the last "i" on my first masterpiece.

> *Does the Spearmint lose its flavor on the bedpost*
> *   overnight?*
> *If you paste it on the left side will you find it on the*
> *   right?*
> *When you chew it in the morning will it be too hard*
> *   to bite?*
> *Does the Spearmint lose its flavor on the bedpost*
> *   overnight?*

It was published by Watterson, Berlin and Snyder, and the early ten-watt radio transmitters smallpoxed the air with it. I got an appointment with a Wrigley executive and told him I thought I was entitled to some money for my efforts on behalf of his product. He booted me out of his office without so much as a pack of gum for my trouble.

But I got my revenge. The time bomb I lit in 1922 exploded in 1939 with the Pepsi-Cola jingle. The rest, God help us, is history.

I wrote the first singing commercial.

There, I've said it! And I'm glad. For years I've been walking around with this secret, fraternizing with people who are kind to small animals and bathe every day. Now I've come clean.

Chop me up in little pieces and feed me to the lions. You won't hear a peep out of me.

Besides the Spearmint classic, I was responsible for "You Tell Her I Stutter," and "You Gotta See Mama Every Night." These songs made quite a bit of money, and the following year I invested some of this loot in the nightclub business—principally, I think, because I wanted to wear a black hat and meet some girls. My first waterhole was hidden over a garage on 56th Street near Sixth Avenue. The iron-stomached citizens who survived the Noble Experiment may remember it as the Backstage Club—the place where Helen Morgan first climbed up on a piano to avoid the tables which were advancing upon her across the dance floor.

The Backstage Club represented an outlay of $4,000. It amortized itself the opening night.

A few months later I opened a second trap on Fifth Avenue—I wanted to meet a better class of girls. It was called the Fifth Avenue Club, and it exhaled so much fake swank that on opening night my French head-waiter suggested I stay out of sight in the office. The show was written by a couple of kids fresh out of Columbia—Rodgers and Hart. I felt I had really arrived socially. My new neighbors included Samuel Untermyer, the Union League Club, and John D. Rockefeller, Sr.

Eyebrows shot up all over the neighborhood the night we opened. John D. was at the age when he needed his sleep something fierce, and when my bug-eyed musicians erupted with "Somebody Stole My Gal" at four in the morning, he hollered copper at the top of his ancient lungs. A dozen of New York's Finest roared up on motorcycles, but when they found I wasn't selling whiskey, they compromised on making me mute half my trumpets.

To keep the club exclusive, I slapped on a $5 cover charge. Well, that did it. Pretty soon it was so exclusive the waiters were playing penny casino with each other. In a couple of months I was feeling through the pockets of old suits for lunch money.

One night I got an idea. I would sell my club to a blonde who was running a speakeasy in Greenwich

Village. Her boy friend was one of our leading bathtub chemists.

I went down to the Village to see her. "Queenie," I said, "this speak is no showcase for a woman of your talents. You belong on Fifth Avenue."

"You can say that again, dearie," said Queenie, "but what would I do up there? I can't sing and my gentleman friend made me give up hoofin'."

"All great women of the world have had salons," I said airily. "Du Barry, Pompadour, Marie Antoinette. Princes and statesmen flocked around just to hear these women talk."

I moved in for the kill. "Get your boy friend to buy my club for you. Advertise yourself as 'Mistress of Conversation.' Wear a stylish gown—something transparent and expensive. And when the customers arrive, talk to them—just talk to them. It'll be tremendous!"

Queenie bought the dream, and next morning the bathtub chemist bought my sick little nightclub. He ran big ads, billing her as "Mistress of Conversation." But the place folded in a few weeks.

Poor Queenie! Though she was willing to talk to anybody, nobody wanted to talk to *her*.

After the Fifth Avenue Club, I went back to songwriting. You may remember one of the ditties I wrote around that time—"Barney Google with the Goo-Goo-Googly Eyes." Deems Taylor said it was probably the worst song in the history of the music business—but Deems always was a jealous fellow.

In 1926 I wrote a vaudeville act for Fanny Brice. During its out-of-town tryouts, I found that Fanny and I liked the same jokes and disliked the same people. In 1928 I persuaded the great comedienne to become Mrs. Rose. The day she did, I automatically became known as Mr. Brice. You see, in those days, Fanny's house was

"Bolingbroke," "Peru," "Erin," "Sleepy Hollow," "Fairfield," to name some of them—to which they sent their surplus slaves to be worked under overseers. Many of these slaves came from the eastern coasts of Georgia and South Carolina and spoke a dialect known as Geechee, a cross between English and Gullah, very hard to understand.

Practically every white person among us was of English, Scottish, or Irish stock. Since money was scarce, all our people lived simply; but there was none of the squalor and low-livedness of the "Tobacco Road." Many of the amenities were denied us, but the decencies and necessities were not. There was little education in the sense of schooling. I do not recall a single man or woman in the county, who, in my early years, had a college degree, except the physicians. (My uncle, Walter Perry, was graduated at Mercer University, but died soon thereafter in the War.) Yet these people were not ignorant. They educated themselves and acquired culture by self-help and in the school of experience.

Old Blakely

BLAKELY, AT THE TIME I WAS BORN THERE, OR PERHAPS I SHOULD say at the time of my earliest recollection, was a typical small-town, piney-woods county seat. By its charter, it was laid off as a square, with the sides a mile long and with the courthouse at its center; it had a population of about three hundred. From 1818, when Early County was created, to 1825, the superior court was held in various residences. In 1825, a commission was appointed to select a "more permanent county seat." It selected a spot somewhat central to the county, as its territory was then bounded, and named it Blakely, in honor of Captain Blakely, of the United States Navy, who distinguished himself in the War of 1812.

The courthouse square, or the Square, as it was commonly called, consisted of four acres, which means that there was about four hundred feet of frontage on each side of it. The courthouse stood in the center, and along the sides of the Square were stores, offices, hotels, livery stables, and dwellings. The first courthouse, I have been told, was a log structure, but the old courthouse which stood there when I was born was a square, two-storied building, facing west, with a wide porch in front extending the entire height of the building and supported by large columns. It was built of pine lumber and painted white, with green blinds. The ground floor was divided by a broad hallway, which ran from north to south, and by a front hallway that ran from the central hallway to the front of the building. The rooms on the ground floor were occupied by the clerk of the superior court, the ordinary, the sheriff, and other county officers. From

each side of the front hall a stairway ran to the floor above, where were the courtroom occupying more than half the space, a grand-jury room, and a petit-jury room.

At the rear of the courtroom was the judge's stand, about eight feet wide, with a broad board at its front constituting a desk, with the witness box connected to it at the right, and with the railed-in clerk's desk in front of it and below it. Against the wall, on each side of the judge's stand, were the jury boxes, slightly raised above the floor. At the wall between the judge's stand and the jury boxes were the two chimneys with their large open fireplaces. Across the room, at about a third of the distance back, ran the bar rail; and behind that were the benches —those in the rear slightly raised—where sat spectators, witnesses, and parties in cases not on trial. Inside the bar were several plain pine tables, usually cluttered with random volumes of the Georgia Reports or copies of the Code. Very early in my life a revolving bookcase was bought, and the books were supposed to be kept in it. Just inside that portion of the bar rail which fronted the judge's stand was the "mourners' bench," a long seat on which the prisoners who had been brought from the jail sat while waiting for their cases to be reached for trial or for sentence to be imposed.

On the judge's desk, the clerk's desk, the mantelpieces, and the tables, were candlesticks, all smeared with tallow drippings. Occasionally an important case, usually a murder case, would be prolonged into the night; then the candles would flicker and the tongues of shadows would leap across the room. If, while the walls were reverberating from the voice of counsel appealing for the life of his client or of the solicitor general demanding a sentence of death, a breeze sprang up and came through the windows, there would be signs of flinching and gooseflesh all over the room as the candlelight wavered and the shadows danced. Kerosene lamps came later.

The walls and the high ceilings of the courthouses of south-west Georgia in my boyhood were made of pine boards, twelve inches wide, cut rough in the small local sawmills, planed down by the local carpenters with the big jack planes, smoothed with the other bench planes, and then rabbeted and joined and nailed to the studding and joists. The floors were carpeted with jute bagging.

The echoes and reverberations that came back from those walls and ceilings are still to me a vivid part of my recollection of the old court scenes. The echoes of any old building are a part of its history. In these old courtrooms they became a part of the lawyers as they addressed the juries. They became a part of the tread of feet as the sheriffs and the deputies led the prisoners to and from the court. They even gave tone to a woman's scream which rang out when the verdict was pronounced finding her son guilty of murder. They seemed somewhat to hush themselves in awe as the judge solemnly sentenced the prisoner to die.

It is still easy for me to construct in memory the odor of the jute floor coverings saturated with tobacco juice—ambeer we called it—and loaded in the corners with tobacco quids, generations of them. Most judges did not allow smoking in court, but no judge seemed willing to endanger his popularity by forbidding the jurors and the spectators to chew tobacco in the courtroom and spit on the floor.

At the front of the second story of the courthouse, projecting into the porch, was the court crier's balcony. From it the sheriff or one of his deputies would cry out so that it could be heard all over the Square: "Jurors come into court; jurors come into court," or "John Jones, John Jones," according to whose presence was wanted—the jurors, who were allowed to wait outside the building until they were needed, or John Jones, who was a party or a witness. The phrase for this was "being called at the door."

It was told of one of our young lawyers from Blakely that when he came to Atlanta to be admitted to the bar of the Supreme Court and filed his application, the clerk told him that the Court was then engaged in other matters, but would take up admissions to the bar later in the day. "All right," he said, "I will stroll around the Capitol, and when they need me have the Sheriff call me at the door."

Scattered about on the Square, usually under the large oaks which grew there, were the horse racks, to which the people from the country hitched their horses, mules, or oxen, when they came to town. They were built by driving into the ground stout upright posts, about five feet high, and morticing into the tops of them a horizontal log, say six inches in diameter, with pegs driven into auger holes bored into it. There was also a well, with windlass and bucket, and a watering trough.

The only Confederate flagpole in the South still stands on the courthouse square at Blakely. It was erected during the War Between the States. It was originally nearly a hundred feet high, but from time to time it has been necessary to cut away parts of it which have rotted in the ground, so that its height is now only about sixty feet. Except on Memorial Day, the banner that flies from it nowadays is the flag of the United States.

Out of the middle of the north side of the Square ran the Cuthbert Road (now Cuthbert Street); out of the northwest corner, Fort Gaines Road (now College Street); out of the middle on the west side, Howard Landing Road (now River Street); out of the middle of the south side, Bainbridge Road (also called Main Street, till it made the turn westward near the town limit); and there was an alley in the middle of the east side. The reason why there were no roads leading to the eastward was that a dense swamp or hammock came up almost to the Square on that side. The Arlington Road, which also led to Morgan and Albany, turned off the Cuthbert Road near the northern limits of the city. The Bainbridge Road was also the road to Colquitt. The Columbia Road (now Columbia Avenue) leading toward Columbia and other points in Alabama, came into the Bainbridge Road about two hundred yards south of the Square. The Cedar Springs Road came into Line Street (now Church Street), which ran along an original land-lot line from the Negro Methodist Church at the northern limits of the town to the white Baptist Church on the south side; and the Sheffield

Mill Road came into the Cedar Springs Road just below the Baptist Church. Our home was at the corner of Line Street and the Fort Gaines Road, about two hundred yards from the Square.

Years later the town council appointed Frank Jones and me as a commission to give official names to all the streets in the town—or city as it had then become—in accordance with a charter amendment. I recall that there was a street the name of which no one seemed to know, which ran from the Negro Methodist Church to Tom Chandler's home on Fort Gaines Road. We named it Washington Street—for Booker at one end and for George at the other. The street which zigzags its way from River Street to Columbia Street near where the new public school building stood until it was recently burned, we christened Zig Zag Avenue.

Down Main Street, about a hundred yards south of the Square, were our two largest general stores—Bolling H. Robinson's on the east side and J. M. & R. W. Wade's on the west side. According to the signs on them and their advertisements in the county paper, the general stores carried in stock, "dry goods, notions, clothing, groceries, boots, shoes, hardware, household remedies, and general farm supplies." A subsidiary sign on Dr. Hunter's store at Colquitt several years later used to read, "Ice cold soda water, onions, apples, and potatoes. Fresh ice, just received today."

All the general stores in the days of my earliest recollection sold liquor under the head of groceries. The whiskey barrel, with its quart and pint measures, and with the jugs on a near-by shelf, stood beside the syrup and vinegar barrels at the rear of the store or in a shed room. Not the slightest opprobrium attached to the sale of liquor. Many of our best people, including church leaders, engaged in it; and no one thought it wrong.

However, before I was ten years old, for what reason I do not know but probably because of license laws, the general stores gave up their liquor business, and it was taken over by the saloons, which we did not call saloons or barrooms, but "groceries." The word "grocery," as we then used it, meant what

the word "barroom" now means. I notice that the dictionary
still carries that definition of the word "grocery" as a localism
of the "Southern U. S.," but I have not heard it used that way
in many years. Nowadays, at the various conventions I attend,
as the cocktail parties begin to come thick and fast in the shank
of the evening, my mind calls up, out of the old days, the ditty
the country Bacchanalians used to sing:

> "On the wings of love I fly
> From groceree to grocery [final "y" long.]"

Below B. H. Robinson's store was Uncle Fleming's printing
office. Just below that, Dr. Dostor's Drug Store, with the Masonic
lodge on the second floor. When I was about ten years old
Colonel Buchannon's store at the junction of the Square and
Main Street burned. Doctor Dostor bought the lot and had his
office and the Masonic lodge rolled, on round logs, to it. My
father bought the Dostor lot and built on it the two-roomed law
office we used till after his death. Next down the street came
the Sam Howard store building, vacant for most of the time I
knew it; then the Fleming home, and then the Old Blakely
Academy lot, where the schoolhouse stood.

Practically all the houses in the town had wide porches—
we called them indifferently porches, piazzas, or verandahs, and
sometimes porticos—and the dwellings, including Negro cabins,
usually had both a front and a back porch. When the Wades'
old colored yard man had a spell of dizziness, he insisted that he
had a "portico" in his head—that the doctor had told him so.

Though Blakely is near the crest of a watershed—the water
on the west side flowing to the Chattahoochee River and that
on the east side to the Flint—the ground on which it stands is
nearly level. Its physical landmarks, in my boyhood, were the
Baptist Branch, the Tanyard Branch, and the Big Ditch.

The Baptist Branch came into town on the west side, crossed
Sheffield's Mill Road and Cedar Springs Road just below the
Baptist Church, and made its exit near the southeast corner of

the town. There was no stream close by deep enough for baptizing; so the Baptists dug and ceiled with lumber a pool at the edge of the branch, and in this they baptized. We boys frequently used it as a swimming pool, and the community was once shocked to hear that some of the girls had slipped down there and had also used it.

The Tanyard Branch was a sluggish stream that rose in the northeast part of the town and ran eastward. Before my day, there had been a tanyard on the branch; and a few public hangings had taken place there. I have been told that in those days, when a man was to be hanged, the sheriff placed his coffin on an oxcart or a one-horse wagon and put the rope around his neck; and thus they rode to the place where the gallows stood. I was a good-sized boy before public hangings were abolished in Georgia. I once passed the spot where a hanging was to take place and saw the condemned man on the gallows with the black cap over his head. I had gone but a short distance, just far enough to be out of sight but not out of hearing, when I heard the trap fall and the Negroes screaming. As I passed by, I noticed that the trees all around the gallows were filled with Negroes, who had climbed up to get a better view. When the trap fell, they fell too; hence their screaming. I was told that they would do this at every hanging.

Dr. Dostor used to tell—whether he made up the story or not I do not know—that a man, who lived out on the Arlington Road, near the tanyard where the hangings took place, had been convicted of murder and sentenced to be hanged. When the verdict was received his lawyer told him not to worry, that the judge was sure to grant him a new trial. When the judge refused the new trial, the lawyer still told him not to worry, that the judge was a fool and that the Supreme Court would reverse him. When the Supreme Court decided against him, the lawyer told him not to worry, that the Governor was his friend and that he would get the Governor to commute the sentence. On the morning set for the hanging, a message came from the Governor refusing to interfere. So at high noon the sheriff led the prisoner to the coffin on the one-horse wagon, put him on it, put the rope around his neck, and drove toward the tanyard. As they were going down Arlington Road and passed the culprit's home, his wife came to the door and said, "Good-bye, John," and he called back, "Good-bye, Sally." Just as the wagon was about to pass the turn in the road, Sally called out, "Oh, John, where must I plant the inguns [onions]?" "Plant 'em where yer dern please," John yelled back, "I'm getting a little down-hearted about this whole business."

The Big Ditch was our chief drainage facility. It started in the western part of the town, south of Howard Landing Road, but turned and crossed that road just east of Line Street, angled across Line Street not far south of our home, crossed Fort Gaines Road, between our home and the Square, continued northeast till it crossed Cuthbert Road, and then lost itself in the swamp that lay in the eastern part of the town. It was fed by a small spring and there was nearly always water in it; and how we children used to love to play in it. It is a wonder that we did not get snake-bitten, for there used to be moccasins in it. I believe that my brothers and I got more thrashings for playing in the Big Ditch than for any other cause. However, we got almost as many whippings for playing with Ed Chancey. Ed was the bad boy of our street. In but a few years, he was one of our prominent merchants, and for many years he has been one of Blakely's moral and religious leaders. You cannot tell about boys.

In those early days, there were no waterworks or sewers in that part of the country; but there was a public comfort station on the Big Ditch at Blakely. It was a small but commodious structure, erected by some artisan of the Specialist's trade upon timbers laid across the ditch. It was the daily habit of our good old postmaster, Mr. Crawf Fryer, after he had sorted the morning mail, to take his Macon Telegraph in hand and walk down to this secluded spot on the Big Ditch. Others used it occasionally; he used it regularly. His niece had a cottage on Cuthbert Road which she put in his hands for sale. He had a sign painted and posted on the cottage,

"For Sale—This Neat Little House—Apply to H. C. Fryer." It disappeared one night, but next day was found posted upon the little building on the Big Ditch.

I have spoken of the Baptist Church. I do not mean the brick church building that now stands on the corner of Church and River streets; I mean the old wooden church with its wide verandah and columns and square belfry and gallery for the Negroes, which stood with its graveyard around it in the middle of what is now the Blakely Cemetery. There cannot be many who still remember it, because it was torn down about sixty years ago; but I do. There I first went to Sunday School. There I heard my first preaching. It had no musical instrument in it; the preacher lined out the hymns and the congregation sang them— "On Jordan's Stormy Banks I Stand," "Nearer My God to Thee," "Rock of Ages," "Jesus, Lover of My Soul,"—all those great old hymns that no lack of melody in the voices singing them could rob of their uplifting spiritual force.

One night my parents took me with them to preaching there. It was a summer night with the moon shining. I could look through the windows and see the gravestones, especially the tall one having the angel with the outspread wings on the top of it, and could catch glimpses of the mimosa leaves trembling in the light breezes that played among them. The wide boards of the church walls had reverberations in them—echoes that imitated and enhanced the special reverential tones the preacher assumed as he read the Scriptures or prayed. It was too much for my childish imagination; I came back home all aquiver with awe and emotion. My parents must have noticed it, for I was much older before I went to church at night again.

The Methodist Church was only a few hundred yards from our home. It was smaller than the Baptist Church. There was a wild clangor in the bell in its steeple; and the front door of the church was left open, so that if a fire broke out at night, some one could run to the church and ring the bell to arouse the people. Oh, the excitement of standing in one's childish nightclothes and hearing people running through the streets crying out "Fi-yer! Fi-yer!" and listening to the Methodist Church bell ringing out wildly into the night. When the Baptist Church bell was tolled for a funeral, it gave out a solemn tone that emphasized death itself; the Methodist Church bell spoke a more earthy language.

Before my day and time "singing treble with the hick" was pretty commonly practiced in the churches in the small towns of our section; and until I was a good-sized boy there were two old maids who still sang it at the Methodist Church. Treble was sung higher than soprano. The hick was a mere artificial addition. They used it thus:

> "Rock of ages cleft for me—hick!
> Let me hide myself in thee—hick!"

One of these good old sisters unthoughtedly perpetrated this:

> "Sweet prospects, sweet birds and sweet flowers—hick!
> Have all lost their sweetness but me—hick!"

The Negro Methodist Church was at the northern end of Line Street, about five hundred yards above our home. The services there began early in the evening and lasted till after midnight. Especially on a clear night, we could hear them quite distinctly—the preacher with his high-pitched voice and his many "er-er-er's"; the loud "Amens" of the stewards; the singing, very good, especially the singing of the spirituals; and then, when the emotions had been sufficiently stirred, the shouting of the congregation and the screaming of the women. The shouting was part of a sort of trance in which the worshiper leaped upon the floor, danced up and down the aisles, with arms waving and head shaking, and wildly cried out a conglomeration of utterances supposed to be spiritual in their nature. Of course, it was somewhat of a nuisance to have the Sunday evening's calm thus intruded upon, but no one attempted to prevent it. We realized that it was the Negroes' way of worshiping God according to their choice, and none was willing to deprive them of that right. The Negro Baptist Church was to the west of the town, nearly a mile from the courthouse; so I am not so familiar with what went on there.

This Nazareth of a backwoods in which we lived was not deemed worthy to have located in it any of the State's institutions—the Capitol, the State's colleges, the School for the Deaf, the School for the Blind, the Experiment Farm, and the other eleemosynary institutions—and this was true until after I was grown—with one exception. About the beginning of the present century, the State began to establish branches of the State penitentiary, convict camps, in our part of the State. One of these was located just across the road from the Negro Baptist Church. Then, in order that the convicts could hear the services at the church—for they were allowed to come to the windows and look through the iron bars—the services were held on Sunday afternoons. The preacher often addressed his remarks through the open church window to the Negro convicts peeping through the bars; and when the congregation began to sing that good old song,

> "We have brothers over yonder,
> We have brothers over yonder,
> Bye-and-bye we will go and meet them,"

the convicts heartily joined in the refrain.

The jail at Blakely was burned when I was a very small child. I remember seeing the charred body of the prisoner who, in attempting to escape by burning a hole in the wall, burned up the jail and himself with it. I think it was just off the Square. The first jail I really remember, the jail in use during my boyhood and my teens, sat near the Big Ditch, between our home and the Square. It was built of hewn sills doubly sheathed, both on the inside and the outside of the walls, by planks two inches thick, stoutly spiked into the hewn logs, the layers of the planks running diagonally, the first layer slanted in one direction and the other in the opposite direction. The floors and ceilings were laid in the same way. There were two rooms—one for the Negroes and one for the whites—with a hallway between them.

Each room had two windows, one at the front and one at the rear—square holes in the wall, about two feet high and two feet wide. They were not open windows, for they were closed with heavy steel or iron sheets, perforated with a number of holes about two inches in diameter. The prisoners could look out through these holes, without anyone's being able to see them from the outside.

The Negro prisoners usually whiled away the time by composing songs and singing them. We boys used to sit upon the fence around the field in which the jail stood, and the Negroes would come to the windows and sing. I still remember one of the songs, in part:

"When I went to bed I was covered with rugs
When I woke up I was covered with bugs.
It's hard times in jail, I know;
It's hard times in Bla-ker-lee jail.

"Yonder comes the jailer with his old corn bread,
As hard as a rock, and as heavy as lead.
It's hard times in jail, I know;
It's hard times in Bla-ker-lee jail.

"I asked the jailer to pity my case.
He hawked up and spit in my face.
It's hard times in jail, I know;
It's hard times in Bla-ker-lee jail."

And thus it went on at great length, the Negroes often improvising as they went.

Livestock roamed at large upon our streets, such as they were. Hogs made mudholes in the streets and around the well and watering trough on the Square and wallowed in them. Cows slept at night in the streets or on the makeshift sidewalks. To be protected against their depredations one had to build stout fences. Most of the stores and offices had fenced-in yards at their back doors. In watermelon season, bunches of hogs, boars, sows, shoats, and litters of pigs, hovered around the verandahs with which most of the stores were provided, waiting for the rinds to be thrown out to them when the melons were cut. The women, and some of the men, protested against this condition; the Early County News constantly inveighed against it; but the municipal authorities did nothing.

There were no waterworks, no sewer system, and hence no bathtubs. We washed our faces in bowls or tin washpans, and took our regular Saturday night baths in big tin tubs—there were no water closets, but to the rear, usually in the corner of the vegetable garden, stood the old-fashioned privy, screened from the view of the neighbors by high picket fences on which, in spring and summer, butterbeans grew. Until I was grown, I did not know that butterbeans would grow anywhere except upon a picket fence leading to a privy.

Wood was the only fuel for heating or cooking. Lightwood, pine knots, and oak wood were to be had in abundance.

It was twenty miles from Blakely to Fort Gaines; fifteen to Arlington; twenty-seven to Morgan, thirty to Cuthbert, fourteen to Columbia, Alabama, sixteen to Cedar Springs, forty to Bainbridge, and twenty to Colquitt. Sam Morton, of Colquitt, who had a column in the Early County News, once wrote that Colquitt was twenty miles from Blakely, twenty miles from Bainbridge, twenty miles from Newton, twenty miles from Arlington, and twenty miles from Cedar Springs, and was estimated by some to be twenty miles from Hell, but that he considered that an overestimate.

The conditions I have spoken of were those that existed in the pioneer days of this town and this people in the early seventies—about seventy years ago. Nowadays when I go back to Blakely—the Blakely of beautiful homes, brick buildings, neatly-parked courthouse square, even a stream-lined modern jail, and other marks of culture and progress, it is hard for me to believe that this is the same spot I once knew; but the Baptist Branch, the Tanyard Branch, and vestiges of the Big Ditch are still there to assure me that it is.

However, even in the old days the unkempt condition of the streets and public buildings was offset by many neat, though simple, homes, usually with flower gardens in the front yards, in which grew roses, cape jessamines, violets, heartseases (as we called pansies), larkspur, yellow jessamine, honeysuckle, pinks, tuberoses, lilies, and other flowers, and by homes, where, though there were but few flowers or none, the yards were kept scrupulously swept, and the walkways were strewn with a coarse sand mined at near-by sand pits and having the texture and whiteness of granulated sugar. It was only a little town, but there were those of us who loved it.

Forebears

MY FATHER WAS RICHARD HOLMES POWELL. HE WAS BORN in Crawford County, Georgia, near the old town of Roberta, in October, 1841. He was the son of a Baptist preacher, the Reverend Hiram Powell. His mother was a Cheeves, of the same family as Langdon Cheves, of South Carolina. My grandmother's father pronounced it Cheeves to rhyme with leaves; but one of his sons who had been graduated from the Southern Baptist Seminary at Louisville, Kentucky, came back pronouncing it as if it were Chevis. I have heard the old folks tell that when he came back to Roberta to preach his maiden sermon, one of the deacons introduced him to the congregation as "Reverend James Chevis, the son of our good old friend, Grief Cheeves."

My grandfather Powell, who came to Early County shortly before the War, died some ten years before I was born; but, to borrow a phrase from Albert Greene's "Old Grimes," "Everybody said he was a fine old gentleman." In his daily walk, he was said to have been quite jovial, and they called him "Uncle Hi"; but when he was in the pulpit he enforced the precept, "The Lord is in His Holy Temple; let all the earth keep silence before Him." A number of the old people who knew him during his ministry in Crawford County have told me of the one occasion when he, himself, violated this precept. He was conducting revival services and had called up "mourners." A number of them had come to the front seeking spiritual consolation, and my grandfather was going from one to another, patting them on the head and giving such advice and consolation as he could. A drunken old fellow was in the congregatioin and had come

24

to the front with the other "mourners" and was kneeling with bowed head, weeping profusely. My grandfather came to him, and not noticing who he was or what his condition was, patted him on the head and asked, "How do you feel, my brother?"

The old fellow looked up with his maudlin eyes and sobbed aloud, "Uncle Hi, I feel like a God damned son of a bitch."

My grandfather exploded with laughter.

I feel a shock as I see the phrase, "son of a bitch," upon the page. Yet, on reflection, I realize that this feeling is merely a throwback to that Victorian prudery which in my early days often characterized our speech and conduct. Though this phrase may be a vulgarism generally to be avoided in the interest of good taste, unless the point of the incident or story inheres in the words themselves, or unless a raucousness of style is necessary to support the mood or the theme of the writer or the speaker, yet there is nothing inherently obscene or indecent in it. In the South, and perhaps elsewhere, it has a special use and meaning. When one wishes to use, of or to another, insulting language of such intensity that no known word or combination of words is opprobrious enough for the purpose, the phrase, "son of a bitch," seems to satisfy. It thus takes on a transcendental meaning capable of expressing insult or opprobrium to an infinite degree.

Yet there are those who would extend infinity. During the lifetime of my law partner, John Little, there came into the office one day an old farmer friend of his from near Talbotton, Georgia. John asked him if he knew Mr. So-and-So.

"Yes, Colonel Littles, I knows him well."

"What sort of man is he?"

"Colonel Littles, he is a son of a bitch, and has other faults besides."*

---

*Recently a lawyer from New York told me a story which was the same in substance as the one I have just related, and attributed it to the repertory of Henry Breckenridge, another New York lawyer. I make this note to say that, while the incidents and stories contained in this book fell within my own knowledge or experience, except where the context indicates otherwise, some of them have gotten into wider currency, and it is not at all impossible that in some

Now, going back to Grandfather Powell, he was born soon after the Revolutionary War in Edgefield District (County, they now call it), South Carolina, where, in the old days, fighting was said to have been so much in vogue that on almost any Sunday morning you could gather from the ground around the country stores where the fights had occurred the day before, a basket full of teeth, fingers, ears, eyeballs, and other parts of the human anatomy, and almost enough hair and whiskers to make a pillow.

Often when I am asked if I am kin to So-and-So Powell, I have a way of replying, "How can I know? My grandfather had twenty-four children, sixteen of them boys that lived to rear large families." And that is true. I used to have, and my brother, Wade Hampton Powell, now has the old family Bible with the names and dates of birth of all twenty-four of them duly set down.

My father was about nineteen years old when the War Between the States came on. Organization of volunteers was too slow for him in Early County; so he rushed back to the part of the State where he had been born, and, at Fort Valley, joined Company C of the 6th Georgia Regiment, along with his cousins, the Gray boys. (My middle name "Gray" is for them.) For nearly four years he was on the march and in one battle after another—Sharpsburg, Seven Days, The Wilderness, and many others. He got a minie ball through his left thigh at the battle of Ocean Pond, or Olustee as it is also called, and was home on furlough for a while; but he got back to Virginia in time to have his right leg blown off, in the last year of the war, by a bomb shell at Petersburg. He spent several months in the hospital at Richmond, and after the surrender he came back to his home in Early County, penniless, one-legged, ill-clad, and hungry, to find that his father had died and that he had on his hands an invalid mother and six younger brothers and sisters.

Despite his handicaps, especially his educational handicaps,

instances history may have repeated itself. While I assert my own freedom from plagiarism, I make no charge of it against anyone else.

he decided to be a lawyer. He used to tell us that from his earliest days he had an ambition to be a lawyer, but his father had told him that, unless he would forego this ambition, he would not send him to school, as all lawyers were liars.

From an old attorney in Blakely he borrowed Blackstone's Commentaries, Cobb's Digest, and one or two other text books and studied them at night and at such odd times as he could snatch from his farm work. At the October term of Early Superior Court, he appeared and asked to be examined for admission to the bar. He told me that this was the first time he had ever seen a court in session. He stood the examination in open court. I suspect that the examining committee which recommended him for admission was more moved by his manifest earnestness and his record as a soldier than by the amount of legal knowledge he displayed.

In many ways he was a very remarkable man. I have never seen any one possessed of any greater intuition for law than he had. Despite his limitations and handicaps, he was a successful lawyer for his day and time—successful not only in the trial courts but in the Supreme Court. Following the old custom, he rode the circuits and attended courts in a number of counties.

The people of this section were poor and fees were small. I doubt that he ever made as much as five hundred dollars in any year prior to the time I joined him in 1891, when times were getting better; yet he owned his home, paid his debts, paid the preacher, contributed liberally to all civic enterprises, and gave more or less of education to all his five children. Without any schooling in the formal sense, he continued his education to the day of his death. He loved poetry; he loved music. His great love was for men, women, and most of all, for children. He knew no fear; he would fight, but he harbored no ill will. I once saw him knock a man down, and, in doing so, he fell and suffered a compound fracture of the stump of his amputated leg. He got up, lifted his adversary, who was bruised about the face, and took him in his buggy to the doctor's office; not until his adversary's wounds were dressed did he take the doctor home with him. There, without anesthetic of any kind, he held his leg for the doctor to set the bones, and helped dress and bandage the places where the fractured bones had pierced through the skin.

Soon after he was admitted to the bar, his mother died, and his younger brothers and sisters married and moved away. Relieved of these responsibilities, he married Kittie (Keturah Rebecca) Perry, on December 3, 1872.

My mother—"Miss Kittie" everybody called her—was one of the sweetest, gentlest women that ever lived. She was better educated than my father, though she never went to college. She wrote a beautiful hand and was a good speller.

My father was the most versatile speller I ever knew. A saying of his was, "It is a mighty poor speller who cannot find more than one good way to spell a word." He once filed a suit for a horse. Opposing counsel said that he had spelled the word "horse" six different ways in his pleadings. My father challenged the statement, and a bet was made. He lost. He had spelled it "hoss," "hause," "hors," "hous," "horce," and "horse,"—but he won the case.

My mother must have been a pretty girl. The old photographs so indicate; but as she was nearly thirty when I was born, I naturally remember her as she was in middle life and old age. To me, her chief beauty was her hair, which in her girlhood she wore in long natural curls; but when I knew her it was a mass of short ringlets all over her head. It was brown originally, but in the years I best remember her it was a mass of lovely gray curls.

She was the daughter of Colonel Joel W. Perry, who on week days was the clerk of the Superior Court, and on Sundays, the clerk of the Baptist Church. He came to Blakely from Laurens County, and was kin to the Perrys, the Hightowers, and the Hickses there, who, so I have been told by people coming from that section of the State, thought themselves better than common folks. As he died at the age of about seventy-five, when I was around ten years old, I knew him only as a quiet, dignified old gentleman. He must not have put on any aristocratic ways after he came to Early County; otherwise he could not have been elected to public office, as he was throughout fifty years.

He was married twice and had sixteen children. Counting his sixteen and Grandfather Powell's twenty-four, I had thirty-eight uncles and aunts.

Here is a little incident throwing light on this good old man and his times. There is a letter (I think Wade Powell has it) from my uncle, Frank Perry, to his father, written about 1860, from Columbus, Georgia. The substance of it is: "I am sending to you by a friend a small bottle of bitters. You sweeten a toddy of rye whiskey with a little sugar, put in a few drops of the bitters, and shake it up together, and you have what they call a 'cocktail.' " Frank was killed in the War Between the States.

In our home, my father was the head of the family. He took the responsibilities; he shielded and protected my mother as if she were a child instead of a grown woman; to the extent of what little money he had, he did everything he could to make her life happy and comfortable. She loved, honored, and obeyed him. The utmost affection existed between them. She bore the children, kept the house clean and neat, and often did the cooking with the help of my father, and, as we grew older, of us boys. She made most of our clothes, darned our stockings and socks, patched our breeches, and saw that we were bathed; and, as we grew older, she saw to it that we got to school and to Sunday School on time. She spanked us occasionally, but if the mischief or badness was serious enough for a switching she turned that over to Father for attention.

Servants were cheap. One of my earliest recollections is of seeing my father write out a contract between himself and a middle-aged white woman, whereby he hired her to cook and do the family washing—her eighteen year old daughter to nurse the baby—for forty dollars a year, they eating at our table, but lodging elsewhere. Even after I became grown, one could hire a Negro woman cook for a dollar a week and such food as she ate in the kitchen. (They "toted," of course; but they didn't consider slipping out a little food, cooked or raw, and toting it home as stealing.)

Most of the time we had a cook, but father and we boys helped with the chores. I, being the oldest, was given the job of milking the cow when I was about ten years old. I never did like that job, though I think I did it pretty well. The day I was sixteen years old, they asked me what I wanted for a birthday present, and I said, "to quit milking the cow." They gave it to me; and thus my brother, Dick, became the family milker.

Mother was quiet and unobtrusive; but she had a genius for universal friendship. She nursed in her heart a passion for people. No matter how uninteresting a person was, she was interested in him; no person was so low that she did not care for him; no person so high that she was embarrassed in his presence. She was never forward, but there was something that attracted people to her and would cause them to come up to her and speak to her without an introduction—a thing that most women were immune from in those days. Being the wife and then the widow of counsel for the railroad, she traveled on passes and could have ridden in the Pullmans as well as in the day coaches. But she usually traveled by day, and preferred the day coaches because, she said, she met so many more interesting people there than she did in the Pullmans. If she ever met a person, she was interested in him ever afterward—and not only in him but in all his folks and in the place where he lived.

Modern psychologists are pretty well in agreement that the personalities and characters we develop in our lives are more largely due to environment, especially early environment, than to heredity. I think this is true. By inheritance, I got a sound body, a capacity to work, to grow, and to develop. But what I am, my personality, the results of what I have thought and done, are the end products of my environment.

Environment, as here used, includes much more than mere immediate surroundings. My environment, for instance, includes the fact that in the cemetery at Blakely are buried all my grandparents, both my parents; and my conscious and subconscious realization of this fact has been a stabilizing influence in my life and has created in me an abiding love for Blakely, for Early County, for Georgia, and for America. It also includes the fact that practically everybody I knew in my childhood and youth was of British stock; and this accounts for my political conservatism and for my belief in government under law—law developed, as the common law of England was, out of the time-tried experience of mankind under evolutionary processes, as contrasted with those theories of government, developed in Continental Europe, of the supremacy of the State or ruler over individuals, now exhibited at its worst in Hitlerism, Naziism, Fascism, and other forms of dictatorship. It accounts for my reluctance to give up too rapidly old ways of doing things, for my fear of New Deals, and, in the present crisis, for my intense desire, even before we entered the war, to see the United States give every aid to Britain and to see Britain win the war.

What was true of me in these respects was true of most of the other boys I grew up with. I merely use myself as an example.

I have now reached the age when I can look back upon my life objectively and study it apart from myself, as I might study the life of someone else with whom I had been associated intimately for the same length of time. I now see as never before the great influence of my father upon my life and upon my personality.

From the day I was born, my father's pride in me knew no limits. In the files of the Early County News, still preserved in the courthouse at Blakely, is the issue of September 4, 1873. I haven't it before me, but the general tenor of the news item I have in mind is this: On last Tuesday morning, citizens on the north side of town saw a strange phenomenon in the cotton yard, near where the depot is to be built when the railroad arrives. It appeared to be a windmill revolving rapidly, with some of the sails longer than the others. Those who investigated found that it was our esteemed fellow townsman, Colonel R. H.

Powell, standing on his head, whirling in joy and excitement. As his friends would draw near, he would cry out, "It's a boy, the finest, smartest boy that ever was born—a future President of the United States."

There is still extant a tintype of me taken before I was a year old. When I look at it and see what a sorry-looking, tallow-faced country baby I was, I cannot understand how, even in his prejudiced imagination, he could believe that a child that looked as I did could ever have any intelligence. But my looks did not daunt him at all.

He made me his constant companion. He took me with him everywhere he went. He was always teaching me things; always expecting me to understand things beyond the mental range of an ordinary child of the age I happened to be at the time. He trusted me to do things that most people would not have entrusted to anyone nearly so young. The result was that I developed not only precocity but self-assurance and a belief that I really was smart and could do things which other boys of my age could not do.

I developed an egotism—an egotism which I found it necessary to hold down later, lest it become too immodest and offensive. These experiences also developed in me a great amount of curiosity about things around me, and a desire to know the how and the why of things.

Certainly the most important factor in my early environment was a most remarkable father.

4

An Original People

I HAVE NEVER SEEN A MORE ORIGINAL PEOPLE THAN THOSE OF Blakely and the surrounding country in the old days; all of them were full of human interest; no one of them was like any other of them. Naturally, all the men and women of that time have long since passed away—many of them when I was so small a child that I retain in memory no accurate picture of them. But some of them I do remember.

The old men who had fought the Indians, such as Colonel Buchannon and Mr. Winn Sheffield, died too soon after my birth for me to remember much of them. Colonel Buchannon had been married three times, and his second set of children were my mother's nephews and nieces. He had an attractive house in a large lot on the east side of the intersection of Main Street with the Square, and his large general store was on the west side of the street.

I remember Mr. Palmer, the shoemaker. He sat all the day long at his cobbler's bench making or repairing shoes, mostly brogans. We boys would gather around to see him work. He rarely talked, replying to our questions in monosyllables, if he could. It was a pleasure to see him driving pegs into the sole of a brogan. My father always spoke to him in passing and told me that he was a very respectable citizen because he was a brave Confederate soldier.

Then there was that quiet, white-haired old lady whom we looked upon with awe-tinged admiration—our Niobe, Mrs. Griffin. In succession, her husband and five sons went to the Confederate Army; in turn each and all met death "where the bravest love to die." When she buried the last of them, her baby boy, she broke down and wept—because she had no more to send.

The richest and most prominent family in the town were the Wades—J. M. and R. W. Wade. Their general store was on Main Street, and Captain Wilk Wade's residence was a few hundred feet farther down the street, separated from the store by a small orchard. The dwelling and the yard around it have been kept, until now, almost exactly as they were at the time Mrs. Wade died some forty years ago.

Captain Wade was a tall, handsome old gentleman, with a long, white, neatly-kept beard—a Southern gentleman of the old school. It was as superintendent of the Baptist Sunday School that I knew him best. His wife Petrona, Cousin Pete we called her, was my mother's niece; she and her children, John, Wilk, and Pearl, were my cousins.

Mr. John Wade, the elder of the brothers, was a quaint old-timer. He was a tall, heavy man, weighing about 250 pounds, and he too wore a long white beard. He had a thin voice with a slight whine in it, and it contrasted comically with his huge body. Captain Wade kept in his home a room for his brother; but Uncle John, as almost everyone called him, usually slept in the back room of his store. Though kerosene oil came into use a few years after I was born, Uncle John would have none of it; he still used tallow candles. He wore a long white nightshirt, which covered him from neck to feet, and in this he would walk about the store at night with a tallow candle in his hand, assuring himself all over again that the doors were locked and everything else was safe. Sometimes he would hear us boys on the street and would call us in to talk with him and keep him company. When asked why he still clung to his tallow candles when in the other stores and homes, including his brother's, kerosene lamps were used, he would say, "I am afraid of that new-fangled stuff. It's too dangerous. Some careless nigger is going to set fire to a tank of it someday and blow the whole town up."

The family physician of the community had long been Dr.

W. M. Standifer, but he retired about the time I was born, and his son, Dr. Will Standifer, came along several years later. Old Dr. Standifer lived to be a very old man, and the boys of my day knew him only after he had retired. He was the most taciturn man I ever knew, and he had the reputation of having been so all his life. In his home he had two grandchildren of my age, Gene and Mary Ashley Hightower, and we boys and girls would frequently go there. He would sit in his rocking chair on the front porch or in his room, slowly rocking, and would never say a word to us. At Columbia, Alabama, fourteen miles away, he had an old friend, who was a physician and who was also noted for his taciturnity. One morning the friend from Columbia drove up in front of Dr. Standifer's home. Dr. Standifer called a Negro servant and told him to take the visitor's horse and see that it was fed and watered. He shook hands with the visitor and motioned him to take another rocking chair. There they sat and rocked, neither saying a word, until Mrs. Standifer rang the dinner bell. They went in, ate, came back to the porch, and sat there rocking in silence till late in the afternoon, when the visitor asked that his horse be brought. As the servant brought the horse and buggy, the two men shook hands again. "I have enjoyed very much being with you today," said the visitor, "and I hope you will come to see me soon."

"I enjoyed it, too," said Dr. Standifer, "and I will try to spend a day with you as soon as I can."

That was all.

At the time of my birth, Dr. B. R. Dostor was our family physician—indeed, the physician for most of the town and surrounding country; and he ran the drugstore. Dr. Dostor put on a mask of sternness, but he had a keen sense of humor, which often broke through, and beneath the mask he had a very kindly spirit. He was one of the few men in our town who "cussed out loud." He had been a captain in the Confederate Army and was severely wounded in the Battle of Monocacy in 1864. Despite these wounds, which never ceased to pain him, he did not spare himself. Night or day, in fair weather or foul, you might see him in the buggy behind "Old Rattler," his big, swift-footed roan, driving, driving, till the sick and the suffering had been ministered to. On many a cold night did he rise, sleepy and tired, from a warm bed, and go from his home to his drugstore about a block away to supply medicine for some sick Negro, who, as he knew, would never pay him.

Yes, he cursed as he did it; but he did it. One cold night about eleven o'clock, he heard a knocking at his door.

"Who's that?"

"Hit's Ole Si, Doctor."

"What the hell do you want at this time of night?"

"My poor little baby, she so sick wid de diarrhee."

The doctor dressed and went to the drugstore, cursing Si all the way for being so lazy and not coming sooner, and prepared the calomel and sugar of milk, standard remedy of the day for the diarrhoea in babies, and gave them to the old Negro, who rode off on his mule.

About half an hour later, just as the doctor was dropping off to sleep again, came another rap at the door.

"Who's that?"

"Hit's Si, Doctor."

"What the hell do you want now?"

"My poor little baby, she so hongry I thought I'd ax you ef we could give her some of de cold collard greens we got lef' from supper."

The torrent of profanity which greeted this simple remark was such as to awaken the neighbors and to let them see that Si's old mule could take on new life in an emergency. Yet next day the doctor went by the old Negro's cabin to see the sick baby and to leave more medicine.*

---

*I have made no attempt at complete uniformity in representing dialect, for dialect itself is not uniform. I have mentioned that our Negroes were the descendants of slaves who came from the eastern coasts of Georgia and South Carolina and who spoke a dialect known as Geechee, much modified, of course, in their descendants.

Not long ago I was filling in an application to take training as a sector air raid warden, and one of the questions on the blank was, "What language do you speak?" I hesitated to say English, for I had to swear to it. I did not like

Dr. Dostor had a large repertory of stories which he was always ready to tell us boys at the slightest urging. We shall see more of him later.

Major T. F. Jones was a quiet, undemonstrative gentleman, with a subtle sense of humor. He had been an officer in the Confederate Army and in the State Militia. He ran a general store and was the county school commissioner. His eyes would dance with glee as he would show his friends a note he had received from a Negro schoolteacher named Whitaker. Whitaker had a Negro woman cooking for him. She demanded her wages and he told her that he had no money. She then asked him if he would give her an order on Major Jones for three dollars' worth of goods, and let Major Jones take it out of his salary as teacher. Whitaker gave her the order. It ran thus:

"Major Jones, please let this woman have three dollars' worth of goods and look to her for the money. Respectfully yours, J. W. Whitaker."

I have already spoken of our postmaster, Mr. Crawford Fryer, who was also justice of the peace. He had a long red beard, which became streaked with gray in his later years. He was superintendent of the Methodist Sunday School and was popular with us boys because he had four pretty daughters of about our ages. He was a very genial old gentleman and kept a hospitable home.

Judge W. W. Fleming—the title came from his having served as a judge of the inferior court, a court of considerable jurisdiction in the early days of our State, though presided over by laymen—was the husband of my mother's sister, Aunt Bina (Albina). She and Aunt Rona (Angerona), with whom Grandfather Perry lived, were our favorite aunts. Uncle Fleming, as we called him, was the proprietor of the Early County News; because of his getting old, his two sons, Will and Jeff, relieved him of much

---

to say Negro or Geechee, though I realized that my speech, especially my informal speech and my dialect had been strongly influenced by the Negroes I came in contact with in my childhood and young manhood. Though it did not entirely satisfy me, I compromised on "Southern English."

of the harder work in the office. He was a short, round little Pennsylvania Dutchman, but as he had come South before the War, had married a Southern girl, and had been in the Confederate service, he was one of us. He and Dr. Dostor were great friends, and the doctor was constantly playing pranks on him. One morning he came up the street, saw the doctor and said, "What's the news?"

"Have you heard of the big fire?" the doctor asked.

"Where?" Uncle Fleming inquired eagerly, taking out the reportorial notebook he always kept with him.

"In Hell," Dr. Dostor replied. "You ought to read about it in the Bible."

"Tut! Tut!" ejaculated Uncle Fleming, and then sat down and chatted with him for an hour.

Mr. Dave James came to Blakely from southeast Alabama. When I first got old enough to know about the things around me, he was running a barroom on the Square. He must have prospered in this business, for soon he had a large general store on Main Street, near J. M. and R. W. Wade's, with a large cotton warehouse in the rear. He dealt largely in farm supplies and had many mortgages on farms. If the mortgages were not paid, he foreclosed, and in course of time he owned a number of farms. In 1895 he organized the Bank of Blakely, with a capital of fifteen thousand dollars, and made my schoolmate, John Wade, cashier of it.

He had so many people of the county in debt to him and his bank that most people were afraid to oppose him. I recall that in 1905, Mr. E. Hilton, who lived at Hilton Station ten miles southwest of Blakely, and who had made considerable money in turpentine, sawmilling, and other timber operations, came to me and said that he would like to open a National Bank in Blakely with a capital of fifty thousand dollars if I would become vice-president and give it personal attention. He put a few thousand dollars of the stock in my name and let the dividends on it pay him back the money he thus advanced. Certain other business men were allowed to subscribe for blocks of the stock, but Mr.

Hilton put up most of the fifty thousand dollars. While I was engaged in the groundwork of getting the organization together, a friend of mine who had heard of my activities came to me in great secrecy and, with alarm apparent in his face, took me into a back room and asked if it were true that I was helping to organize a bank. I told him that I was. "Aren't you afraid to do it? Don't you know Mr. James will ruin you?" he whispered.

Well, the bank we organized is still there. The Bank of Blakely is not. Figuratively speaking, Mr. James lived by the sword; and he died by the sword. At the height of his career he had amassed about half a million dollars, but he began speculating in cotton futures and suffered heavy losses. He had long litigation in the United States Court with the brokers, and finally large judgments were rendered against him. When he was forced into bankruptcy and his bank failed, most of the community turned on him like wolves. He was thrown into jail, but, as to this transaction, the Supreme Court exonerated him. The last few years of his life were sad. All in all, he was a remarkable man. He came to Blakely with little or no money and with little or no education. His general reading and his knowledge of things beyond the confines of his own business were extremely limited. I recall that during the Spanish-American War, the papers came out one morning with a news item stating that a number of regiments had been encamped at Tampa, Florida, for several weeks, waiting for boats to take them to Cuba, and it had just been discovered that no one had thought to order the boats to transport them. Someone mentioned this in the presence of Mr. James. "All that money wasted!" he remarked disgustedly. "Why didn't they make them march, as they did in the last war?"

Andrew J. Singletary, Colonel Singletary they called him because he was once admitted to the bar, was a rare character. His father was well-to-do, and had two sons, Andrew and Luke, the former of whom he educated to be a lawyer, the latter to be a physician. According to my best recollection, Luke never practiced medicine but spent his life at farming and sawmilling. Andrew did open a law office at Arlington, fourteen miles from

Blakely. His first client to come in was an old darkey who had been arrested for stealing one of Mr. Rawls's hogs.

Colonel Singletary said to him, "Now, Josh, you know I am your lawyer, and you must tell me the whole truth."

"Yazs'r, Marse Andrew, I knows I'se got to tell my lawyer de truth. I did steal Mr. Rawls's hog, but dey cain't prove it on me."

Colonel Singletary flared into outrage and indignation. "Josh, what do you mean by stealing Mr. Rawls's hog? You are just a common thief, and you ought to be in the penitentiary. I'll quit practicing law before I'll defend you." And quit he did—permanently.

Although he was a young man of means and education, he led a very simple life, marked with extreme frugality in so far as the satisfying of his own needs was concerned, but with extreme liberality in so far as private charity and the needs of the community were concerned. About this time, the railroad was being constructed from Arlington to Blakely, and numerous trestles were to be built through the creek swamps. He contracted to build a number of them. By day he walked in the mud and the water, often putting his hands to some of the tasks of the job, and at night he slept in the camps with the other laborers. He acquired large farms in the county and a water mill about two miles from Blakely. He worked long hours by day and often into the night in giving them his personal management; and, as if this were not enough for any man, he became a partner with Major Jones in a general store and helped run that. He slept in the back room of the store, paid no attention to his food or attire, and indulged himself in no bad habits.

Then he fell in love with one of the sweetest young women I ever knew, beautiful, gentle, and refined, and they were married. His manner of living became entirely changed. He bought himself new clothes, dressed neatly, and lived well. He and she were a model young couple. He was in process of building a large, well-planned dwelling, admirably located, when his wife gave birth to a son and soon afterward died.

He never got over the shock of his wife's death. He stopped work on the uncompleted house, left it just as it was on the day she died. The son, who is today one of the State's best citizens, he cared for and educated; but he himself went back to his old frugal ways of living, working hard, and denying himself the comforts of life. There were some who thought he was a skinflint, because he would rarely join publicly in raising funds for any charitable or civic enterprise. I came to know better. As I grew up he frequently talked with me about his personal affairs and when I was admitted to the bar, I became his legal adviser. I had access to his books of account and from them I learned that throughout many years he had been furnishing the necessities of life to the poor of the community, chiefly old people, white and black. On his books he would charge the amounts against them, but would never make any effort to collect from them, though the indebtedness ran into thousands of dollars. Soon after I was grown, I served with him on the board of trustees of the public schools in Blakely. Times were very hard, and the State was behind in sending in our part of the school funds; yet our treasury was a widow's cruse—it was never exhausted—and the schools were run. I knew from the public records that he was mortgaging his land, but I supposed that he did it to get the money to run his farms. In part, that was true, but to the extent of about a thousand dollars he was using this money for the schools. He made no professions of piety, but he was a Christian gentleman.

And Luby—I forget his given name—was a part of the picture. He did not come into prominence until I was fourteen or fifteen years old, but he was there all the time. He was one of those who lived on the Chattahoochee River and got their livelihood by catching catfish on trotlines and selling or bartering them to the neighbors—a very low scale of living. He had a broad-bottomed bateau, with which he tended his trotlines, and on it he had a tarpaulin, arranged in the likeness of a wagon cover, under which he and the woman who lived with him—he called her his wife, and perhaps she was—could sleep. However, on the bank of the river, near a spring, he had a tent, and usually at night the bateau was moored adjacent to it.

One morning he notified the nearest neighbors that his wife was dead. They came and found the woman's body lying in front of the tent; there was a gash in her scalp and a fracture in her skull, and Luby's hatchet was under her. Luby, seeing her dead, must have rushed off to alarm the neighbors without waiting to ascertain the cause of her death. When they called to his attention the wound and the hatchet, he said, "Why, I must have killed her myself. Last night I was in the bateau and she was in front of the tent. She kept mouthing and I told to shut up and when she wouldn't quit, I threw the hatchet at her. I didn't know I hit her, but she shut up."

They seized him and brought him to Blakely. The superior court was in session; the grand jury immediately indicted him for murder; and on the following Monday morning the case was called for trial.

He had no friends; he wanted none. Doubtless, to him life was not worth living. The only human relationship he had maintained was with the slovenly woman who now lay in a pauper's grave, where she had been sent by his act. Trotlines and catfish; more trotlines and catfish—that was all he had to live for, and he was tired of that.

When the judge inquired if he had counsel, he said that he had none and didn't need any, that he had killed the woman, was ready to be hanged, and please make it snappy. The judge, nevertheless, appointed my father to defend him, and he did the best he could with his client giving him no assistance. The jury convicted him, and the judge sentenced him to be hanged. Much to Luby's disappointment, my father appealed to the Supreme Court, but that court affirmed the judgment.

The day for the hanging came. It was to take place between the hours of ten in the morning and three in the afternoon. Promptly at ten o'clock Luby began to urge Bill Hodges, the sheriff, to go ahead and get over with it. "Hurry up and hang me," he said. "I want to get to Hell in time for dinner." Before eleven o'clock he was taken to the gallows, the noose adjusted around his neck, and the black cap put over his head. The sheriff asked if he had anything to say, to which he replied, "No, Hell, no!"

It was Hodges' first hanging and he was very nervous. He drew back the axe and cut the rope. This was supposed to release the trap of the gallows, but the trap stuck and did not fall. The sheriff was all up in the air, when Luby called out, "Oh, Hell, don't you know how to hang a man?" and with that he jumped against the floor of the gallows, sprung the trap and sent his body hurtling through space to dangle at the end of the rope until he was dead.

The fact is that Luby was probably not guilty of any higher offense than manslaughter. For several years there were many in the community who had the feeling that he met an undeserved death. A result of this was that for a long time thereafter juries were very cautious in assessing the death penalty.

Among the old-time Negroes of Blakely was Cleve Robinson, who lived and ran a small store in Negrotown, near the Negro Methodist Church—Colored M. E. Church they call it now. He chiefly sold mullet, especially on Saturdays. There were white storekeepers in and around the Square who also had a large Saturday trade in mullet. Our Negroes always have been very fond of this salt-water fish; and, on every Saturday morning's train there would come by express a dozen or so barrels of them. The reek that persisted all day Saturday in the neighborhood of the southwest corner of the Square came from the frying of mullet in "Kizzie Dawson's Select Restaurant for Colored People." As soon as the country Negroes arrived in town, they would flock to the places where the mullet were sold and buy their string of fish—two or three of them strung on bear grass or palmetto fiber. Beneath the summer sun these strings would be toted around all day by the proud possessors—and thus there was another foul smell that vied with the one from Kizzie Dawson's Restaurant. At the beginning of the business day, the price was twenty-five or thirty cents a string, but if by late in the afternoon it became apparent that some of the fish were likely not to be sold, the price dropped; and some frugal ones waited for the drop.

They tell it of a Negro woman who was a witness in a case: "Now what time of day was it when you saw what you have just told about?" the lawyer asked.

"I dunno, suh, I don' have no watch."

"Was it morning or afternoon?"

"It wuz along in the evenin'."

"Was it before sundown?"

"Yazs'r, I can tell you when it wuz—the price of mullet fish had just drop to fifteen cents."

Cleve Robinson was a crafty old darkey, given to many of the venialities, but he managed to stay out of jail. One time the sheriff almost got him. The local express agent reported to the sheriff that a barrel of mullet consigned to a small storekeeper had been stolen from the place near the railway station where the express had been put off the train. When the sheriff went to Cleve's place, which was not far from the station, the barrel of fish was there.

"What are you doing with Mr. Smith's fish?" the officer demanded.

"Dem's my fish. I paid de express agent for 'em at de depot and brang 'em here in my cart. Dey's got my name on de barrel," and he pointed to the letters, plainly stenciled there, "C.O.D."

"Why, that's 'C.O.D.,'" the sheriff said.

"Yazs'r, dat's de way dey spells my name, 'C.O.D.—Cleve Robinson.' All my fish comes marked dat way."

When they found at the express office Cleve's barrel which he had paid the express agent for, the matter was amicably adjusted by Cleve's letting Mr. Smith take that barrel and pay for it.

Ed Hutchins, a young Negro who ran a small shop near Cleve's and who had been taught to read and write, said that

Cleve should have known his name was C. R. Robinson, just as his own name was E. H. Hutchins. It is true that, in those days, practically all the Negroes who could read and write constructed the names of themselves and other Negroes by taking the initial of the given name and the initial of the surname, and then adding the full surname; for example, Joe Thomas was J. T. Thomas; Henry Powell, H. P. Powell; Alonzo Stamper, A. S. Stamper; Oscar Wade, O. W. Wade; and so on.

Jake Holmes, stout, tall, coal-black and proud of the fact that he did not have the taint of a drop of white blood in him, was one of our good citizens. He was the local Republican Committeeman and had the approval of appointments to local postmasterships, but he always consulted his white friends—Democrats, of course—before approving an appointment. He paid his taxes and voted as he pleased, and no one attempted to hinder him. He had a good influence in the community and was highly respected. For a while he rented my father's farm near Blakely and later bought it on time. One of his sons now runs a school for Negroes in Atlanta and is well respected. My annual budget for charity always carries a small sum for Holmes Institute.

Then there was Aunt Sallie Meriwether, our colored washwoman, of the old-time Mammy type. She was almost as broad as she was long. It was a pleasure to see her balance a big bundle of the family wash on the top of her head and walk away with it, smiling benevolently as she went. She was so calm, so placid, so good-natured that, despite her obesity, no one thought of her dying of apoplexy. I remember the day when she died. Several of us boys were sitting on the front porch of Dr. Dostor's drugstore, and he was entertaining us with his yarns. We saw Aunt Sallie's lazy son-in-law, Oscar Wade, coming across the Square at a pace unusually lively for him. When he arrived, he was all out of breath, but he managed to blurt out, "Come, Doctor; come quick! Aunt Sallie Meriwether have fell spokeless in the road."

I think that Aunt Jane Powell, and such of her children as

were born before or during the War, were the only slaves my grandfather Powell ever owned. She refused to be set free. She had no white blood in her; nor did her children have any. When my grandmother Powell died, she wanted to come and "take care of" my father, but he bought 125 acres of land about nine miles south of Blakely, with a cabin on it, and gave it to her, and persuaded her to go there. But if my father or any member of his family became sick, no one could keep her away; she came and made her pallet at the foot of the sick bed and, though she was very old, was ready for any task.

To my childish mind, an old Negro, Albert Jeems, was an interesting character. He had a small farm two or three miles from Blakely and would come to town on Saturdays and drink cheap liquor at the barrooms until he was drunk, and then he would go slowly staggering down the street singing decorously his one and only song—only two lines of it—which he repeated over and over again:

> "Shout and go round! Shout and go round!
> Shout and go round the walls of Zion."

He molested no one, and no one bothered him.

Saint Maryland was a Negro Baptist Church three miles south of Blakely on the road to Colquitt. The pastor of the church was called Elder Hudson Williams. He was a long, tall, gingercake-colored Negro, with a loud voice and but little sense, and probably no education. He once created a commotion among the Negroes by a sermon he preached. He came into Blakely one Saturday afternoon and stayed in one of the barrooms until it closed at midnight. Already drunk, he took a quart of whiskey with him. He would walk a while, lie down beside the road and sleep a while, wake up and take a nip and walk some more. He tried to get to Saint Maryland by the time appointed for the morning service, but he was a few minutes late, and, as he entered the church, the congregation was singing. He mounted the pulpit and without much ado gave out his text.

"Brothers and sisters, my text this morning is from the thirty-third verse of the thirty-third chapter of the Book of John, and it reads as follows, 'God Damn the World.' "

The versions of his sermon, as the members of his congregation brought it back to the white folks, varied in slight detail, but the tenor of it was as follows:

"You get up in the morning and start to hitch the old mule to the plow; he kicks you in the belly and lands you back on the prongs of the pitch-fork: and that's 'God Damn the World!'

"You see the 'cycloon' coming through the woods, blowing down the trees and tearing down the houses, and the thunder rolls and the lightning flashes and all you can do is to fall on the ground and hold onto the tall grass; that's 'God Damn the World!'

"You give the landlord all your cotton and you kill your last pig and meat is getting scarce, and you look up the road and you see Mr. Sim McGlammory [the local constable] come riding down the big road in that rattly old buggy of his with that little old horse of his frisking around in the shafts, because he is too little to fill them, and he puts his eyes on you and he comes down on you like a tilly hawk on a jay bird and he say 'Where's that corn?' and you show him the crib where you got the five bushels left, and he levies on that; that's 'God Damn the World!' "

He went on to describe sickness, and death, Hell and damnation, till he had the congregation in a frenzy of fear and desperation, and then walked out as suddenly as he had come in and went to find the quart bottle which he had left hidden in a fence corner and which had one more drink in it.

Blakely and the people in and around it were typical of the rest of our section. Fort Gaines, twenty miles away on the Chattahoochee River, with a branch line of a railway running into it, had advanced a little further commercially and was considered a sportier town than Blakely. Colquitt, twenty miles to the south, and Miller County, of which it was the county seat, were not quite so far advanced as Blakely. I have been told that at the time of my birth only three men in Miller County wore white shirts and black neckties on week days as well as Sunday; and one of them, Dr. Wilkin, did not need the tie as he wore a long beard.

5

Mayhaw Jelly and Ginger Cakes

D R. BOSSARD, IN HIS *Problems of Well-Being*, SAYS SENTEN-tiously, "Being an infant is a dangerous occupation." That was doubtless my first occupation, but I do not remember it. Booth Tarkington in his recent autobiographic sketches professes to remember a great deal more of what occurred in the very early years of his life than I am willing to claim for myself.

They say that I "learned my letters" when I was three years old; and I seem to have a dim memory of being with my father with the big family Bible open on his lap and of having him teach me the names of the large initial letters at the beginning of chapters. However, this may be an ex post facto memory, acquired from what I was told in later years.

I still recollect several things which occurred when I was about six years old; for example, the Sunday afternoon when my parents could not find my younger brother, Holmes (Dick, we called him later) and me until they finally discovered us in the back yard in an iron wash pot. In our childish fancy, we had converted the pot into a carriage and were driving in state a fine pair of horses which our imagination had hitched to it; but our smutty faces, hands, and legs, and soiled Sunday clothes made us look like two little Negroes in a tar bucket.

The mind of a child stores things, the meaning of which it is not able to compass at the time. One afternoon, when I could not have been over six years old, several gentlemen were sitting in front of Dr. Ewell's drugstore. My father was there, and, as usual, I was with him. Dr. Ewell said a thing that made them laugh. While I did not know what he meant, I can still repeat his words. "A widow," he said, "is a woman who knows what's what, and desires further information on the same subject."

I remember the game of "peep house" some of us small boys invented. We found a large white-pine drygoods box near the sidewalk at J. M. & R. W. Wade's store, and hid ourselves in it. We would watch for someone to come down the walk and as one appeared we would crouch down in the box, and as the passer got alongside of us we would pipe out at the top of our voices, "Peep house! Peep house!" Aunt Bina came by and when we "peep-housed" her she pretended to be greatly frightened and thereby gave us great amusement. We were thus engaged one afternoon, when up the walk came a tall, erect gentleman, wearing a long-tailed, cutaway coat. We were getting ready to peep-house him, when John Wade struck terror into us by whispering, "Hide! Hide quick! That's Professor Dozier, the schoolteacher, and he has switches hidden under his coattails!"

This may be as good a place as any to explain the use we made of the title "Professor." With us, all male schoolteachers were called Professor, just as all lawyers were called Colonel. I was once a professor myself. While we did not intend this title to carry all the meaning that attaches to it when properly used to indicate rank in a college or a university, yet it had none of those sinister implications that attend its use when applied to a mountebank or even to a professor of boxing or dancing.

I remember the Grier's Almanacs that hung on a nail at the side of the fireplace—there was one in almost every home. They were distributed from the drugstore and paid for by the patent-medicine companies who put them out. They contained tables in which were given not only the information found on an ordinary calendar, but also the times the sun and the moon rose and set each day, the hour, minute, and second when tides would be high and tides would be low at Savannah, the changes of the moon, a full account of all the eclipses which were to occur during the year, and other astronomical information including prophecies as to the weather. We had only one time in those days—sun time—and we set our clocks by the sun and Grier's Almanac.

There were other almanacs put out by other advertisers, with grotesque pictures in them, forerunners of the comics of today. I still remember the first comic I ever saw in one of these almanacs. There was a picture of a small boy scratching his head and of his mother correcting him. The dialogue under the picture ran thus:

> "Mother—Johnny, quit scratching your head."
> "Johnny—Well, Ma, they bit me first."

A few days after my sixth birthday, I entered school. I remember that day quite well. I remember the schoolhouse, a large rectangular building sitting near the center of a three-acre tract, on which there were a number of magnificent oaks. It had a front and a back room, a wide, columned verandah, and a belfry on top.

Professor John W. Dozier was the principal and only teacher. There were no desks, but some tables were provided; and the pupils sat on long benches, which formerly had done service somewhere as church pews. My father gave me a homemade pine desk with a hinged top and a cowhide-bottomed straight chair; but as Professor Dozier had no desk and no chair, and as I was only a little fellow needing no such equipment, he took the desk and chair for his use; and I sat on the long benches with the other children.

On the opening day, the teacher faced us, about thirty boys and girls, as I recall, of all ages from six to twenty, and read out the school rules. He read out one, "No talebearers allowed."

The word "talebearer" challenged my curiosity, as well as my imagination. When he finished, he stated that anyone who did not understand the rules should make it known. I promptly arose and piped out, "What is a talebearer?"

On Friday afternoons we had "speaking" by the boys and the girls; sometimes compositions by the older ones.

At the close of the school next spring, we had the "Exhibition," with charades, dialogues, recitations, and so forth. My recitation was "All Quiet Along the Potomac." The chief feature of the program was "The Charade of the Flowers." Miss Mollie

Robinson, Miss Trudie Smith, and others of the older girls represented various flowers and spoke their parts; Charlie Robinson, Gene Dozier, and others of the older boys had their roles; and four of us youngest boys, Bob Dostor, Jim Cartledge, Perryman DuBose, and I, stood at the corner of the stage and represented little anemones. One of the girls recited a poem containing the line, "And the little anemones peep and peep"; it was our part to chime in with "Peep! Peep!" My children have frequently laughed, as I have told of this incident, at what seems so funny to them—my ever being a little peeping anemone.

I was under Professor Dozier for but one year. Next year several changes took place. Dr. B. R. Dostor, Major T. F. Jones, and my father became the school trustees. During the summer, they found the money to provide a number of desks, which may be described as embryos of the modern school desks, with small benches on which to sit at them. They were made of plain pine boards by local carpenters. There were not enough of them, and some of us had to sit on the long benches as we had before; but a step forward had been made.

Professor Granberry succeeded Professor Dozier as teacher. He was not the disciplinarian that his predecessor was; but he was kindly, and, though somewhat languid, perhaps somewhat lackadaisical, we liked him. How much education he had, I do not know, but I suppose it was slight as compared with modern standards. Yet, during the two or three years that he ruled over the Blakely Academy, the pupils made progress.

The big bell rang at half past seven in the morning, and the small bell rang at eight to call us into the schoolroom. From ten to ten-thirty was morning recess. At twelve o'clock we "took out" for dinner; and school "took in" again at half past one. Afternoon recess came from three to three-thirty; and at half past four, "school was out."

I remember this period best for the games we played: marbles (the four large marbles on the circumference of the ring with the middler in the center, and taws to shoot at them with);

knucks (also played with marbles that we shot from hole to hole, with many ground rules and quaint jargon of "vincher roundance," "flat knucks," and so forth); bull-pen (the boy with the ball threw at the boys in the pen, marked on the ground); town ball (rudimentary baseball); and many other old games, most of which have been superseded or discarded.

The railroad reached Blakely about this time, and we played train. The paths through the woods behind the school grounds were the railway tracks. The boys, lined up in tandem, were not only the train, but also the crew. The boy at the front was the engine and the engineer. It was his job to imitate the train whistle. Next came the fireman, who imitated the engine as it blew off steam from the cylinder cocks. Then came the conductor, the baggage master, and the flagman; and the rest of the boys trailed along as coaches or boxcars. Often the front of the train arrived at its destination considerably in advance of some of the cars.

Our railroad, which ran out from Albany, was not much of a railroad in those days. Most of the way, if not all the way, from Albany to Arlington, it was laid with 20- or 25-pound rail, supported on wooden sills, or stringers as they were called. From Arlington to Blakely the rail was a little heavier and laid on crossties. Necessarily the trains ran slowly. The schedule for the fifty miles from Blakely to Albany was a little over four hours.

One of the hazards of travel between Arlington and Albany was the snakeheads—the thin rail, under the weight of the train, would buckle, pull loose from the spikes that held it to the stringers, and strike against the bottoms of the cars and occasionally would punch through them. A derailment generally ensued in such instances; but the country was flat and the trains ran slowly, so that usually the damage was slight.

Soon after the railroad reached Blakely the Negroes requested that an excursion train be run to take them to and from a picnic a few miles above Arlington. The railway official notified them that they could not supply passenger coaches, that the only equipment available was a number of flatcars, that if they were willing to ride on these, they would run the train. The Negroes promptly consented, and the train was run. Most of the passengers sat at the edges of the cars with their feet and legs hanging over the sides, others sat or squatted in the middle of them. A few miles beyond Arlington a snakehead rose up under one of the cars. It tilted the car into the air and pitched the passengers off on to the berm of a cut through which the train was passing.

They used to tell it of a fat good-natured old Negro woman, who was enjoying the experience of riding on a train for the first time, and who was squatted in the middle of a flatcar when the snakehead struck it, that when she was thrown from the car she plumped down on her fat buttocks on the edge of the cut and sat there grinning contentedly.

"Aunt Phoebe," someone asked, "What do you think of that? Did it hurt you?"

"Naw," she said, "I allus gits off de train dis way."

During this period my brother Dick entered school. I remember the soda fountain that he and I ran in the woods near the path that was our railroad track. Two large pines had fallen parallel to each other and so close together that we could lay short planks from one to the other for shelves. Our only stock in trade was soda water. This was made by taking sweetened water with cooking soda in it and pouring into it a small amount of vinegar to make it foam. Our price was one pin a glass. Despite our limited stock in trade, we fastened upon one of the logs a large cardboard sign bearing the words "Messrs. Powell & Powell —General Merchandise." Trudie Smith, one of the large girls, came along, saw the sign, read it, and caused much merriment by remarking, "Messers Powell & Powell; messers is right."

One year, just after "big court" had been in session, we boys decided to organize a court. Wilk Wade was the judge, Bob Dostor was the solicitor general (the prosecuting officer), Lucius Granberry was the sheriff, Will McDowell was the clerk, I was the lawyer for the defense, and Johnnie Williams, Dick Powell,

Frank Jones, Perryman DuBose, and other boys of the group were jurors. We tried Jim Cartledge. I defended him. The jury convicted him, and Judge Wade sentenced him to be spanked with a paddle. I gave notice that I would move for a new trial and asked that the execution of the sentence be postponed till next day. The stay was granted. That night I asked my father how to make out a motion for a new trial. He gave me an outline, which I followed as best I could, writing it out on a piece of legal cap, which I got at his office. Next day I presented my motion and demanded a new trial. Judge Wade did not wish to display his ignorance by refusing my demand; so he ruled, "I will grant it this time; but if he does it again, I will have him spanked before you can write out any motion for a new trial."

Most of us lived within a few hundred yards of the schoolhouse, though the Boyd children walked in from their home three miles away in the country and the Carmichael children walked in from their home four miles away. There were three of the Carmichael children, Ozro, Roscoe, and Florine. We boys nicknamed Ozro "Cowmiddlings" and Roscoe "Calfmiddlings."

We were so anxious to get to the school grounds and start playing, that usually the big bell had hardly ceased ringing before the school grounds were crowded with children playing at the various games. Mother Goose would probably have said of us:

> "A dillar a dollar, a ten o'clock scholar,
> What makes you come so late?
> You used to come at ten o'clock,
> And now you come at eight."

The children who walked from any great distance to the school brought their dinners in tin buckets, to eat at the noon recess. It seemed to many of those who lived near by that it was fun to eat from a bucket, in the shade of the oaks—that it was akin to a picnic; so a number of us persuaded our mothers to let us carry our dinners to school in tin buckets. There was much swapping of food among the boys. To each boy the other boys' food seemed better than his own. If one of the boys from the country had some good country sausage and I had none, and I had ginger cakes and he had none, I would swap him a ginger cake for a sausage. My mother had a great reputation for her ginger cakes. They were so popular with the other children that often I would carry nothing but a bucketful of ginger cakes, but by barter I had my choice of whatever the other buckets held. In the fall of the year fresh syrup made from sugar cane, especially ribbon cane, was a delicacy. At that season, I would usually carry a biscuit or two, as well as ginger cakes in my bucket. I would punch a hole in the top of my biscuit and bid for syrup. The syrup was brought in small bottles. One of the boys would pour the hole in my biscuit full of syrup from his bottle and I would give him a ginger cake in exchange.

In the spring there was mayhaw jelly to be bargained for. Even now with my experience with foods greatly broadened from what it was then, I know of no jelly that equals mayhaw jelly. It is made from a haw, of that reddish yellow color that one sees in the pomegranate, hardly as big as the end of one's thumb. The haws grow on small bushes in ponds and ripen in May. This particular species grows in southwest Georgia, in southeast Alabama, and the adjacent parts of northwest Florida, and it may grow elsewhere, but I do not think so. The juice is pressed from the haws, sweetened with sugar, and boiled down till it jellies, which it does without the addition of pectin, if the cooking is properly done. No attempt has ever been made to exploit it commercially, though it is still made for private use, and comparatively few outsiders have ever heard of it. My mother usually made up a supply of it for our home use; otherwise I might have swapped away all my ginger cakes when it appeared in the other school buckets.

We needed no kindergartner to invent plays for us. We just played out of the exuberance of our own spirits and enjoyed ourselves.

The girls played their games, and the boys played theirs. We were too young for matters of sex to trouble our heads. It is true that occasionally on Friday nights, or during vacations, we would have mixed parties at some of our homes, but even then the minds of us boys were more on the refreshments than on the girls.

I remember the time I took Clifford Taylor to a party. I was taught to offer her my left arm; and she put her right arm through the crook of my elbow. We started out at a moderate pace, but both of us were greatly embarrassed by even this much intimacy, and we kept getting faster and faster, until by the time we had arrived at the party we were almost running. Going back it was the same way, except that, when we passed the cemetery, we broke into a trot.

As I have said, my father frequently took me on trips through the county with him from the time I was able to sit on the buggy seat. However, when my brother Dick came along I had to share these trips with him. Out in the country in those days many of the small farmers or tenants had sweep-pole wells.

To make a sweep-pole well, one starts somewhat as one does to make rabbit hash. In the directions for making rabbit hash, the first is "Catch the rabbit"; and in making a sweep-pole well, the first thing to do is to dig the well. Then the parallel ceases; for, in making rabbit hash, the rabbit is thrown away and everything else in the camp is made into the hash, but in making a sweep-pole well, one keeps the well, and adds a curb. A few feet back of the well a post is set firmly in the ground, standing about ten or twelve feet above the surface. A mortise is cut in the top of the post, and an auger hole bored in each of the jaws of it, so that an iron rod or a wooden dowel may be inserted in it to act as an axle for the sweep, which is usually a sapling with a heavy butt. An auger hole is bored through the sapling, and fitted to the axle in the top of the post; the sweep pivots on it; being so arranged that when it is not in use, gravity holds the butt end of it to the ground. At the tip of the sweep, which is so placed as to be over the well, a slender pole, long enough to reach down to the water, is tied to it with a chain or a rope; and to the other end of the pole the bucket, usually the old oaken bucket but sometimes merely a tin pail, is fastened. By pulling on the pole the bucket is lowered into the well and, when it is filled, the sweep, by reason of its greater weight beyond the axle on which it pivots, pulls it up. I haven't seen one in many a day.

I made a trip to Fort Gaines with my father one day and when I got back I boasted to Dick that I had seen two sweep-pole wells. A few days later he went with my father and put it over me by bragging that he had seen "lots of sweep-pole wells and a dominicker deel-doll-dell." His imagination surpassed mine, and to this day he has never told me what a "dominicker-deel-doll-dell" is.

Even in those days before we had reached our teens, it was not all play; at least, not with my father's boys. He was a firm believer in the doctrine that boys should be taught to work. We might go fishing on Saturday afternoons; but on Saturday mornings we had our task of working the garden or sweeping the yard, or something else that had to be finished before we could go fishing.

Before I was ten years old my father bought a piece of land about a mile and a half from town, and in clearing it up a lot of wood was available. On Saturdays and during vacation time my brother Dick and I would haul wood to town and sell it. My father would have the farmhands cut the lightwood into lengths suitable for burning in the fireplaces or stoves. Dick and I would load it on the two-horse wagon, bring it to town, and sell it for fifty cents a load (about half a cord) if we merely dumped it into a back yard or woodpile; but Judge Thomas Williams, who was the local justice of the peace and also a watchmaker, had an office upstairs over Mr. Jim Butler's barroom, and he paid us a dollar a load, including the labor of toting the wood up the stairs. It was thus that we earned our spending money.

It was back in those days that my legal education and my practice of the law began. Starting even before I was six, my father would take me to the justices' courts in the various parts of the county. I would sit for hours listening to what went on, and coming back in the buggy with him, I would ply him with questions as to what I had seen and heard; and he always took the pains to answer me. By the time I was ten years old, he was using me a great deal in his office to do copying and other writing for him. I soon learned some of the simpler matters of pleading and practice. For example, he would turn over a note to me and tell me to sue it in a justice's court. I would make out a summons, attach the note, or a copy of it, to the summons, and mail it or take it to the justice of the peace. When the court day arrived, I would go to the court, usually some six or seven miles out in the country, and ask the justice to enter up judgment. Sometimes the maker of the note would appear and ask that the case be continued. In similar circumstances, I had heard my father tell the magistrate that no one could defend a suit on a promissory note unless he filed a written plea under oath; and I would make the same point. Usually I got my judgment, but if the defendant produced a sworn plea, I would ask for the continuance the law entitled me to, and my father would handle it from then on. This is why, when someone asks me how long I have been practicing law, I answer that I do not know—that I can tell the date of my law license, but that I cannot remember when I was not practicing law.

I would not have anyone think that I was the only one of our set who displayed precocity. Precocity was the rule rather than the exception. Very early in life Will McDowell was a skilled pharmacist. Gus Jones and Tom McDowell were first class bookkeepers and minor business executives when they were in their early teens. Gene Hightower, generally regarded as a little dull, was an excellent railway mail clerk when he was sixteen years old. Gene, one of the Boyd children who used to walk three miles to school, was hardly twenty-one before he served on the grand jury—as foreman as I now recall it. Edgar Paullin, who was a few years younger than I, was born at Fort Gaines, twenty miles from Blakely. Today he is Dr. James Edgar Paullin, the president of the American Medical Association, but at a very early age he had been graduated from Johns Hopkins and had become one of the leading physicians of Atlanta.

6

Old Fitz

W<small>E WERE UNDER</small> P<small>ROFESSOR</small> G<small>RANBERRY UNTIL</small> I <small>WAS ABOUT</small> ten years old; and then came Professor Zeno I. Fitzpatrick. Professor Fitzpatrick ("Old Fitz" we sometimes called him), was as self-assertive as Professor Granberry was self-effacive. Certainly he was not given to assentation; nor was he one of those old schoolteachers who boasted that they taught the "flat or round system [that the world is flat or is round] according to the wishes of the school trustees." He was of Scotch-Irish lineage, tall, robust, and rather handsome, and was in his early thirties. His family was of the former slave-owning aristocracy of middle Georgia. He himself was still a Morgan County landowner. He was land poor, as we say, and taught school to keep up the ancestral holdings. He had been graduated from Mercer University. He was proud and impetuous, nervous and high-strung. In school he sat in an armchair, and when he wished to rap for order or call a class, or to emphasize a reprimand, or even to punctuate what he was saying with a gesture, he would beat down on the arm of the chair with the jaws of a large closed Barlow knife he always carried. He thus beat out such a large hole in the arm of the chair that he had to get another.

Under Professor Granberry we had studied Webster's Blueback Spelling Book, McGuffey's Readers, Smith's English Grammar. I have forgotten whose arithmetic and whose geography we used then. Not only do I remember the Blueback Spelling Book for the fables in the back of it and the McGuffey Reader for the poems we used to recite from it, but I also remember Smith's English Grammar for its technical aspects, especially such statements as: "Grammar is divided into four parts, Orthography, Etymology, Syntax, and Prosody," which four "graces" we boys had renamed "Orthogravy" (with long "o" in the second syllable and long "a" in the third), Etymology (with long "o" in the third syllable, short "o" in the fourth and "g" hard in the last), "Swine-Tax," and "Possum Grease."

Even back in the professorships of Dozier and Granberry we had blackboards—the wall between the front and the back rooms was painted black—and crayons of chalk. We wiped them off with rags, but under Old Fitz we had erasers. We had no scratch paper or pencil pads; we had slates, on which we wrote and figured with slate pencils. Some of the girls had tiny sponges with which they cleaned their slates; we boys merely spat on ours and wiped them off with our hands, or by rubbing them against the seats of our trousers. We did have a few sheets of ruled paper, which we used as copy books to learn to write. The teacher wrote the copy at the head of the sheet and the pupil was supposed to copy it, over and over again, till the bottom of the sheet was reached. Old Fitz introduced store-bought copy books, with the line to be copied stereotyped at the head of the page in Spencerian.

Each room had in it a cast-iron stove, around which teacher and pupils huddled in cold weather. There was a well in the schoolyard, and a pail with a tin dipper (sometimes a gourd) sat on a shelf in the schoolroom. It was the job of us boys to bring wood for the stove and fresh water in the pail.

There were no grades in our school in those days. We were classed into groups and advanced as fast as we seemed able to go. We were no "Quiz Kids"; most of us were just healthy, life-loving boys and girls; and yet, comparing us with the boys and girls of similar ages that I see in the modern graded schools, I think that we were just about as far advanced in true education as they are, and, in many cases, further along.

When Professor Fitzpatrick came, he put us into Swinton's Word Book, Appleton's Readers, Reid and Kellogg's English

Grammar, and Sanford's Arithmetic; and for the boys of my approximate age and advancement, he added Bullion's Latin Grammar. When I was eleven, he put us into Bullion's Greek Grammar. We had geography, I am sure, but somehow I do not remember much about it.

It may seem that a boy of ten is too young to study Latin, and a boy of eleven too young to study Greek. We did not find it so. Perhaps the reason was that Professor Fitzpatrick did not stress formal grammar, but paid more attention to translation and to developing the relation between the Latin and the Greek words and the English words derived from them. It is true that we were taught to decline nouns and adjectives and to conjugate verbs, and we went through the form of parsing what we had translated, but many of the finer points of the grammar, which I have known some other teachers to stress, were neglected.

Tete Hester never could decline the Greek word "kakos," meaning generally bad, and being the root of so many of the "cac" words in the dictionary. He would begin "kakos, kaka, kakon." By the time he got to the genitive case, he was cuckoo, and from then on it was just "cack-cack-cack," till he bent over in a paroxysm of cackling laughter. I got the impression that onomatopoeia was working in reverse when the Greeks acquired their word meaning bad. Kakos should be associated with glee and laughter.

In the three years I was under Professor Fitzpatrick, I translated into English a number of the Latin classics and several of the Greek. I hope that I have retained some of the exactness of thought and speech inherent in the Greek language.

Professor Fitzpatrick taught us to use what is called the English pronunciation of the Latin. After he had been at Blakely for a year or two, he went up to Macon and visited his alma mater, Mercer University. He came back filled with disgust. Professor Manley was teaching the Roman pronunciation. Old Fitz seemed to take it as a personal insult. When he told us of it, as he did with great frequency, his blood would boil; he would almost rave. "The idea of calling Cicero 'Kickaro!' I wish I could kick his roe."

By the time Professor Fitzpatrick came to take charge of the Blakely Academy, the number of pupils had increased to nearly a hundred. It was plain that he would have to have an assistant. He solved the problem by making a trip to Brooks County and bringing back with him as his bride a lovely, well educated South Georgia girl about seventeen years old, Miss Ida Hester, of Hickory Head, near Quitman. The back room of the school was fitted up, and she took charge of the teaching of the younger children. Today she is one of the most prominent and best beloved women in Georgia. Her work among the mountain girls of north Georgia, as head of the Tallulah Falls Industrial School, is second only to that of Miss Martha Berry.

The school grew. The trustees were still Dr. Dostor, Major Jones, and my father. Three good men they were. They worked hard for the school.

Practically all of the pupils now had desks and seats. However, the chair with the cowhide bottom, which I had brought with me when I first came to school, was still there; but the seat was split and the stiff cowhide jutted downward in irregular strips. Florine Carmichael was allowed to use it, though she had to sit on the edge of it to keep from falling through.

The last thing in the afternoon was "Spelling." This was a spelling bee in which several of the classes competed. If a speller missed his word he was sent to the bottom of the class. The boy or the girl who was at the head of the class today, had to go to the foot of the class tomorrow. The game was to see how quickly the one at the foot could make it to the head. It was exciting, so exciting that when the spelling was over, the floor around where I had stood for most of the time often had a pool of water on it; and I was not the only one.

Exciting as it was to the participants, it affected Florine otherwise. One drowsy spring afternoon, right in the middle of the spelling, we heard a crash. Florine, plump and roly-poly, had gone to sleep and had fallen through the chair. She had not fallen through head foremost nor feet foremost, but seat foremost. Nor had she fallen completely through. She hung halfway through in the tentacles of the projecting cowhide. Professor Fitzpatrick ran to extricate her, caught her by the hands and tried to lift her up; but when he pulled, she screamed with pain as the stiff cowhide cut into her flesh. So, as the rest of us roared with laughter, he picked up the chair and shook her through it. It was a breech delivery, her rear middle emerging first, and her head, clamped between her feet, coming out last. This ended the career of the old cowhide-bottomed chair that came to school with me on my first day.

Old Fitz frequently sent some of us boys to the woods back of the schoolhouse to get the switches when some of the other boys were to be flogged. It is interesting to note that we always brought good ones. It seems to be an inborn trait in every normal boy to take delight in seeing one of his fellows get a licking, though he fully realizes that it may be his turn next. Something akin to this must underlie the maxim of experienced criminal lawyers—"Never take a Negro on the jury to try a Negro defendant."

My brother Dick earned under Professor Granberry and maintained under Professor Fitzpatrick the reputation of being the dullest and most mischievous boy in the school. One day when the algebra class was working at the blackboard, Professor Fitzpatrick noticed Dick and Ozro Carmichael ("Cow-middlings") with their heads together. He slipped up behind them and saw that they had tied their big toes together. He went back, got his switch, came up silently behind them again, and began to frail down on their backs. They squalled and they leaped and somehow got to the middle of the floor. Hobbled as they were, they could only dance around each other in their respective attempts to avoid the blows; each striving to throw the other into the line of fire. Professor Fitzpatrick, seeing how amusing these antics were, made no attempt to restrain the laughter with which the rest of us greeted them.

Dull, mischievous Dick Powell had a rebirth, so to speak, when he was about fourteen; he went to Mercer University, was graduated with first honor, and, after some graduate work at the University of Chicago, entered the field of teaching. He recently retired as Dean of the Coordinate College of the University of Georgia. I often use his career as an example to cheer some fond mother in despair for her young son, who wishes to play through, rather than to study through the early years of his school life.

Let it not be held against me at this late day when I confess that, under Old Fitz, for some reason or other, I became "teacher's pet." He dubbed me, "Judge," an appellation that I have worn ever since. It is true that I later earned the title through judicial service, but I first got it from Old Fitz when I was ten or eleven years old.

Very few people have ever called me "Mister," the title I like best of all. During the short while I was at Mercer University, my college mates coined the nickname "Gracie" from my middle name, Gray, but Judge Warren Grice of our Supreme Court is the only one who so calls me now, as far as I know. Especially in the old days and somewhat now, the title of "Colonel" has by common consent attached to the license of every lawyer in Georgia upon his admission to the bar. Thus some people have called me "Colonel Powell," and occasionally I now get a letter so addressed.

On one occasion, a spirit of devilment came very near to getting the "teacher's pet" in bad with the teacher. It was Friday afternoon; and on Friday afternoons we usually had exercises which our parents attended. The older girls would have essays (we called them compositions) on "Poetry," "Music," "Spring," or one of the other seasons; but "Spring" was the favorite; and Clifford Taylor gave us "Poeta Nascitur, Non Fit." The younger girls would recite bits of poetry. We boys would "say speeches": "The Boy Stood on the Burning Deck," "On Linden When the Sun Was Low," "The Burial of Sir John Moore," and so forth; and, occasionally, a translation from one of the classics. Professor Fitzpatrick had a number of speeches on various subjects which he had composed and spoken when he was in college. He usually gave one of these to me to memorize and to speak.

For the particular Friday afternoon in question, he had failed to give me a speech, and I selected one for myself. It was one of those composites much in vogue among the newspapers in those days. One editor would put forth a stanza; some other editor would print this and add a stanza; and so on until the theme would be treated with considerable length and variety. One of these which had progressed to ten or twelve stanzas under the title, "Because She Ain't Built That Way," caught my eye, and I memorized it throughout.

The school trustees and a larger number than usual of other parents were present. Toward the close of the exercises, Old Fitz gave a prideful clearing of his throat and announced: "We will now have something good. I do not recall the theme of the speech Arthur is to say, but I know it will be good"; and, nodding toward me, he added, "Give it to us, Judge."

I took my place upon the platform, made my bow, and began:

> "A girl can sing and a girl can dance,
>   And a girl can attend the play,
>   But she doesn't have hip pockets put in her pants
>   Because she ain't built that way."

At that moment, I cut an eye toward "Old Fitz." Already he had his long finger out, motioning me down. He never sat on the platform, but in the middle of the room. I made a hasty bow and attempted to get off the stage and to the back of the room; but he kept motioning me to him till he got me to a seat near him, when he said, "You remain here after the exercises are over."

Dismissal soon came, and he took his switch and carried me into the back room, which was so high off the ground that the other boys could not peep through the window. He said, "I ought to give you a good whipping. The idea of you shaming me by getting up here in the presence of all these ladies and gentlemen and talking about girls' pants and how they are built. Now I am going to thrash this desk instead of thrashing you, but don't you tell the other boys that it was the desk and not you that got the licking. But, if you ever do such a thing again, you are not going to have any hip pockets in your pants, because I will thrash the whole seat of them off."

To the day of his death, he was my friend, though there were times when his undue praising of me was embarrassing. From Blakely, he went to Albany, the leading city of southwest Georgia, and became principal of the schools there. I learned that I was thoroughly hated by the boys who were under him there, as he was constantly holding me up to them as a model. Many of the boys later became my friends, but they have often told me of the great handicap over which the friendship was attained.

Some time before he died, my old preceptor and friend made his will. He had no children. He willed all his property to his wife, except the old Morgan County plantation. This he willed to his wife for life, with remainder, after her death, to me and my wife as a token of esteem and affection for us. Neither Mrs. Fitzpatrick nor we got the plantation; for the expenses incurred in the illnesses of his later years were such as to make it necessary to sell it to pay his creditors. We did not get the land he devised us, but the love he bequeathed us will ever be more precious than the land; and this legacy is beyond the reach of any creditor, and beyond the power of the law to adeem.

7

Roman Candles

OUR PEOPLE WERE A HARD-WORKING PEOPLE. WE TOOK FEW holidays, but Christmas we did celebrate. Its holiday season extended from Christmas Eve until after New Year. Even before the season itself arrived, we children and the Negroes were full of excitement and expectation. Toys and other Christmas goods began to appear in the stores. On the streets and on the porches of the stores, stands were set up in advance of Christmas and kept open until New Year for the sale of fireworks—firecrackers, cannon crackers, skyrockets, and Roman candles. Oranges, big red apples, and bananas were not in our market all the year round as they are now; but they were there at Christmas.

Of course, we children hung our stockings by the hearth on the night before Christmas and went to bed, all full of excitement, early after supper. We were awake on Christmas morning at the first streak of dawn. I cannot believe that present-day children, to whom fruits and candy are no novelty at any season of the year, can possibly feel the thrill that we experienced when we saw at the top of our stockings a big yellow orange, flanked by sticks of striped peppermint candy. We had hardly emptied our stockings and taken the count of the presents in them, when the voices of the Negro servants crying out "Christmas gif' " rang through the house. All got something.

In addition to the fruits, we also had nuts at Christmas— almonds, English walnuts, Brazil nuts, and cocoanuts, besides the pecans, the walnuts, the hickory nuts, and the peanuts which we raised at home or found in the woods. Everyone called the Brazil nuts "nigger-toes."

We did not celebrate Fourth of July in those days, but celebrated Christmas with fireworks as if it were the Fourth of July. A few could not wait until Christmas day to begin shooting them, but Christmas day and the ensuing night was the real time for them. Kept somewhere throughout the year, I do not remember where, nor do I know the history of them, were two small cannons, about a foot long and a little over an inch in diameter. On Christmas morning they were placed upon the Square, and all day long they were fired—just to make a noise, I suppose.

Down at Colquitt one Christmas the boys—I could call their names, but since some are dead and others are now dignified old gentlemen, I will refrain from doing so—included a gentle old mule as a part of the paraphernalia of their fireworks display. The old mule was browsing around on the dry herbage of a pasture just off the courthouse square. He let the boys tie to his tail a twenty-ball Roman candle and light it. He paid no attention to it as long as it was merely spewing, but when the first ball blew out with an explosive sound, he gave a leap, threw his tail into the air, and ran to the other side of the pasture, where he unconcernedly began his browsing again. "Pop," another ball went out, and back to the other side of the pasture went the mule, waving his tail as before, and then starting again to browse; and so on till the last ball was discharged. Spectators gathered, other Roman candles were provided, and the performance continued for some time. The old mule, instead of being pestered or really frightened, seemed to enjoy it.

None of us ever saw Santa Claus, though we often tried to keep awake on Christmas Eve to get a glimpse of him, but we had no intention of offending him by letting him know that we had seen him; none of us ever saw him in the flesh, though we had seen pictures of him as we had seen pictures of Jesus, with whom he stood in somewhat similar position in our minds. In our day, he did not stand with long white beard, bulging paunch, and false face on the street corners or in the stores and talk to little boys and girls. We did not expect any such familiarity from him; and I think that our respect for him was thereby increased.

On the afternoon of Christmas day, the young men and the young women of the town would "ride fantastic." They would array themselves in grotesque garb, put on one of those comical papier-mâché masks, which we called "door-faces," and, in groups, would ride on horseback around the streets, coming through the Square from time to time at a wild gallop, singing and shouting.

In the homes, usually at about eleven o'clock on Christmas morning, eggnog would be served. Friends were expected to make their calls at about that hour. Even the children had a little of the nog, considerably weakened from the original, of course. So universal was this practice that eggs which usually sold at from five to ten cents a dozen, rose to from thirty to fifty cents a dozen just before Christmas.

Then there were the Christmas trees—not in the homes as now, but as community affairs. Sometimes separately, but often jointly, the Methodist and Baptist Sunday Schools would have their Christmas trees, sometimes in the churches, oftener in the courthouse, and occasionally in Howard's Hall. These exercises were held on some night between Christmas and New Year. The young men and boys would go to the woods and select a cedar or a large holly. All the morning would be taken in erecting the tree and decorating it. In the afternoon the presents would be brought in, and early that evening the candles would be lighted, and presents for the people young and old would be "called off," usually by someone selected because of his ability to make jocular remarks. Every girl above fourteen years of age expected one or more presents from her boy friend or friends, but always giggled excitedly when her name was called out, as if she were not expecting it. Likewise every boy expected to get one or more presents from his girl or girls. A favorite present from a girl to a boy was a mouchoir case—a case for the boy to hang in his room to keep his handkerchiefs in. It looked as if it were made by taking two of those false shirt bosoms occasionally seen in the past, sometimes called dickeys, and fastening them back to back, with the top left open and decorated with ribbons.

Every child had to have a present, and often things which Santa Claus had brought on Christmas eve did service again at the Christmas tree—usually to the same recipient.

Frugal as we were, and had to be, at other times of the year, we all splurged a little at Christmas. Our chief feast of the year was the Christmas dinner, served at midday. There was an absence of some of the "fixings" one might expect nowadays, such as celery, olives, sauces, and ice cream, but in most homes there were the big fat turkey, the brandied peaches, and the fruitcake; and in some there would be venison; perhaps also a hunk of bear meat. Game was still plentiful in those days.

In the summertime there would be Sunday School picnics and the "all-day sings"—minor festivals as compared with Christmas but pretty good. For our picnics we liked to go to the woods. to some place where there was a good spring of water and a branch running off for the children to wade in. On the day before, the carpenters would go to the place selected and build a long deal table for the food. No seats were provided at the table, but rough benches would be made and placed under the trees. We would begin to arrive at the picnic grounds at about ten o'clock in the morning; and our parents brought with them the baskets of food. At noon this food would be spread on the table —fried chicken, baked chicken, chicken pie, baked country hams, perhaps a leg of mutton or barbecued goat, which we called "kid," potato salad, chicken salad, salmon salad, hard boiled eggs, home-cooked loaves of bread, biscuit, tea cakes, ginger cakes, jams and jellies, dried-apple pies, peach pies, custard pies, pound cake, angel-food cake, devil's-food cake, sponge cake, and layer cakes of various kinds. There would be a barrelful of lemonade. All was free to everyone. When the blessing had been asked, the food spread on the tables was no longer the personal possession of the one who brought it. Everyone ate what he liked wherever he found it.

After all had eaten as much as they wanted, the fragments and the plates and dishes were put back into the baskets; the children played games, the old folks looked on benevolently, and late in the afternoon we went back to our respective homes; and for a week or ten days thereafter we kept busy scratching redbugs.

The all-day sings were themselves a form of picnic, except that the food, instead of being shared in common, was eaten by the ones who brought it or their invited guests, and instead of being held in the woods, they were usually held at a country church or schoolhouse. The leader, with tuning-fork in hand, stood prominently to the front. The system of singing was, I presume, the diatonic, with the use of what the dictionary calls the sol-fa syllables; but we never heard it called by any name like that. We called it "do-ra-me" or "fa-so-la" singing.

The leader would announce the song, catch the key from the tuning fork, and lead off, carrying the tune, and the rest of us followed, whether we could sing or not. We all knew the words of the good old songs they sang: "Sweet Bye and Bye," "All Hail the Power of Jesus' Name," "Hold the Fort for I am Coming"—the church songs, the Sunday School songs, and, if the sing was not held on Sunday, such secular songs as "Sweet Alice, Ben Bolt," "Maggie," "Old Black Joe," and "Suwanee River."

If a larger crowd was expected than the church or schoolhouse could accommodate, seats on the outside would be improvised by placing, in front of the building, pine logs cut for the saw mills or for rafting down the river, and laying planks from one log to another. I remember being at a sing one day when the seats were thus provided, and the planks extended beyond the logs. A country swain came along, gallanting his sweetheart, who was a tiny, slender girl, weighing not over ninety pounds. He decided that there was room enough on the plank where it extended beyond the log for him and the girl to sit. As he motioned her to the seat, Mr. E. Hilton, one of our prominent citizens, who weighed over two hundred pounds, had climbed over the log and was getting ready to sit in the middle of the same plank; indeed Mr. Hilton and the girl sat down at the same moment; and the swain had the experience of seeing his sweetheart catapulted four or five feet into the air and of catching her as she came down. Mr. Hilton did not see it at all and did not know why the people around him were laughing.

We were not wholly without other public entertainment. Occasionally a magic-lantern show would come along; or some public entertainer would give an exhibition. (Irvin Cobb did not visit us, but if he had done so, it would have been an entertainment of the kind of which I am speaking. We did have Willoughby Reed, Charley Lane, and others not so famous as Cobb, but pretty well known in their day.)

It is the patent-medicine shows that stand out clearest in my memory. One of them, the "Kickapoo Indian Show," presided over by a fakir who called himself "Doctor" and who sold "Sagwa Indian Tonic," and "Kickapoo Indian Salve," stayed about two weeks and held performances twice a day, afternoon and evening, on a stage built on the Square. The Doctor had with him two Indians—at least the fakir said they were Kickapoo Indians—all dressed up in Indian clothes and feathers, who performed war dances and other antics to music, which he provided on a banjo. The Doctor joined with the Indians in singing the Indian songs. He was also a ventriloquist, and had a dummy named "John Watt." John could not only sing and carry on conversations with the Doctor, but he was a great speller. The Doctor would give out "huckleberry pie," and John would spell "h-u-huckle; b-u-buckle; h-u-huckle; h-y-high; h-u-huckle; b-u-buckle; h-u-huckleberry pie."

Circuses came occasionally. I need not describe them; for whoever has seen one circus has seen all circuses; and everybody has seen a circus. The coming of the circuses was not favored by our merchants because they took considerable money out of the community.

Speaking of money, I am reminded that in those days nearly all our money was either gold or silver coin. There was some paper money, but no bills of less than five dollars in circulation. We had silver dollars, half-dollars, quarters, dimes, and half-dimes. There were some nickels, and a nickel three-cent piece was seen occasionally; but pennies and other copper money were not in general use. There were twenty-dollar, ten-dollar, five-dollar, two-and-a-half dollar, and one-dollar gold pieces in circulation, though those who were able to own them tended to hoard them.

There was not much money among us in those days. Farming and other occupations were carried on almost wholly on credit. In the stores, articles carried two prices—the cash price and the credit price; and the credit price was usually twenty-five per cent above the cash price. Accounts were paid in the fall when the crops, chiefly the cotton crops, were harvested. The maximum legal rate of interest was eight per cent, but no one could borrow money locally at that rate. Even the banks, after they came, charged a minimum of one per cent per month.

When John Wade was cashier of the Bank of Blakely, he went to one of the school exhibitions. The teacher gave out to the pupils the problem of calculating the interest on three hundred dollars for one year, one month, and ten days at six per cent. John immediately protested that there was no such rate of interest as six per cent, that the rate was one per cent. He calculated by the month; and fractions of a month counted as a whole month. Private lenders charged higher rates than that— two and three per cent per month. I have often paid one per cent per month and was glad to get the money at that rate.

Many look upon usury with odium, and yet, in those times after the War, usury was the salvation of many of us in the South. That slow but steady advancement we made in the seventies and eighties—and perhaps later—would not have been possible if we could not have obtained some financial aid beyond our own resources. There were but few among us who had collateral. The merchant who advanced money or supplies to a farmer to make a crop took practically all the risk. Farming is always a gamble against the weather, against storms, floods, and droughts, and unless the farmers made the crops, they could not pay the merchants. The proof of the pudding is in the number of merchants who went broke through the furnishing of farm supplies never paid for. We were poor, and there are doubtless many who would consider us underprivileged, but we did not have spastic colons. Our troubled world today sometimes seems to have a spastic colon.

I have mentioned that I was born in the tallow-candle days. However, it was not long until kerosene and gasoline (which we called naphtha) superseded the candles, and lamps and lamp chimneys took the place of the candlesticks. When I was twelve to fourteen years old, the municipal authorities decided to light the streets. Lampposts were erected on the Square and on street corners throughout the town and were fitted with gasoline lamps that burned with a flare. I remember Tom Jones, the lamplighter, who late every afternoon went from post to post to fill and light the lamps and went again early next morning to turn them off. It made us feel progressive to have a public lamplighter.

The street lamps were not very reliable; occasionally they went out of their own accord. I recall that one night about midnight I had gone across the Baptist Branch to take one of the Odum girls home from a party and was returning, when I came to the cemetery. There was a road around it, but there was a path through it. I decided to use the path—it afforded a short cut, and the street lamp at the cemetery gate was burning. Just as I got in the middle of the graveyard, that lamp began to flicker. I do not like for the light to flicker when I am in a graveyard. And then it died down entirely and left the ghosts to darkness and to me.

Outside of things spiritual and excepting ghosts and other superstitions in which we faintly believed in a subconscious and inherited way, we boys and girls took but little stock in the supernatural. I did once have the supernatural experience of being suspended in space. I was doing some surveying with an old-style surveyor's compass, supported on a jackstaff—a rod with a steel-shod pointed end to stick into the ground, and with a joint fitted to the top to hold the compass. I was standing in a small clump of oak runners sticking the staff into the ground, when I felt something striking against the leg of my trousers. Thinking it was a twig, I paid no attention to it, until I happened to look down and see that I was standing on a ground rattler and that with his head, which was free, he was attempting to bite me. I jumped straight up into the air, and it seemed to me that I remained suspended for at least five minutes, and even now after all my ratiocination on the subject, I cannot bring my mind to think of it as being less than thirty long seconds. As I came down, the snake was moving off in one direction, and, as I hit the ground, I was making good time in the other.

8

Old-Time Printing Office

SCHOOL KEPT ONLY ABOUT THIRTY WEEKS A YEAR, BUT THE REST of the time was not spent in idleness. When I was about ten years old, I became printer's devil in my Uncle Fleming's printing office, where the Early County News was published and general job work was done. I washed the forms, rolled the old Washington hand press, worked the job press, and set pi at first. Later I became pretty expert at setting and distributing type, and even in setting display ads for the newspaper or matter for the job press.

The Early County News was established in 1868 and is still one of the leading county weeklies in Georgia. Then it was a little four-page, seven-columned sheet. It is much larger now. Throughout all the years I have known it, it has been run by members of the Fleming family, and has carried at its masthead this slogan, "Success to all who pay their honest debts—Be sure you are right; then go ahead." For a short time Dr. T. M. Howard owned it, but most of the editing was done by his wife, who was Judge Fleming's daughter.

The old printing office was always an interesting place to me. In the small front room was the "sanctum of ye editor"; the printing was done in the larger back room. There were the racks on which the fonts of type were placed. For the ordinary printing of the paper there were fonts of pica, long primer, bourgeois, and nonpareil, with bold face, small caps, and italics in all these sizes. We did not call them 12-point, 10-point, 9-point, and 6-point, as they are now called. Other fonts held the types of various sizes and faces needed in display advertisements and job printing. All typesetting was done by hand. The typesetting machine was not installed there until the early part of the present century.

There were racks of galleys. The type was first set into the stick and then emptied into the galleys, which, when full, held about enough to make a column. Then there was the big table with the heavy stone top on which the forms were made up for printing.

On this were the chases, the quoins, the rules, and other apparatus used in making up the forms and holding the type secure for printing.

Then there was the old Washington hand press. The chases, with the type in them, were laid on the bed of the press. Extending out obliquely above it was the tympan, on which the sheet to be printed was placed, and over this the frisket was folded to hold it in place and to keep the ink, except that on the faces of the type, from smearing the paper. The tympan and the frisket were then folded down upon the type on the bed of the press. A roller pulley then drew the bed with the type on it under the press. The strong-armed pressman then pulled the press handle which controlled the knee-joint, or toggle-joint lever, and this sent type and paper together under controlled pressure. Back the press bed was rolled, the tympan and frisket raised, and the printed sheet removed.

While the printed sheet was being taken off, the printer's devil, standing behind the press, rolled the forms with the inked cylinder, which was furnished with printer's ink by being rolled back and forth upon two other cylinders upon which the ink was spread from time to time.

Thus it went on until one side of the paper was printed and then the other.

When the printing was done, the forms were taken to a rectangular vat of lye which sat just outside the back door and thoroughly washed and scrubbed with coarse brushes. As this was the job of the printer's devil, and as none of the hand lotions which nowadays are so lustily advertised over the radio were then in use, a printer's devil could usually be identified by the condition of his hands. On a nail at the back door hung the office towel—the old printing office towel, the brunt of many a joke in the country newspapers in those days. It was made of some heavy, close-woven material—possibly duck—originally white but soon a dark dull gray, nearly black. On it the printer's devil wiped his hands after washing them as best he could to remove the ink accumulated in rolling forms and in washing them. The old towel was washed, but the smudges never came out.

I have mentioned only those things which stood out prominently in the old printing office. There were hundreds of others. One may look upon the little old county weekly newspaper and call it paltry, but it took many detailed operations and much labor to produce it. Nowadays the Early County News office is equipped with powered machines which set the type and roll the forms and do the press work, and great saving in time and in labor results; but I do not begrudge the time or the labor I put into the work there in the old days.

My job in the Early County News office was my first steady pay job—five dollars a month, not including board and lodging. We began work at seven o'clock in the morning and worked as long as necessary. On the publication day, Thursday, we often worked all night to get the papers in the mail in time to catch the star routes which went out at about six o'clock in the morning.

These were among the most enjoyable days of my life. We looked forward with pleasure to the Thursday nights, to the hustle and bustle of getting the paper out, and to the feasts we would have along about midnight, when we would stop to eat canned salmon and sardines with soda crackers and with vinegar or pepper sauce.

After a short apprenticeship, I was required not only to set up in type what others had written but also to compose and set up local items, such as, "Misses Mattie and Clifford Hightower, two charming young belles of Damascus, are visiting their cousin, Miss Mary Ashley Hightower, in Blakely this week."

And here is a society note which I did not write. At Colquitt, in Miller County, twenty miles south of Blakely, a widow, Mrs. Zula B. Cook, established and edited the "Miller County Liberal." In course of time she married Mr. Joe Toole, and had the privilege of writing up her own wedding. She wrote as impersonally as if she had no interest in the affair until she got to the end of the column, and then concluded, "The bride, who was ye scribe, though not very pretty was very happy."

Uncle Fleming knew the rules of English grammar and of English composition. He knew how to frame a sentence and how to punctuate. He inculcated these rules into us; and woe to the one who violated them. He considered the usual, ordinary, and orderly printer's methods then in use as quite adequate to express every form and mood of thought. I am sure that if he were living now he would look down his nose at some of the modern writers for the typographical devices and abuses of punctuation they use to attract attention, to claim a novelty, or to express a mood—such as the overuse of small capitals or all capitals, the discarding of initial capitals, weird paragraphing, inverted interrogation and exclamation marks, and even one-legged parentheses.

Jeff and Will Fleming were enthusiastic amateur baseball players, and the local items in the Early County News were then and still are carried under the title "Short Stops." It was not long before I had progressed beyond being a short-stop writer to being a reportorial and editorial writer. I do not mean that all this progress came immediately; for, in addition to the few months I worked regularly as printer's devil at five dollars a month, I kept up my contact with the printing office and worked sporadically there throughout most of my teens.

I conducted, for a while, under the pseudonym "Sol Eli," a column which carried the headline "Guess Who?" It was juvenile and personal. For example, "Guess who sent his best girl two large watermelons last Saturday, and when he called to see her that night, found her too sick from eating them to see him?"

Along in my middle teens, the paper put on a campaign to get the city council to clean up the cemetery. We succeeded to the extent of getting them to whitewash the board fence which enclosed it. The next week, under the pseudonym "Sol Eli," I wrote a special article about a citizen who happened to be passing the cemetery about midnight and saw two spooky figures on the cemetery fence and heard their conversation. It ran about this way: Said Ghost One to Ghost Two, "My friend, what is that I see on thy shroud-tail?" The shroud-tail was examined. "It is whitewash! They have whitewashed the fence! The weeds and grass still grow rampant over our graves; but they have white-washed our fence!"

As the conversation progressed, the two ghosts condoled with each other over the fact that, despite the great display of grief with which friends and relatives brought them out there and laid them in their graves and erected monuments with lovely epitaphs above them, they soon forgot the dead and let the grass and weeds cover them over. In the course of the conversation, I had one ghost say to the other, "Why do you suppose the boys all laugh when they look over the fence and read the sentiment my widow put on my monument?"

"No, what is the sentiment?"

"Gone to his just reward."

I have sampled the article enough to give the tenor of it. Reactions were immediate.

First, as Bird DuBose, who had been given the job of setting it in type, put the final stick of it into the galley, he turned to the other boys in the office and said, "You know, I believe this is all a damned lie."

Next, the widows came into action. They said the article was disgraceful—that the use of the word "shroud-tail" was sacrilegious.

Third, the city council put men to work and cleared the cemetery of the grass and weeds and made many other improvements.

On another occasion I wrote a fanciful article stating that a few days before, about nine miles west of Blakely, a party of gentlemen came upon a large stream of a very useful substance known to the scientific world as "protoxide of hydrogen." I went on to extol this valuable substance saying that when properly applied it stimulated the growth of crops and flowers; that beef cattle could be increased in weight by the liberal use of it; that it was often used as the base of many beverages; that it was absolutely indispensable to navigation, and so on.

The next morning after the article appeared, the local banker (for by that time we had a small bank in Blakely) came to Will Fleming and asked for details. Will referred him to me. The banker took me into the back room and told me that we should not let the Yankee capitalists exploit so valuable a find; that, if it could be proved to be as valuable as I said it was, he would finance a local syndicate to buy it up and would let me in on the ground floor. I tried to hold a straight face when I told him that "protoxide of hydrogen" is another name for water, and that the stream of it nine miles west of Blakely is the Chattahoochee River.

As early as I can remember, there were many well-bred game chickens in southwest Georgia. Fred Grist, at Fort Gaines, was a gamecock breeder with an international reputation. Jeff Fleming stayed a year or two in Fort Gaines with Mr. Grist, and came back to Blakely and also achieved a wide reputation along the same line. There were professional cockfights held in our section during my boyhood but I never attended any of the mains. About the time I was sixteen years old the legislature outlawed cockfighting in Georgia.

Jeff Fleming shipped many cocks to mains held in other States and in Mexico. I frequently was with him when he was preparing the cocks for shipment. Every one was gone over carefully to see that he was in prime physical condition; the spurs were sawed down to where the gaffs or slashers could be securely fastened upon them. Occasionally with their spurs thus shortened, a pair of them would be tried out to see if they were game. They usually were, and had to be separated before they did each other harm. A gamecock is always ready for a fight to the death.

Jeff printed and published at the office of the Early County News, under the title of "Southern Pit Games," a monthly magazine devoted to gamecocks and cockfighting. It had a circulation all over the United States, and some copies went to France and Mexico.

One morning Jeff came to me in distress. He showed me a ten- or fifteen-line Associated Press dispatch in one of the daily papers, telling of a cockfight in one of the lower Mexican states, which had broken up in a general melee among the Señors and their retainers. "I am in a fix," Jeff said. "I knew that main was to take place; in fact, I shipped some cocks there to participate in it. I intended to ask a friend at San Antonio to go down there and send me an account of it, but I just forgot all about it. It is too late now for me to get it before I go to press, and my subscribers are going to wonder why I didn't get it."

I asked him how much he wanted, and he said about a column and a half. I suggested that I would try my hand on it. I had been in Mexico shortly before; I knew that the Mexicans attached slashers, which were knifelike blades, to the spurs of the cocks when they pitted them, instead of the awl-like gaffs used in the States; I knew something of the geography of the place where the fight occurred; and the news item gave certain names. For the rest, I drew on my imagination. I described the setting of the main with the mountains rising high around it. I described, in general language, the haciendas in the valley. I described the colorful scene when the Señors arrived with their retainers; described the serapes the men wore and the gay-colored mantillas worn by the women, who also came along. I pictured the cocks, the pit, the slashers, the fight of the cocks, the quarrel, which I said was over some trifling detail, and the fight.

I turned in my column and a half, and Jeff printed it. Within the next few days he got several letters from persons who had attended the fight congratulating him upon the scoop he had made and upon the accuracy of his report of what had occurred. I still do not believe all I see in the newspapers!

Boys and Girls Together

I WAS ABOUT THIRTEEN YEARS OLD WHEN OLIVER BUSH CAME UP from Colquitt and entered our school. In the spring, he invited me to go down one Friday afternoon and spend the weekend with him, and I went.

Miller was then known as the "outfightingest" county in Georgia. I still have in my scalp the scars of the wound I received in an affray in court there several years later, but I will not tell about that now.

Oliver and I had just gone to bed on my first night there, when I was awakened by the firing of pistols and the screams of a woman, crying, "Oh, Miss Chloe! Oh, Miss Chloe!"

Oliver didn't seem to pay much attention to it, so I shook him and asked, "What's that?"

"Oh, nothing," he replied. "Just a bunch of fellows teasing Mrs. Hunter's cook."

Further inquiry developed that the teasing consisted of firing pistols into the air above the roof of the cabin in which the Negro woman cook slept, just behind the Hunter Hotel fronting on the courthouse square.

The next day Oliver and I were walking around the town and came to the opposite corner of the Square, where we started down the side street. A side yard came down to the street. I looked into it; and for the first time in my life, I looked twice at a girl.

Up till then, girls had just been objects or things not worthy of much notice. It is true that I would give one look (but not two) at the Fryer twins, Lilian and Lena; but that was because they looked so much alike and not because, as I later observed, they were very pretty girls.

But this girl in the side yard at Colquitt was different. She was about eleven years old. She was barefooted. She was feeding the chickens from a pan of dough. I knew as soon as I laid eyes on her that she was the prettiest, sweetest-looking girl I had ever seen. She had brown hair, hazel eyes, a slender boyish figure; and there was something about her that made me think of the princesses I had read about in the story books. I saw all that at the first look—the look which made my heart start beating faster.

In bashfulness I looked the other way, but when I turned my eyes toward her again, intending to take only a peep and not a look, I saw something that made me take the second look. A big red rooster was trying to take the dough away from her; and she was fighting him off. Every instinct of chivalry within me commanded me to leap the fence and go to the rescue, but I suddenly remembered that I had on my new blue suit and I was afraid the rooster might spoil it. That was the fear I admitted to myself. The real fear was that I was afraid of the girl. She solved the problem by running into the house, but I took a vision back to Blakely with me. Later I asked Oliver who she was. He said, "Her name is Annie Wilkin."

I then recalled that a year or so before a young man named Eager Wilkin, the son of Dr. Wilkin, of Colquitt, had come up to Blakely and had been coached by Professor Fitzpatrick in preparation for his entering medical college in Baltimore; so I inferred that Eager was her brother and Dr. Wilkin her father, which proved to be correct.

When the next fall session of our school opened, Dr. Wilkin brought Annie up and entered her as a pupil. She was shy and timid, especially so at first, but the boys and girls welcomed her; indeed, all took special pains to be nice to her because we learned that her mother had died only a few months before.

Some of the other boys began to make up to her, but I claimed her as my girl by right of prior discovery. This was made easy by the fact that she boarded with a relative of hers,

Mrs. Stewart, whose granddaughter, Berta Smith, also lived with her. Will McDowell (Will Mc., we called him), though a little older than I, was my boon companion in those days, and Berta was Will Mc's girl. So "Little Annie," as Old Fitz called her, became my first sweetheart.

I was too bashful to go to the Stewart home at first, but since they lived at the edge of the town, in the direction of my father's farm, I soon acquired a new interest in the farm and found myself making frequent occasions to go out there in the afternoons after school. Usually, Berta, Annie, and Berta's unmarried aunt, Miss Leila Stewart, would be sitting on the porch. I always made an awkward bow to them as I went by, and then broke into a run as soon as I was out of sight.

One Friday night Will Mc. was going to call on Berta, and he persuaded me to make an engagement to call on Annie at the same time. The note asking for the engagement was penned with effort, was carefully folded with the corner turned down, and was sent by a Negro boy. It read, in the stilted style then prevailing:

> "Mr. Arthur Powell presents his compliments to Miss Annie Wilkin, and requests the pleasure of calling on her this evening."

Her reply was equally prim and formal.

Will Mc. and I would have been glad to take candy with us, but the total cash of both of us was not enough for that. We did have a dime between us; and so we decided to take fruit. We bought four bananas. He took two and I took two. We put them in our pockets. I put mine in my hip pockets.

The girls received us in the parlor. After the ice was broken and the initial embarrassment had subsided, I suggested to Annie that the night was warm and the full moon was shining, and that it might be well if we let Will Mc. and Berta have the parlor to themselves by our going out on the porch. We went out and sat on the banisters. This was the critical moment at which I had planned to present the fruit. I reached back to my hip pockets to get the bananas. Oh, tragedy of tragedies! I had been sitting on them, and they were mashed into a pulp. The presentation of the goodwill offering died a-borning. It was a few years later before Annie found out why Berta got a banana that night and she did not.

At first, we were more or less disturbed to find that Annie's father, Dr. Wilkin, was a New York Yankee, but this was made all right a little later when we learned that he had come South before the War and had served as a surgeon in the Confederate Army; that when he married Annie's mother, she was a widow of a Confederate soldier, with four small children, her former husband, Mr. Fudge, having been killed in the early months of the war.

It also raised Annie's standing somewhat when we learned that, though she came from the backwoods town of Colquitt, she had a sister Nellie who had been graduated at Wesleyan College. Very few of our young ladies were able to go to college in those days.

Sex life had not come to any of the boys of my set at the period of which I have been speaking, except in that crepuscular way in which the dim streakings of dawn portend the coming of day. Not only sex but all the overtones of sex were mysteries to us. With us sex was budding, but not yet in bloom. We were passing from the age at which boys write gross words upon school walls or plank fences, not because they know what they are writing about, but because they know it is something bad, and it affords an outlet for the spirit of devilment that possesses them.

I may say in passing that I do not believe there ever existed anywhere finer relations among boys and girls than in the set I was brought up with at Blakely. I do not mean to say that none of our boys ever put his arm around a girl, or kissed one of them; but I do mean to say we never made a habit of it. Even in those days, in some places, considerable "lallygagging" and "gum-sucking," as it was called, went on; but that was not generally true at Blakely when I was a boy.

This honoring of the person of our girls may have been due in part to a spirit of chivalry, but there was another reason why our boys were not roues. For the most part our girls did not lead us on. I have observed that in the affairs of sex-life, both sanctioned and unsanctioned, courtships, meretricious affairs or mere "petting," the female of the species is the aggressor, usually an artful aggressor.

If a stranger to the ways of this world, say a visitor from Mars, were to come upon a fisherman just after he had cast out the lure when the bass was attacking it, he would get the impression that the fish was the aggressor. I have no doubt that the bass thinks he is the aggressor, even after the hook is in his jaw and the reel is gradually leading him in. So, when a girl, young or old, desires to catch a man as husband or lover, she throws out the lure carefully so as not to frighten the intended victim; he grabs it, and from then on he thinks he is the aggressor; thinks he is having such a big time wrestling with the bait, tugging against the pulling of the line, rushing back and forth, leaping into the air, and doing everything that a poor fish does; but all the time it is the girl, who, unnoticed by him, is winding the reel.

Another reason occurs to me why our boys and girls behaved themselves as well as they did. Fathers and brothers had horse whips and shotguns which they did not hesitate to use in the preservation of the chastity of the female members of their household. This is a matter as to which we Southerners are accused of being hair-trigger; and maybe we are. A few years ago I was attending the American Law Institute in Washington. The work of the Institute is the restatement of the law, in an attempt to get a reconciliation and a uniformity among the decisions of the various highest courts of the country upon general principles of the law. The reporters had presented their draft of the restatement on the subject of alienation of affections and crim. con., to use the technical phrase. An eminent jurist, one of the Justices of the Supreme Court of Massachusetts, earnestly objected to the inclusion of a restatement of the law on these subjects into the work we were doing. Said he, "Suits of this kind have no place in our jurisprudence. Usually they are instrumentalities of blackmail. We have abolished them in Massachusetts," and so on.

The reporter explained that while Massachusetts and a few other States had abolished such suits, some forty-odd other States had not, and that there was a considerable volume of law on the subject. The distinguished Judge still protested, but he was voted down.

That afternoon, I met the Judge at one of George Morris's famous cocktail parties in the garden of his home on Kalorama Road. He immediately asked me if I had heard his remarks that morning. I told him that I had. He then asked what I thought of them. I told him that while I presumed that the actions against which his remarks were directed still exist in a theoretical way in Georgia, since it is a common-law State, we have another statute, as a result of which they are practically abolished. He inquired as to the statute. I told him that it is a code section which provides that causes of action of that nature abate with the death of the defendant.

"Yes," he replied, "but you Southerners are more given to homicide than we are in our part of the country."

"Why, certainly," I responded. "And you must realize that the free use of homicide is a *sine qua non* in every effective civilization."

"What!"

"Yes," I continued, "and that is why the civilization of the South is so much more virile and effective and so much more universally highly thought of than the effete civilization of Boston and the East."

He shut his eyes and fled to keep from having a stroke.

The next year, we met at George Morris's again, and to the party around us, I related the incident, and added, "I had just enough cocktails in me to play a prank of that kind on him."

"And," he broke in, "I had just enough cocktails in me not to see that you were playing the prank; but that night on the sleeping car it dawned on me that you were spoofing me."

While I did say it in a spirit of persiflage, still there is more food for thought in what I said than there is in most mere cocktail talk.

10

Busy Youth

I WAS UNDER PROFESSOR FITZPATRICK FROM THE TIME I WAS
ten until just before I was fourteen. During this time, besides
going to school, working in the printing office and in my father's
office, and going to justice's courts, I finished my education,
without diploma or degree, in agriculture. There was a clearing
on the tract of land I have mentioned as having been bought by
my father, about a mile and a half from town. He decided to
clear up more land; and then I became a farm hand.

Have you ever hauled fence rails in a wagon pulled by an ox?
I have; and that ox was named "Snip," and he was the biggest ox
I ever saw; and my father believed the bigger the rails, the better
the fence; and the rails I hauled on that one-ox wagon were
almost large enough to be called logs; and there was a cypress
pond on the place, and when Snip got hot he would make a
break for the pond and roll over in it; and, often as not, he rolled
me and the rails into the pond with him.

Have you ever chopped oak runners in new ground with a
light hoe? I have; and the hoe would spring back from the tough
fibers of the oak runners and would stretch and sprain every
muscle in my body; and I would go home at night so tired and
so sore I could not stay awake because of the tiredness and yet
could not sleep because of the soreness.

Have you ever plowed new ground, or pulled fodder in
July, or picked cotton in the fall? Have you ever made cane
syrup on an open evaporator? I have; and when the cane juice
began to boil and the sugar-laden steam began to rise and it was
necessary to ladle fast and to keep the foam-skimmer working

furiously, I found myself full of goo. "Goo" sounds just the way goo feels when it gets into your clothing, your hair, your eyebrows, all over your skin; and you feel it, smell it and taste it; and you can wash yourself and scrub yourself, and for a week later you still feel it, smell it and taste it.

I escaped at the first opportunity, and I have never had any desire to go back to the farm.

A few days after the school closed in the summer just before I was fifteen years old, Major Jones, the county school commissioner, asked me to come to his office and stand a special examination. I did so; and he gave me a second-grade teacher's license and told me that he had appointed me as assistant principal of the school at Urquhart's, five miles north of Blakely, at a salary of five dollars a week. I taught there from early June until the last of August. Many of the boys and girls I taught were older than I was.

I boarded at the excellent country home of Mr. Henry Hayes, and paid one dollar a week board. So I saved some money that summer. It was there that I learned again not to believe all I see in a newspaper. Mr. Hayes had some beehives. I saw in the paper an item stating that if you held your breath a bee could not sting you. I tried it. The statement was not true.

On my fifteenth birthday, Mr. Jim Alexander, the clerk of the superior court, offered me a place in his office, at one dollar a day. Principally, I was to do copying (by hand, for we had no typewriters then), recording deeds and mortgages on the record books, or copying suits to be served. He expected to look after the more important duties of the office himself, but he had me take the official oath as a deputy clerk. A few days later he became seriously ill, so ill that Dr. Dostor would not allow anyone to see him. When the fall session of the Superior Court met, I was the only person qualified to act as clerk.

Though I can see now that this was a large responsibility for a boy of my age, frankly the thought of running away from the situation never entered my head. When the court convened

I was at the clerk's desk in the courtroom, with the case papers, the jury lists, and the other papers the clerk was supposed to have there. Throughout the two weeks the court was in session, I handled the impaneling of the grand jury and the petit juries, administered oaths, issued writs and processes, kept the minutes; in fine, did all the clerk was supposed to do. The kindliness of the judge and the lawyers is evidenced by the consideration they displayed toward my youthfulness and inexperience. All congratulated me; none complained.

I also acted as clerk of the county court which met once a month or oftener, with jurisdiction over misdemeanors. The county judge was Thomas Williams. One day that winter, he said to me: "Arthur, can you draw an accusation against a Negro for carrying a pistol?"

"Yes," I said, "I have plenty of forms of accusations for concealed weapons in the office and I know how to fill them in."

"Bill Jordan (the county solicitor) is away," he said, "and there is a Negro in jail to be tried. You draw the accusation and question the witnesses, and I'll do the convicting." I did; and he did.

This happened several times during the winter and spring. One day Bill Jordan was there and drew an accusation against four Negro men and a Negro woman, named Hester Brown, who was so twisted up with rheumatism that she used both her hands and her feet in walking. He charged the five with riot at the Negro Baptist Church. The defendants came to me and offered me a dollar apiece to defend them. I asked Judge Williams about it.

"That's all right with me," he said. "I can convict them with you defending them just as easily as with you prosecuting them."

I took the five dollars and commenced looking up the law, as I had seen my father do when he had a case.

The evidence was that Hester was sitting on the back seat near the door, when the four other defendants started the fight in the church. She tried to get out, was run against, knocked down the steps, and lay there yelling for help till the fight was over.

At the conclusion of the testimony, Judge Williams announced, "I will find the four men guilty, but all that Hester did was to holler and I will discharge her."

That was the turn in the case I was waiting for. "One moment, Your Honor," I said, "this is a joint accusation for riot, and under a decision of the Supreme Court, all must be convicted, or none."

He took the decision and read it carefully; he knew enough about law to see that my point was well taken. He hesitated but a moment. "I will take back what I said about Hester. She hollered too loud. I will find her guilty, too."

The fall I went to work at the courthouse, Captain Wade having died Mrs. Wade took the three children to Macon, entered John and Wilk in Mercer University, and either that year or the next, entered Pearl at Wesleyan. So when Professor Fitzpatrick opened the school at Blakely that fall, several familiar faces were absent. The important thing to me was that Annie Wilkin came back. Of course, I did not have the opportunity of seeing her at school, as formerly, but the girls were allowed to have company during the weekends.

Frequently, we would have parties at the various homes of the town. We were not allowed to dance—that was against the rules of the churches—but we played "Tucker" and "twistification." The former was simply the old fashioned square dance under another name, and the latter a somewhat modified version of the Virginia Reel.

In the late fall we would go to the cane-grindings. The farmers would be cutting their sugar cane, grinding out the juice, and boiling it into syrup. Frequently a farmer would invite us to a cane-grinding on Friday evening. We would drink the juice fresh from the rollers or would skim the foam from the newly made syrup on a cane peel and eat it. The glow of the pine fires under the kettles or evaporators into the hushed night cast a spell, which, to our young minds, smacked of the mysterious. In the dim outer glow of the firelight were piles of the stalks that had come from the mill after the juice had been squeezed out of them. We did not call them bagasse as they do in Louisiana, but called them "pummies" (pomace). There was a special thrill in getting your girl and slipping off with her to sit on one of the pummy-piles and exchanging with her such conversation as puppy-love inspires.

About this time, many pretty, attractive girls of our approximate ages from near-by towns began to visit in Blakely —Mattie and Cliff Hightower and Evie Layton from Damascus, Dickey Beckom from Arlington, Annie and Sammie Beauchamp from Bluffton, Dita Bostwick from Albany, and others.

I liked the girls from other towns and paid them a good deal of attention, and I was not quite so attentive to Annie as I had been. Perhaps this was natural, since in my new work I felt myself quite a man, and she was just a little schoolgirl. Yet I have reason to believe that down deep in my heart, she was still my sweetheart. One afternoon, some of us boys were sitting on the side steps of Dr. Dostor's drugstore watching the girls as they came by from school. Annie came along, her body erect, her head high, looking straight ahead as usual. One of the boys said, "There comes Annie Wilkin, biggity as ever"; and before I had time to think, I had knocked him down the steps and into the street. He apologized, saying he meant nothing derogatory to her; and I am sure he did not.

Let me explain that word "biggity." I do not think any lexicographer has ever caught its exact meaning, as it has long been and still is used in our section of the country. The definition "saucily independent" approaches it; but "saucily" is not exactly the right adverb. The word does connote a spirit of independence, a sort of hands-off-ness and touch-me-not-ness, a headstrongness, a tendency to display temper, to have one's way, a soupçon of pride and vanity, a regal bearing, and other notions of this kind. It may be slightly reproachful, but is not contemptuous; indeed, one can easily admire or love a biggity girl. I am sorry; but I cannot define it. You will have to see Annie to know what it means.

11

Saints and Sinners

IN MY EARLY TEENS I JOINED THE BAPTIST CHURCH. IT CAME AS a surprise to everyone except to me. I have never been pietistic, and hope I never shall be. I was brought up in a time when the churches, especially the Baptist churches, were full of dogmatism. I have never cared for dogma or creed in the formal sense. I have never been able to worship the Bible, as many do, though at that period of my life I was quite familiar with its text. The church has never appealed to me as it does to many. I have never been able to speak to God of the church as "the place of thine abode," as distinguished from any other place.

However, from earliest childhood, I have had a reverence for, a belief in, and an abiding faith in the everlasting God—the God who is Love. As I became older, the sense of duty to Him began to be awakened.

I thought it out for myself, weighed the pros and cons; and one evening, when, at the conclusion of the service, Brother Corley, our old pastor, gave out the hymn, "Just as I Am Without One Plea," and "opened the doors of the church," I went forward and offered myself as a candidate for baptism and for membership in the church. On the next Sunday afternoon, I met Brother Corley at the millpond a mile and a half north of Blakely, and in the presence of my parents and a few friends, was baptized by him.

Our people young and old were for the most part church-goers, and the prayer meetings were usually well attended. It was a neglected child who did not attend Sunday School. In Blakely, there was a Methodist and a Baptist church, and in each of them there was an ordinary parlor organ, but on the days in which Old Lady McCan, who was the oldest person in the county, attended services, the organ in the Baptist Church could not be used. She said that such music "was not Biblical" and that it offended her.

The superintendents of our Baptist Sunday School, during my childhood and boyhood, were Captain Wade, Mr. Jim Hobbs, and my father, in the order named. Miss Minna Collins, a blind music teacher, was our organist, and carried the tune for our singing. Mr. Jim Hobbs would sit or stand near the organ and give out the number and title of the songs for her. He also sang. His voice was strong, but not exactly musical.

I remember now how Miss Minna in her high soprano voice would start the song off,

> "When all thy mercies—

and Mr. Hobbs, in his deep voice, would join with her in ending the verse,

> "O my God,"

Will Mc. said that it was difficult to tell whether he was singing or swearing.

A part of the exercises every Sunday morning was for each pupil to recite a verse from the Bible. One day Bob Dostor's mother was sick and she forgot to give him a verse; so as he saw his turn approaching he whispered to Wilk Wade, "Give me a verse." Wilk whispered back, "Bread is the staff of life." Bob said it. Dean Swift seemed to have equal standing with the Bible; for the superintendent passed it without comment.

As long as I lived in Blakely, there was a prayer meeting at the Methodist Church every Wednesday evening, and at the Baptist Church every Thursday evening. Some member of the church, usually a steward or a deacon, would conduct the service. The program ran about thus: an opening song; a prayer by the leader of the meeting; another song; the reading of a selection from the Scriptures; a prayer by someone designated by the leader; another song; the reading of another passage; another prayer by some other member of the congregation, and so on.

One Thursday evening, as Brother A. M. Irwin was conducting the Baptist prayer meeting, a stranger came in and took a seat near the front. In course of time, the leader looked toward him and said, "My brother, will you lead us in prayer?"

The stranger seemed to be a little surprised. He rose to his feet, blurted out, "You will have to excuse me. I don't live in this county." Brother Irwin, being a justice of the peace, sustained the point as to the venue and called on someone else.

A constant attendant at the Baptist prayer meeting was a timid, though earnest, Christian gentleman, who was nearly always called on to pray in the course of the evening. He spoke haltingly and Will Mc. said he had the "Oh Gods." In his efforts to overcome his stage fright, he would punctuate his prayer with "Oh God," much as the Hardshell preachers and the Negro preachers, as well as some other inexperienced speakers, would punctuate their sermons or public speeches with "er-er-ers"; for instance, "Oh, God, we come here tonight, oh God, to pray to you, oh God, and to worship you, oh God. Oh God, hear us," and so on.

There were others who prayed with more fervor than meaning. I recall a visiting deacon from one of the country churches, a gray-headed old Saint in Israel, as he called himself, who in the midst of his prayer exclaimed with fervor, "Oh Lord, unlock the wheels of Zion and let her roll." Not content with that, he added, after a pause, "Down hill backwards, Lord."

One evening at the services at the Baptist Church, there sat in the space behind the pulpit along with our pastor, the Reverend Zack Weaver, an elderly gentleman who had been ordained to the ministry and who preached occasionally in the country churches. He had no regular charge but ran a farm about eight miles from Blakely. He was a good old man, with only a meager education. I recall that he was a justice of the peace on the side. Brother Weaver had preached a most excellent sermon from the text, "And ye would not!" taken from Christ's lament over Jerusalem. He turned to the visiting preacher and said, "Will you please conclude the service?" thinking that he would give a short prayer and dismiss the congregation with the doxology. But the visitor had more in mind. He wanted to preach a little himself.

He arose and began, "Brethren and Sistren, in this world there are many kinds of nots. There is the plain slip knot, and there's the bow knot, and the double bow knot, and there's the hangman's knot, and the woods are full of lightwood knots, but the worst not in the world is the 'ye would not.' On and on he rambled in this style for about twenty minutes until he had the congregation tittering and the spiritual effect of Brother Weaver's fine sermon almost wholly dissipated. He stopped for a moment to get his breath and to take a sip of water to clear his throat. Brother Weaver, pretending to think he had concluded, arose quickly and said, "Thank you, my brother, we will now have a short prayer and be dismissed," and he himself gave the prayer and made it short.

In the town we had only Methodists and Baptists, but out in the country, we had also Hardshell (Primitive) Baptists and Freewill Baptists. Most of the Hardshells, including the ministers, were uneducated, and considered it no sin to drink liquor; but a member who did not pay his debts, who engaged in any worldly activity on the Sabbath Day, or who was caught lying was promptly turned out of the church. The Methodists preached the doctrine of "falling from grace"; and they practiced what they preached. The Baptists preached against that doctrine; but they also practiced what the Methodists preached.

They used to tell of a member of one of the Hardshell Baptist churches, who went to Macon soon after artificial ice began to be manufactured there. He came home and stated that he saw them hauling hundred-pound blocks of ice in July, and was promptly turned out of the church for lying.

One of our Hardshell Baptist ministers, during Farmers' Alliance days, preached from the text, "Ho, every one that thirsteth," and made the point that none but farmers could go to Heaven, because everyone gets thirsty but only the farmers hoe.

Another of the preachers of this denomination was attempting to describe to his congregation the horrors of Hell. I will leave out the "er-er-er's" and give only the substance of what he said: Hell is so hot that no man can know how hot it is until he gets there. If you will take a log heap of beechwood, and fire it with lightwood knots, and keep piling on the wood and firing it till the log heap gets seven times hotter than any log heap you ever saw, and keep heating it until it is seventy times that hot, and then heat it seven hundred times that hot, and if when you get it seven million million times that hot, you should take a poor soul out of Hell and cast him into that log heap, the change would be so sudden that he would freeze to death in less than a minute.

Uncle Charlie Martin, our Freewill Baptist preacher, was a man of great originality of thought and action. When he prayed, he knelt behind the pulpit, but he would interrupt his prayer from time to time to look over the top of it, or to peep around the side. "The Bible says," he explained, " 'Watch and pray.' "

He was once seen sharpening his pocket knife and someone inquired why he was doing it. He replied, "I hear about some folks going around and saying they can't sin and calling themselves perfect. If I come across one of them, I am going to cut a swallow-fork in his ear, because the Bible says, 'Mark the perfect man'."

He was preaching at old Cedar Springs Church one Sunday and was much annoyed by a bunch of "frying-sized" girls who kept going in and out of the church with the obvious purpose of showing off their new Sunday frocks. They would come prancing in with that special twist of their rear ends which the sixteen- to eighteen-year-old country girls used to affect, presumably to show off their dresses, would writhe into a seat, sit for a few minutes, and then twist out again on their way to the spring to get a drink of water, and then back again. This had happened several times while Uncle Charlie was reading the Scriptures and after he had begun his sermon. They had just come in again and switched to their seats, when he stopped abruptly in the middle of his discourse and said:

"I am goin' to tell you a thing that was told me by a preacher as old as I am now, when I was a boy. I don't say it 's so; and I don't say it ain't so. But if it ain't so, I don't see why that old preacher would have lied to me. He told me how the Lord created woman. He said that the Lord was in the Garden of Eden, one day, prunin' the fruit trees, when he come across Adam. The Lord said to him, 'How you feelin', Adam?'

"And Adam said, 'Sorta lonesome, Lord.'

"Then the Lord said, 'How would you like to have a wife, Adam?'

"And Adam said, 'What's that, Lord?'

"The Lord said, 'A helpmeet, a companion.' And Adam said he would like it if the Lord thought he would.

"So the Lord moved his hands before Adam's eyes and put him to sleep, and took his prunin' knife and cut a rib out of Adam's side, intendin' to make woman out of it. He got through sewin' up the hole in Adam's side, and turned around to get the rib, and saw his little yaller dog, which had followed him into the Garden of Eden, trottin' off down one of the paths with the rib in his mouth. The Lord, with the knife still in his hand, took after that little yaller dog, and the faster the Lord run, the faster that little yaller dog run; and here they went buckety-buck right down the path, till the little yaller dog got to a crack in the fence and was goin' through it. The Lord, seein' he was about to lose the rib, made a whack with the prunin' knife and cut the little yaller dog's tail smack off—AND HE MADE WOMAN OUT OF THAT LITTLE YALLER DOG'S TAIL."

Then Uncle Charlie left the pulpit and came prancing and twisting down the aisle in imitation of the girls, exclaiming, "And I believe it's so, because, to this very day, you can see women and gals comin' into this very church, a-twistin' and a-squirmin' just like that little yaller dog's tail used to twist and squirm."

Peter Porter, an old Negro, used to come from Cedar Springs to Blakely, occasionally, and stand around the stores and regale us boys with his experiences. He once told us of a powerful sermon he "heared" preached.

"I wuz a young feller, not much older'n you boys is, an' wuz a-courtin' uv Liza, the gal I married. I tuk 'er ter de bush-arber meetin', an' a big yaller nigger preached de mos' pow'rfulest sermin I ever heared. He tuk his tex', 'Seek ye fust de Kingdom uv God, and all things shall be added unto yer.'

"He says, 'No matter what yer doin', or whut yer think yer gwine ter do, stop right whar yer is and come here ter dis moaner's binch and seek till yer gits yer 'ligion, an' den all de things yer wuz gwine ter do will be added unto yer. If yer is startin' a crap er corn, stop right whar yer is; leave de ole mule an' de plow in de furrer an' come ter dis moaner's binch an' seek, an' den whin yer gits yer 'ligion, go back an' finish yer crap. If yer is fixin' ter buil' yer a house and got yer logs skunt in de woods, leave 'em right dar and come here an' seek till yer gits yer 'ligion, an' de house will come out all right.'

"Den he look right pintedly at me settin' dere wid Liza an' he say, 'If youse cotin' of a gal and thinkin' of marryin' 'er, leave 'er right whar she is a-settin', and come ter dis moaner's binch an' seek an' seek till yer gits yer 'ligion, and den marry 'er an' all dese things will be added unto yer.' An' he bore down so pintedly dat I got up an' went ter de moaner's binch, an' seeked an' seeked till I got my 'ligion, an' den I married Liza.

"An' fo' God dat preacher wuz right. 'Cause, ef I hadn't got my 'ligion fo' I married dat gal, I never would er got it sence."

One year certain evangelists, who were preaching the doctrine of "holiness," were allowed to use the Methodist Church for their services. They were so sensational in their methods that the Baptists frowned down on them. But Brother Tim Smith, as I shall call him to conceal his identity, though he was a Baptist by profession of faith, was a sensationalist at heart, and went to all these services, sat on the front bench, and enjoyed them, though he refused to participate further.

The theme of these preachers was that under the spell of religious exercises, the chief of which was "storming the citadel of God with a flaming circle of prayer," the "old man" of sin will die in you and the "new man" of holiness and freedom from all sin will be born in you. Repentance of past sins was also a feature of attaining the sinless state. After an impassioned sermon, there would be thronged around the altar rail dozens who were weeping and praying, some silently, some aloud, seeking the death of the old man and the birth of the new man, while those who had professed the attainment of the new life stood around singing psalms of praise and crying "Glory to God!" The preachers went from one kneeling penitent to another giving words of consolation and cheering them on in their struggle with the problem of the death of the old man and the birth of the new.

Kneeling at the altar, sobbing as if her heart would break, was a young widow, who probably in all her life had never committed so great a sin as even to darn her stockings on Sunday. A few months before, her husband was out bear hunting in a dense creek swamp. He was wearing a fur overcoat, and as he quietly pushed his way through the thick undergrowth, another bear hunter, crouched in a blind, mistaking him for a bear, shot him.

The preacher approached the young widow. He patted her on her head, repeating the words, "Oh my sister, is not your 'old man' dead yet? Is not your 'old man' dead yet?"

This was more than Tim Smith could stand, even if he was a Baptist. "Yes, Preacher," he called out from his point of observation on the front seat, "her old man is dead. He got shot for a bear."

We laugh at these old preachers, but we cannot successfully deny that they have been a virile and potent force in promoting civilization and in advancing Christ's cause on earth. And did not Saint Paul say in the first chapter of his First Epistle to the Corinthians:

"Where is the wise? where is the scribe? where is the disputer of this world? hath not God made foolish the wisdom of this world?

"For after that in the wisdom of God the world by wisdom knew not God, it pleased God by the foolishness of preaching to save them that believe."

12

At Mercer

I HAD NEVER HOPED TO GO TO COLLEGE. THAT WAS FOR RICH men's sons; and we were poor. The Wade boys could go, because they had money. However, I had doubted that they would stand very high there, because they came from our backwoods and were in competition with boys from the cities and from the old aristocratic counties of middle Georgia. However, when they came back for the Christmas and the summer vacations and told us of their college activities, of the Kappa Alpha fraternity, the badge of which they wore, I saw they were making good; and I was proud of them.

To my surprise, in the fall of 1889, my father told me he was arranging to send me to Mercer in January. I made application to enter the sophomore class.

January came; and I left home with many misgivings and with some qualms at the sacrifice I knew my father was making. It was an all-day trip to Macon. There I was to spend the night at the Corbett House, run by an old gentleman who had once lived in Blakely, and to go out next morning to the home of Dr. McCall, a retired prominent Baptist minister, where I was to board.

As I changed cars at Albany, I came up with a tall, awkward country boy of about my age, who was making the change from the Coast Line train. He would remember (for he remembers everything) how I came to meet him; but I have forgotten the details. At any rate, I did meet him; and, in so doing, met one of those to whom I owe much. It was then and there that I first

saw Sam Bennet. He told me that he was from Quitman,
Georgia, and that he was going to Macon to enter Mercer.

He was so shy and so timid, and looked so rustic, that I wondered if they would let him into the college. At least I got the
consolation that I would not be the sorriest looking backwoods-
man there. Yet, though he was reticent, when he did say something it showed intelligence.

As we approached Macon he said that he also was going to
the Corbett House. We went there together; and Mr. Corbett
put us in the same room. That night I asked him where he was
going to board. He said "at Dr. McCall's."

The next morning, Mr. Corbett's grandson, a chubby, good-
natured, city-bred boy, Pratt Brown, introduced himself to us
and told us that he had heard of us—of Sam from his older
brother, Stanley Bennet, who had been graduated at Mercer
the year before, and of me from the Wade boys; that he was a
sophomore at Mercer, and would be glad to take us to Dr. Mc-
Call's. Dr. McCall met us at the door, took us upstairs, and put
us in the same room, to occupy the same bed.

In those days, standards were low at Mercer, and after a
cursory examination, we were admitted as sophomores "half-
advanced."

A few days after I entered Mercer, I received an invitation
to join the Kappa Alpha fraternity, which, at that time at least,
was the choicest fraternity at the College. At some other college, I
might have preferred some other fraternity, but not at Mercer.
I was to be initiated on the following Saturday night, and as it
approached I began to think of Sam, and to wish that the others
knew him as I did, knew what a fine fellow he really was, so that
he might also be invited to join the fraternity. I kept my invitation secret from him for fear it might hurt him to know that I
was being taken into a select group into which he had not been
invited, and I wondered how he would feel when the boys came
to take me to the chapter hall for the initiation. But when they
came to the boarding-house for me, he had gone out somewhere
so that I was relieved of the embarrassment of leaving him. As

I walked into the anteroom of the chapter hall, who sat there but Sam Bennet? His delight in seeing me was manifest. We were to be initiated together and neither of us knew it. He had been pledged through his brother Stanley before he left home and had been worrying about me and whether I would feel hurt at his joining the fraternity.

Our initiation into the fraternity brought Sam and me into contact with one of the college leaders, who was a junior at that time, and who afterward exercised a great influence over our lives and methods of thinking. "Kil," we called him; but there are those who may be able to identify him better if I introduce him as Dr. William Heard Kilpatrick, who for twenty years or more was Professor of the Philosophy of Education at Teachers College, Columbia University, New York, and now is emeritus professor there. Even when we were with him at Mercer, he had begun to display that genius which later gave him nationally and internationally the reputation of being one of the world's educational leaders. His philosophical and pedagogical books have been translated into many languages and used the world over, even in the Orient. The number of those whom he has taught in the course of his career runs into the thousands; and I have never seen one of them who did not ever afterward show in his processes of thinking Kil's imprint upon him. Once at a social gathering in Florida, I met a pretty little flapper—at first blush, one would have called her just an ordinary shallow-brained little flapper—but whenever she said anything, there was something in the way she said it that made me ask her, "Where did you go to school?" And her answer was, "I was last under Dr. Kilpatrick at Teachers College."

No account of southwest Georgia in the old days would be complete without references to Sam Bennet and "Kil." While Kil was not born there, immediately following his graduation he spent several years at Blakely as principal of the public school; and his imprint is there to this day. Beyond that, Kil is now so well known to so many thousands of people, that incidents relating to him have, in and of themselves, a general interest.

We had no Easter vacations in those days, but I went home in April to help my father with his papers at the spring session of the Superior Court. He insisted that he needed me, but I suspect that his real reason for wishing me there was that I might familiarize myself with the procedure in the courts.

June and Commencement came quickly enough. To me, college life was no longer a thing apart.

During this spring a vacancy had occurred in the principalship of Blakely Academy by the resignation, in late April, of Professor Wilder, who had succeeded Professor Fitzpatrick. Upon the suggestion of the Wade boys and me, the trustees employed a fraternity mate of ours, Andrew Lane (Major, we always called him) to complete the term. He was a senior and had passed his final examinations.

I thought of Annie Wilkin occasionally during the spring and early summer, but when I came home from Macon she had already returned to Colquitt. I found a change taking place in my thoughts of her. She was still an immature schoolgirl, while I was a college man, soon to be a junior. Occasionally I wrote to her, but, as I had pointed out to me in later days in a very discomforting way, I wrote very patronizingly.

I did drive down to Colquit one Sunday during the summer vacation with the intention of seeing her, but neglected to make an engagement. When I got there, I found that she was out of town for the day, and I had to content myself with going to hear a travelling evangelist preach. He had erected a tent on the south side of the courthouse square, and, with the aid of a professional singer, whom he had brought along with him, was conducting a series of revival services.

Though he preached with great emotion, the congregation sat and listened in respectful silence. There were plenty of good people in Colquitt, but they were not emotional. When he finished his sermon, he asked all who wanted to be prayed for to come forward, and signaled to the singer. The singer sang and the preacher pleaded with all the old-time appeals to both saints and sinners to come forward and seek spiritual uplift and salvation at the altar. Not a person stirred in the congregation.

He rushed dramatically forward and cried out, "For two weeks we have preached the same sermons, prayed the same prayers, sung the same songs, and made the same appeals which, elsewhere, have brought hundreds to the altar and have sent them on their ways to lives of joyful Christian experience; and yet, throughout all these days and nights, not a one of you has approached the altar or has shown the slightest response to our appeals. Somebody, anybody, in all this congregation, tell us what we must do to make the people of Colquitt and of Miller County a God-loving, a God-fearing people. Tell me! Somebody tell me!"

This struck Mrs. Pet Morton as a special challenge to her. She was known for her plain speaking and for her willingness to speak. She arose and said, " I will tell you."

"Do so, my sister, do so," the preacher shouted.

"You will have to kill out the old crowd and move in a new set," stated Miss Pet, and she sat down.

All the preacher could say was, "I think that would be a little drastic."

This trip to Colquitt was my only attempt to see Annie Wilkin that summer. I spent the vacation doing some work in my father's office, writing for the Early County News, earning a little money here and there by collecting delinquent accounts, going to parties, playing tennis, and making trips to the surrounding towns to see the girls. Wilk Wade got some golf paraphernalia from somewhere, and we set up a rough imitation of a nine-hole course in Wade's pasture, where the hazards were more hazardous than the fairways were fair.

When I was born, Blakely was so small a town that little or no social distinctions were made between town folks and country folks; many of the boys from the country were friends of boys in the town. As some of our boys began to go off to college, some of the other boys both in the town and country began to be envious of us. When we built a court and began to play lawn tennis, it created further jealousy, and there were those who, not catching the exact pronunciation of the words "lawn tennis,"

called us, with a sneer, "them long tenants," and would slip in at
night and injure the courts.

A year or two later, I was supplementing my income by doing
some surveying, and on one of the jobs I had assisting me a
young countryman. I have never seen anyone with a keener sense
of direction than he had. As I would adjust the compass, he
would catch the direction by looking at it for the flash of an
eye, and off down the line he would go two or three hundred
yards and turn and face me. I would sight through the compass
and the center of his body would be exactly on the line.

We suspended work one day for lunch. As we sat on the
ground eating it, he remarked, "I never did like them town boys
at Blakely because they are stuck up; but I like you, because
you are so common."

My old chum, Will Mc., was clerking in Dostor's Drug Store;
I spent much time there with him, and in doing so got a good
deal of basic pharmaceutical information. I learned, and strangely
enough, still remember the Latin names for many of the drugs
then in use. Dr. Dostor always wrote his prescriptions in Latin.

Will Mc. also had the job of posting the Doctor's books of
account against his patients. On the face of a number of the accounts in the ledger, we saw that he had put in large letters
"O.D." We discovered what this meant when we came to one
of them where the Doctor had written it out in full, "Ovum
Damnum." This was his way of saying that the debtor was a
"bad egg."

In the late summer, I got a letter from Kil. He wrote that
Mrs. McAndrews, at 723 College Street in Macon, had decided
to take a few Mercer boys to board with her, that he was going
there. He asked me to share the room with him. Though I hated
to leave Sam Bennet, the opportunity of rooming with Kil
could not be neglected; so I wrote quickly and accepted.

When I got to Mrs. McAndrews' at the opening of school
that fall, I found there were two double beds in Kil's room; and
that Sam was already there to occupy one of them with me. I
did sleep in the bed with Kil for a while, and Russell Davis, of

Quitman, slept with Sam; but for most of the year, I slept with Sam.

Several years later, a gentleman inquired of me, "Do you have the same trouble when you go to Atlanta that I do? Does your wife ask you to bring her a pair of shoes, and when you bring them, they do not fit and you have to go to the trouble to send them back?"

"No," I said, "when my wife asks me to bring shoes from Atlanta, I take the salesman into the rear room, and, pulling up my shirt, say to him, 'You will find two sets of footprints on the small of my back; please fit the shoes to the smaller tracks. The larger ones are Sam Bennet's."

This year found us under some new teachers. In Math, we had "Old Shelt," Dr. Shelton P. Sanford, a very kindly, sweet-natured old gentleman, who had once been a great teacher but was then in his dotage. We boys loved him, but we imposed upon him. "Old Joe," Dr. Willet, had us in physics, and we had English under "Old Doc" Brantley.

Willie Lee Duggan had us in Greek, as well as in Latin. His method of teaching Greek was wholly different from what Old Doc's had been the term before. He laid a great deal more stress on our memorizing some note declaring a trifling exception to some general rule of prosody than he did on our understanding the shades of meaning existing, for instance, between the aorist and some other tense. I recall that he used to harp on four little words, which, as I can best recall, were "dos," "es," "sches," and "thes," and some exception to the general rule of scansion that had to be noted as to them. I had forgotten them until years later they came back to me when Frances, my daughter, came home from Wellesley College, and in speaking of her various friends, called them by their favorite nicknames, "Dot," "Sliz," "Het," and "Floss."

Think of trying, as he did, to center attention upon the technicalities of scansion when confronted with some phrase from the chorus of one of the Greek tragedies, such as, "O, Moi, Moi, O, Popoi!" He took no note of how the words, in and of themselves, independently of any translatable meaning—and treating them as if they were only vocables—produce a distinct and specific effect. A few years ago, I used this phrase, as an exclamation, in the presence of my poet friend, Wallace Stevens. He had not heard it before, and neither he nor I knew any translation for it, but he got great and immediate pleasure from it.

Our rooms at 723 College Street soon became the center of a number of college activities. We organized a court—a "Kangaroo Court," we probably would have called it, if we had known the word—for the initiation of the freshmen by what was intended to be a mild form of hazing but sometimes proved to be not so mild. Kil was the judge, I was the prosecuting attorney, and Bill Murrow the sheriff. Some of us would entice a freshman on some pretext or other up to our room. Bill would immediately seize him. I would prefer all sorts of monstrous charges against him and sustain them by the testimony of our professional witnesses. Kil would convict him, and, in an awe-inspiring tone of voice, would sentence him to be laid upon the pillory and soundly flogged with fifty lashes of the cat-o'-nine-tails. The "pillory" was Sam's round-top trunk and the "cat-o'-nine-tails" was the leather strap from around my trunk. Bill, with the aid of an able corps of deputies, would bend the prisoner over the pillory, and while the others held him would apply a few gentle strokes of the strap to the most exposed part of his person. Whereupon we would all burst into laughter and give him the right hand of fellowship. We would then send him out to lure some other victim in.

Haman got hung on his gallows. Kil got impeached in his own court. He came into the room one day and exhibited a curiously shaped block of wood and asked us to guess what it was. We guessed and we guessed, until we got tired of guessing. We demanded that he tell us what it was, and he refused to do so. Someone suggested that he ought to be impeached for treating us that way. We hastily organized a court of impeachment and put him on trial. He was promptly convicted and sentenced to be lashed until he told us what it was. Bill laid on the lash. After each stroke, the acting judge would say, "Tell us what it is," and Kil would answer in a monotone, "I refuse to tell."

The affair went too far. The punishment was too severe, and Kil was hurt and angry, but his answer was always the same, "I refuse to tell." Finally, seeing that he was about to faint, we released him. He was hurt and his feelings were hurt, and for several days his relations with us were very cool, but after a time he forgave us, and then he told us what it was. It was a setting block for preserving butterflies. He would not take the judgeship again; so we elected him Governor, with pardoning powers.

That fall I persuaded some of the other boys to join with me in publishing a college monthly, which we put out under the title of "The Mephistophelian," with the sub-title, "A Devil of a Good College Paper." Though the local merchants took enough advertising to pay the expenses of publication, it lived for only a year. So far as I know not a copy of it is extant.

During the ensuing spring semester, another college activity had its fomentation and integration at 723 College Street. Every year, in late March or early April, a Chautauqua was held at Albany. Several of us boys from south Georgia conferred with the passenger representative of the railway company, and he agreed to make a very low excursion rate there if we could get as many as fifty to go. We conferred with Dr. Nunnally, the president of the College, and he gave his consent to our going to Albany on Thursday night, returning by Sunday night. We easily got the requisite number signed up to go. On Wednesday morning, which happened to be the first day of April, Dr. Nunnally announced at chapel that he had changed his mind; that classes would be held as usual on Friday, that none, except those who had obtained leave of absence upon the special request of parents, would be allowed to go to Albany, and that anyone else who went would be demerited.

Dr. Nunnally had never been very popular with the student body. This announcement certainly did not increase his popularity. Indignation was rife. It did not affect John Wade or me, for we had been granted leave at the special request of our parents; yet we fully shared the indignation. I do not know why John was going to Blakely, but I was going there to be with my father at the spring term of Early Superior Court.

A conference was called in our room at Mrs. McAndrews', and we agreed to "raise hell" that night. We first planned to burn Dr. Nunnally in effigy, but later decided to give him a mock burial, with an appropriate epitaph. We invited into the conspiracy only the four students who stood highest in the senior and the junior classes, respectively; but to make it ten, Sam Bennet and I, who had no such marks, were added to the list. In the eight were included from the senior class John Wade, who was first honor man; Kil, who was second honor man; and two others, whom I have now forgotten; from the junior class, Wilk Wade, with the highest mark; two others whom I have forgotten; and Billy Hardwick (afterwards Governor and United States Senator), whose marks put him among the first four.

We learned that Dr. Nunnally, the only member of the faculty who resided in the college building, was to attend a meeting at the First Baptist Church that evening. The new chapel building was in process of erection, and there one of our number discovered a quantity of green paint and paintbrushes. As soon as we found that Dr. Nunnally had left for the city, the ten of us stealthily went into the new chapel, got the paint and the brushes, and proceeded to the main building. We first painted the door to Dr. Nunnally's office, and then went to his classroom and painted the blackboards. Someone suggested that we paint the blackboards in the rooms of Bobby Ryals and Willie Lee Duggan. No sooner thought of than done. As we left the building, one of the boys added a finishing touch by putting a green streak on each of the granite columns at the entrance. Two others, as an impromptu, climbed to the tower and removed the clapper from the college bell.

We had arranged to have the mock burial on the campus in front of the new chapel, and we decided to add a grave for

"Bobby" and "Willie Lee," in addition to the one we had planned for "Old Gus," as we called Dr. Nunnally.

Kil and I collaborated on the epitaphs and hand-printed them on large cardboards, and when the mounds of the three graves had been heaped up, we tacked the epitaphs to the headboards. I think I can recall them. For Dr. Nunnally, we had:

> "HERE LIES OLD GUS—THAT'S NOTHING NEW—
> HE HAS LIED OFTEN BEFORE."

For Willie Lee Duggan:

> "HERE LIES WILLIE LEE.
> IF HE'S NOT DEAD, HE OUGHT TO BE.
> HERE'S THE LAST OF POOR OLD DUGGAN
> WE HOPE HE'S DONE WITH HIS HUMBUGGIN."

For Bobby Ryals:

> "HERE LIES BOBBY RYALS—
> HE DIED TALKING."

We then quietly departed to our respective places of abode. The backhouses to the rear of the campus were turned over that night; but our crowd was not in on that.

Dr. Nunnally returned to the college building about ten o'clock, and for some reason he went by his office. When he caught hold of the doorknob, he discovered that something was wrong. As this was before we had electric lights, he got a lamp and went on an inspection tour. He had not gone far before he woke up "Dr. Bloom," the colored janitor, and sent him to the drugstore for a gallon of benzine.

I do not know how late they worked, but when we arrived at the college building next morning, all the paint had been removed, except the two stripes on the columns at the front door. It seems that it is difficult to remove paint from granite. The soil in front of the new chapel had been smoothed down and the epitaphs had been removed, but on the spot where the graves had been, a stake had been driven into the ground and on it a cardboard placard had been tacked. It announced:

"RESURRECTION DAY
ALL ARE RISEN."

On the next evening, John Wade and I started our trip to Blakely, but we decided to spend the night in Albany, as we had heard that some of the girls we knew were to be there; and to go down to Blakely Friday afternoon. The Governor and several members of his staff were on the train. We reached Albany at about nine o'clock. Will Mc., who had taken a position in a drugstore there, met us at the station. We were about to take a hack up to the hotel, when we espied two fine horses and a carriage. "For the Governor," Will Mc. said.

A word to the wise was sufficient. Will Mc. didn't dare go with us, for he was too well known in Albany; but John and I walked up to the carriage and asked the driver, an old-time Negro in livery and high hat, "Is this the Governor's carriage?"

"Yas'r; yas'r," he said with a bow.

"The Governor wants you to take us to the Albany Hotel right quick, to have things arranged for him when he gets there," we said, as we jumped into the carriage.

He gave the horses a flick with the whip and up the street we went at a lively gait. When we were about a block from the hotel we told him to stop. We jumped out and told him to go back quickly and get the Governor and tell him that we would have for him at the hotel the liquor he told us to get.

Will Mc., who stayed behind and joined us later, told us that when the Governor, his Colonels and the local committee arrived at the porte-cochere at the rear of the station and could not find the carriage, there was an amusing consternation; but when the driver came back, jumped from the seat and, tipping his hat and bowing toward the most pompous and elaborately uniformed Colonel on the Governor's staff, said "Gubner, dem gentmuns dat yer sont by me ter git yer licker sez dey'll hab it fer yer whin yer gits ter de hotel," the consternation was confined to the Governor and the others shared the amusement. The Governor was a prominent churchman and a temperance leader.

I spent a week or ten days at Blakely, and when, on the return trip, I got to Smithville, a dinner station where the trains passed, I saw Annie Wilkin on the other train. She had gone to Andrew Female College at Cuthbert that year. As I went to speak to her, I saw that she was dressed in black. She said simply, "Papa is dead; I am going home."

Sam Bennet and I finished our junior year. He told me that he did not expect to return in the fall. I doubted that I should do so. I knew that my father was expecting to enter my brother Dick at Mercer that fall, and I realized what a financial strain it would be upon him to have two of us in college. Subconsciously, I sensed then what I later consciously more fully recognized—that I had already gotten out of college nearly everything I could get out of it except the ornamentation of a diploma and a degree. In those days the word "University" in the name "Mercer University" was a misnomer. Mercer was little more than a denominational high school.

What I had learned from the textbooks and from the teachers had amounted to little; but I had joined a first class fraternity, I had been able to associate with boys from all over the State, I had seen enough of city life to get some of the backwoodsiness rubbed off me, I had been to the theatre, I had seen a Federal Court in session with the judge berobed and a tipstaff to call the opening of the court, and most of all I had been intimately associated with Sam and Kil. Sam had taught me some things to think about, and Kil had taught me how to think more clearly than I had ever thought before. So my days spent there were well worth while.

Studying Law and Other Things

THE SUMMER OF 1891, THE SUMMER BEFORE I WAS EIGHTEEN in September, passed very much as the previous summer had, except that I undertook to spend eight hours a day, on the average, reading law. I say "on the average," for I devoted no particular time of the day to it. During all the years I had been about my father's office, I had been browsing around in the law books I found there; but this summer I confined myself to the Code of Georgia, Greenleaf on Evidence, Kent's Commentaries, and Blackstone's Commentaries.

The old lawyers in our part of this State who undertook to prepare applicants for admission to the bar used to require them to read through Blackstone's Commentaries twice, probably on the theory that if the applicant had the persistence to plod through all those dreary pages more than once he would likely have enough persistence to plod through the disheartening days of the first few years of a law practice. So I read through Blackstone twice and memorized the synopsis in the front of the first volume, because I knew, from having seen other applicants examined, that Judge Kiddoo, who usually examined the applicants in the common law, got all his questions from it.

That summer while I was reading law, I put some furniture in the back room of my father's office and used it as my bedroom. We boys also used it, somewhat as a club room or meeting place. We called our quasi-club, "The Villainy Club."

Up to that time I had written only by hand, but that summer I persuaded my father to buy me a Blickensderfer typewriter. It would be difficult for me to picture one of those machines. It had a keyboard somewhat like that of the modern portable type-writer. The letters were on a cylinder attached to a movable arm that rose up in front. When the appropriate key was pressed, the cylinder whirled until its corresponding letter was at the right point and then whacked down and printed it on the paper. It reminded one of a woodpecker in action.

We boys decided that since we had a typewriter at our command we would get out a magazine for private circulation among ourselves. It contained accounts of all the local scandals, and in the joke columns were many things not suitable to be read in family circles. We called it "The Villain." It contained eight letter-sized pages and was illustrated by our making carbon tracings of pictures we found elsewhere. I still think that some of the original jokes were good and were not half as pornographic in suggestion as many of those which one may see any day now in some of the magazines.

For instance, Gus Jones had gone to Macon to take a place with a cotton firm there. From a plumber's catalogue, we traced a picture of an old-style water closet, the kind with the tank above and the chain hanging down. Under the picture, we had this:

"Extract from a Letter from Gus Jones to His Mother. 'I like everything here but the water. When you get it from the waterworks it tastes funny.' "

Our social activities were increasing. Our set had been widened to include a number of the younger group: Dick Powell, Tom McDowell (Will Mc.'s brother), Frank Jones, Wyatt Alexander, and other boys of that age; Pearl Wade, Emmie Howard, the Fryer twins, Gertie Jones, Fannie Alice Jones, and other girls of their group. Our State Senator, Judge Lanier, married a Mrs. Barnum, of Lumpkin, and when they moved to Blakely, they brought with them Posie Barnum, who answered fully to the description, "A Georgia Peach."

Many of the men in our section, young and old, wore long beards; some wore mustaches and chin whiskers; others wore mustaches and goatees; and most of the rest had at least a mustache. Even before Wilk Wade was old enough to vote, he possessed a set of burnsides. A few went clean-shaven and I was among the few; when I tried to grow a mustache the best I could produce was a stubbly growth that looked like a worn-out toothbrush, yellowed with age; nowadays, if I were to try it, it would look like a worn-out toothbrush which someone had used for applying white shoe polish.

Wilk Wade was our *arbiter elegantiae* in social affairs. He had learned to dance at Macon and was anxious for the rest of us to learn. We were willing, but the opposition of the churches was strong. Dancing was strictly forbidden under the rules of both of them.

There were liberals who, like my father, thought the rules against dancing should be amended or repealed; but there were those like Deacon Jim Hobbs, a good man and a good citizen, who was a stickler for the maintenance and observance of every ancient rule, no matter how puritanical. Nevertheless, many of the boys and girls were learning to waltz, more or less on the sly; and I would have learned if I could have done so. Blakely was getting to be a social center, attracting many visiting boys and girls from other places.

The Blakely Academy was fast outgrowing itself. Near the old building there had been erected a new building containing two large classrooms. Formerly, the Academy had but one teacher; it now had a principal and three teachers, and there was a semblance of grades. There was already talk of a new and better school building.

One of our college mates, Major Lane, had come down to finish the 1890 spring term, had come back as principal for the next year, and had been reëlected for the 1891-92 terms. Major was a little older than the rest of the boys in our set, but he was brilliant, handsome, and capable of adapting himself to any company. So he went right along with us, except that, being a teacher, he had to deport himself with a little more dignity and caution than some of us displayed.

As the boys and girls of my set passed from childhood to youth we began to take part in the community life of the town. There were no trained nurses; we sat up with the sick and closed eyelids of the dying. There were no funeral parlors; we sat up with the dead. Doctors needed assistance in their operations; those of us who did not sicken at the sight of blood often helped in these cases.

The experience was valuable. One night, when Will Mc. was working in Dostor's Drug Store, a drunken Negro was found, about to bleed to death in Fryer's livery stable. Some other Negro had cut his throat from ear to ear, probably in a crap game. The large artery was exposed, but not cut; so was the windpipe. Every doctor in town was out in the country on cases. Will Mc. volunteered his services, and I assisted him. We made up in the drugstore an antiseptic solution of bichloride of mercury, and washed the wound with it. We tied off the bleeding blood vessels and sewed up the wound with a large needle and catgut sutures. Three Negroes sat on the victim—one on his head, one on his legs, and one on his abdomen—and held him down while we worked on him. We left him on a dirty floor. If some great surgeon were to operate under such uncleanly surroundings and had to leave his patient there, as we did, he would expect nothing less than general septicemia. But not so with our patient. His wound healed by what the surgeons call "first intention," and in two or three weeks the scar could hardly be seen. I always thought that Will Mc. should have been a surgeon, he was so deft with his hands and fingers.

In those days there was but little to rob death of its grossness or funerals of their lugubriousness. There were no undertakers, and all the attentions needed by the corpse had to be performed by friends and neighbors. We boys or girls helped in all these things.

The news of a death soon spread through the community by word of mouth. The funeral notice was more formal. It was prepared by someone who wrote a good hand. It was written on a sheet of white notepaper, with a bow of ribbon—white in the case of a young person, black in the case of an adult—inserted into it at the top. This was placed in the suitable-sized top of a white pasteboard box and was carried around, from home to home and from store to store, by someone charged with the task.

Usually the funerals themselves were simple, but dignified. Occasionally there were those who gave way to their grief and made spectacles of their mourning. There used to be a saying among us that the widow who mourned the loudest at her husband's funeral was the one who was soonest in beginning to look around for another.

With the Negroes it was different. At the burials of their dead the shrieking and the mourning of the family and even the friends of the decedent were the prominent features. There used to be an old story, fanciful I am sure, of the colored maid who got off to go to the burial of her cousin, and did not return for three weeks. When she did return, the lady of the house told her that her place had been filled. "Yes'm," the maid said, "I knows dat. I jus' come back for my close. You see I mourned so loud at my cousin's funeral I got married to de bridegroom of de corpse."

The funeral of a Negro rarely occurred at the time of his burial. It was put off for a month or even a year until the family and friends from near and far could be present and join in it. When it did take place, it was an all-day affair, with the screaming and the mourning all over again.

When a preacher, white or black, preached a funeral it was no short affair; and many a corpse who in life had not trodden any straight or narrow path was preached right on into glory.

Before We Were Old Enough To Vote

I HAVE DESCRIBED THE PRIMITIVE CONDITIONS INTO WHICH THE boys of my set were born; I have spoken of the lack of school facilities, of how we worked with our hands, of the lack of money. Yet in their early teens many of these boys were in college. I believe I am the only one of those who went to Mercer who did not take first honor in his class. The boys who went to college and those who did not were, nearly all of them, gainfully and successfully employed in men's work before they were old enough to vote. They were the leaders in the community life. They made good citizens. It seems to me that the boys of Blakely demonstrated that formal schooling is not a *sine qua non* to successful living—that education is not to be found in the schools alone. And this is not to disparage a formal education or to deny its necessity in modern times.

Even before we boys were old enough to vote, we were influencing political affairs. One of the things to which we addressed our attention was the liquor problem. For many years liquor had been sold in saloons in Blakely, and it was impossible to vote the county dry, because the Negroes constituted about sixty per cent of the population, and they voted in those days. The Negro vote was almost wholly purchasable in any election; and in a local-option election a pint of liquor had more purchasing power than a dollar.

The saloonkeepers of Blakely were not bad men. Most of the population of the county was not opposed to whiskey as such. I can look back on it now and see that the opposition of a majority of the white people of the county to the saloons was based on two reasons: that liquor had a demoralizing effect upon the Negroes, especially Negro labor, and, more important, that the saloonkeepers, in order to save their businesses from being outlawed, had to control and did control the politics of both the county and the town. They were caught napping when, on the petition of a majority of the white citizens, our representative and senator put through the bill creating a public dispensary— a county liquor store which was conducted under stringent regulations.

As for me, I was classed as an ardent dry. I was not dry on moral grounds; though, as to that, I made the distinction between the use of liquor and the abuse of it. My father was not a liquor-drinker, but there was always in his home a quart of rye whiskey, which lasted about a year, for use in case of sickness, or to make an eggnog at Christmas; and my mother always kept on hand a quart of blackberry wine for the stomach's sake.

I did not drink; none of the boys in my set did—I don't mean never; I mean hardly ever. I think that all the liquor I had drunk up to the time I was fifty years old could have been contained in a one-gallon jug. I do recall that one moonlit night we boys got hold of some wine and drank it and it made Bob Dostor horribly sick. I also recall that one night, at a meeting of the Villainy Club at the Ranch, someone produced a small bottle of Scotch whiskey. Our social referee, Wilk Wade, told us that the proper way to drink Scotch was with bottled water. Bottled water was new to most of us, but one of the boys said that Dr. Strong had just received a shipment of it at his drugstore. A collection was taken up and one of the boys was dispatched for the water. On his return, we made the highballs, and, with wry faces instead of the show of bravado we should like to have exhibited, drank them. There were some after effects. This last statement may be better understood when I add that the bottled water was Red Raven Splits.

It seemed to us boys that the enactment of the dispensary law gave us an opportunity to effect further civic reform in Blakely. Up to this time the usual routine in town government was that three of the saloonkeepers would be elected to the town council; the mayor and other councilman were not important. A bar clerk would be elected town marshal, the liquor license fixed at five hundred dollars, the street tax at three dollars; and that was about all there was to it.

The town had a short, antiquated charter. Under it any person qualified to vote in the county elections was qualified to vote in the town elections, if he lived in the town; and no length of residence in the town was required. A day or so before the election, a horde of Negroes from the country farms would be collected by the saloon group, moved into town and crowded into shanties provided for that purpose. When the election day came, they claimed citizenship in the town and voted. Promptly thereafter they moved back to the farms.

The town was growing rapidly. Improvements, such as lights, water, and better streets were badly needed. We boys decided not to take the situation lying down as the other citizens had been doing. We approached Dr. Strong, and he agreed to head our ticket, as mayor, with four others we could count on as councilmen. Dr. Strong was a quiet, reserved, old gentleman. However, he had a brother living in the country, who was a member of the "Colomokee Nine."

The Colomokee Nine was an organization that existed in the Colomokee District with the purpose of preventing Negroes from voting in that district. The name was derived from the fact that at one election there the members had appeared at the precinct in baseball suits, and each of them carried a baseball bat. They used for the ball the head of any Negro who tried to vote. When Dr. Strong's candidacy was announced, his brother in the Colomokee Nine volunteered the services of his team to attend the election.

The polls opened at seven o'clock. By six-thirty scores of country Negroes could be seen huddled around fires built on the public square, guarded by the town marshals and several deputies. The Colomokee Nine were in the courthouse, standing in the corridor into which the voters had to come to cast their ballots. With them was another brother of Dr. Strong, Mr. DuPont Strong, one of the finest specimens of physical manhood I ever saw.

There were no registration lists, but if a would-be voter offered his ballot, any citizen could challenge his right to vote, whereupon the managers would question him under oath as to his qualifications. I had been selected to do the challenging.

As the polls were opened, the march of the Negroes began toward the courthouse. A little Negro, named Ed Ryals, who as we all knew lived with his mother three miles from town, was the first to approach the balloting place and offer to vote. I promptly challenged. When he was sworn and asked if he resided within the corporate limits of Blakely, he answered, "Yaz, Suh."

DuPont Strong was just behind me, and, as the Negro gave the answer, he called out, "You are a damned liar," and with a mighty swing, struck him under the jaw. I think that little Negro must have sailed through the air ten feet; and when he came down he hit the floor running. Instantly, pistols flashed from hip pockets—from the pockets of the Colomokee Nine on one side of me and from the pockets of the marshals on the other— and there I was right in the line of fire between them, wholly unarmed, as I never carried a weapon.

Not a shot was fired. As the pistols appeared, the Negroes began to run. They ran over themselves and even over a few white men and boys who were in the way. They ran and did not stop running until they were entirely out of town. Even those Negroes who had not yet started to the polls joined the exodus. The suddenness of the stampede and its amusing phases distracted the attention of the armed forces on both sides, and they forgot to shoot one another in their desire to watch the spectacle taking place on the Square and down the streets leading from it. As soon as it was plain that the Negroes were gone, the Colomokee Nine quietly retreated through a back hallway and were gone.

We carried the election. Amendments to the town charter

were obtained, and a new era in municipal government was at hand. Blakely began to grow rapidly.

A little later, I was in Montezuma, spending the day with Roland Daniel, who had been Kil's successor as principal of the Blakely Institute. I found that Montezuma, which was of about the same size as Blakely, had a telephone exchange, and that Roland and a young lawyer I had known for several years, named Jule Felton (not Judge Felton of our Court of Appeals, but his father), owned it. We talked of putting one in at Blakely. It resulted in the formation of The Blakely Telephone Company, into which Roland and Jule put three hundred dollars, each, and Frank Jones and I each put in a like amount. We not only built an exchange at Blakely but also ran lines out into the country and to several of the towns near by.

Several amusing incidents occurred in connection with the building of these lines. We were building a line sixteen miles long to Callahan's turpentine still in the lower part of the county. On Saturday night we had not finished it, and so left a roll of the wire on the ground at the pole where we had quit work that day. When we came back we found the wire leading from the roll to the pole cut in two. An investigation revealed that on Sunday afternoon a crowd of country folks had gathered around and that bets had been made as to whether the wire was hollow or not; some insisting that if the wire were not hollow you could not talk through it; others insisting that the wire was solid and that the voice travelled on the outside of it. The wire had been cut to settle the bet.

When we were building a line through territory in which the Flowers Lumber Company had been making surveys and acquiring right of way for a logging road, called the tramroad, we came down the county road with our construction crew: first, a gang digging post-holes; then two carpenters and two helpers, morticing the poles and fastening crossarms on them with lag screws and raising the poles with pikes and tamping the dirt around them; and just behind them the linemen, climbing the poles and stringing the wire. Such a sight these country people had never seen before. "Law," as one old woman exclaimed when she saw it, "the world sho' do move."

Standing all agape by the roadside in front of a small farmhouse was a little fellow about ten years old, watching the performance. His mother had not heard of the coming of the telephone line, but she had heard of the coming of the tramroad. Seeing all the unwonted activity and noticing her youngster standing in the midst of it, she called out, "You, John Henry, you come in this house this very minute. Don't you know that cramroad will fall on you and squush you to pieces?"

15

Admitted to the Bar

THE FALL OF 1891—THE FALL OF MY EIGHTEENTH BIRTHDAY— came. Dick went to Mercer. Wilk Wade went back, a senior. Others went off to school. Major Lane was conducting the Blakely Academy with increased attendance.

On October 7, 1891, Early Superior Court met. I filed my application for admission to the bar. In those days examinations were conducted by a committee in open court. The questions they asked me were practical questions, the answers to which I knew from my experiences in the clerk's office and in my father's office, from my practicing in the county court and in the magistrate's courts, and from listening to the trial of cases in the superior courts.

On October 8, 1891, I was given a law license, and became a full-fledged lawyer, entitled by the custom of the countryside to the title of "Colonel." Whereas theretofore I had been practicing in the minor courts as a matter of courtesy, I was now entitled to practice as a matter of right in all the courts of the State, except the Supreme Court; and I could be admitted to that Court by the exhibition of my license and a certificate of good character.

It was about this time that I was possessed, in my own mind, of a maximum of knowledge on three subjects. I thought I knew just about all there was to know on the subjects of law, women, and poker. After more than fifty years' experience with all these subjects, I have finally reached the point where I am convinced that I have never known a thing about any of them.

I began practicing as a partner of my father, under the firm name of R. H. Powell & Son. To the day of his death we never had a partnership agreement. We worked together, kept no books against each other, just took what we made and supported our families on it. He treated me as an equal. He pushed me forward into the trial of cases, merely sitting by and volunteering a suggestion now and then.

He told me that he would not be able to send me to law school; but he would send me to a better school—the school of experience. He told me of the old justice of the peace who said, "The justice's court is the place to learn to practice law; it teaches you what is the law and what ain't the law." He advised me, "Never solicit a case; but take every case that is offered to you whether you get any money out of it or not. Get the experience."

He was right. Law is a science, but the practice of law is an art—an art that no school can impart; it is not to be learned from books. It is just as impossible for a baseball player to learn how to bat 400 in the Big League by reading books on the subject, as it is for a lawyer to learn out of books how to try a case. In these things there is no substitute for experience.

A few years ago, in a case involving proceedings both in New York and in Georgia, I became associated with Professor Sturgis of the Yale School of Law, who was then taking his sabbatical leave and was connected with a prominent New York law firm. A hearing in Atlanta was scheduled on one feature of the case. I asked him to prepare a brief on the law question involved and to send it to me a day or so before his coming to Atlanta for the hearing. He did so, and when we met for a conference, he asked me what I thought of his brief. I replied: "The substance of it is that the courts of the country are badly divided on the question; but the majority of the courts and the greater weight of the authorities are with us. Yet, the question is a doubtful one."

"That is a fair thumb-nail sketch of it," he said.

I handed him a paper, and said "This is what we propose to file by way of answer."

He read it carefully. His face lit up. He said, "When we

take that position, the other parties to the case will have to give us what we are asking for before they can get what they are seeking."

"That is the object of it," I replied. Then I told him the old story of the New York policeman who, in the horse and buggy days, when the rule was in force which required a policeman to report at once in writing any dead horse found on any street on his beat, came upon a dead horse on Kosciusko Street. He could not spell "Kosciusko." So he caught the carcass by the heels and dragged it to Canal Street, and reported a dead horse on Canal Street.

I continued: "Up at Yale, Harvard, Columbia, and the other law schools, you are teaching young would-be lawyers to spell legal principles, but it is not humanly possible to teach them how to spell all the law. Realizing this, I try to teach the juniors in my law office how to move dead horses from legal streets the names of which they cannot spell to streets the names of which they can spell. So, anticipating where you would come out with your brief of the decisions, I asked Charlie Reid, one of our juniors, to look the situation over and to move the dead horse; and he has moved it to a street the name of which we can spell."

There is a maxim of Equity, quoted in our Code: "The equity of one who has been misled is superior to that of him who has willfully misled him". We had a justice of the peace, who made this maxim the pole star of every decision he rendered, but he quoted it, "The equity of him who has been mizzled is superior to that of him who has willfully mizzled him"; and the word "mizzle" is naturally a word of wide import.

For a number of years my father had been counsel for the Central Railroad and Banking Company of Georgia, now the Central of Georgia Railway; on January 1, 1892, I received also a contract and an annual pass as local counsel for the company. The chief duty of the local counsel was to defend against live-stock claims; hence they were often spoken of as "cow coroners."

For more than fifty years, I have ridden on passes, with the exception of the five years I was on the bench. I had leave of absence during that period; so I am counted on the railway records as being in continuous service for more than half a century. Mayhew Cunningham, the General Counsel, once said in jest that the company did not count out the five years I was on the bench because that was the only time in all my service that I ever won a case for them. Mayhew was just jealous, because I outrank him in years of service. He did not go with the company until April, 1892. I am the oldest man in time of service in the law department; and I will deferd my seniority in that respect against anyone who attempts to quibble it away.

Soon after my admission to the bar, my Blickensderfer typewriter did me a good turn. A firm of lawyers in Chicago sent me two sets of interrogatories to be taken at Fort Gaines, twenty miles north of Blakely. On the day named, I drove there and called on the first witness, who was the sheriff of the county. As soon as I mentioned my business, he said impatiently, "You can go on back home. They have already sent two lawyers here to take my testimony and I refused to answer the questions and have told them if they sent anyone else I would kill him. I can't kill you, because you and your father are my friends, but I am not going to answer those questions."

I did not have sense enough to know the danger I really was in; for the sheriff, though an excellent officer, was a dangerous man.

I got a copy of the code and began to examine it to find out what to do when a witness refuses to answer. The simplest procedure was to have the ordinary cite the witness and order him to answer, and, if he still refused, to commit him for contempt. I drew the application and presented it to Judge Foote, the ordinary, who, too, was an old friend of my father's and of mine. He looked at the paper, said to me, "You wait here," and went out and was gone about an hour.

When he returned, he said, "The sheriff objects very much to answering these questions, for personal reasons, but I have persuaded him that it is his duty to do so; and he has told me that if I will pass an order commanding him to answer, and if you will attach a copy of the proceedings to the interrogatories to show that he did not testify voluntarily, he will answer them." We complied with his demands, and he gave the testimony. The testimony of the other witness was formal, and was quickly taken.

When I got home I sent copies of the proceedings and the testimony to the Chicago lawyers with a letter giving them a brief statement of what had occurred. I also sent a bill for my services. I intended to charge four dollars. One of the naughts failed to print distinctly. I attempted to make it plainer by hitting over it, but the key did not hit the paper in the exact spot where the first naught had been printed.

In a few days, I received from the lawyers in Chicago a letter of thanks and a check for forty dollars, instead of the check for the four dollars I had expected. They also wrote that my charges were so extremely reasonable that they were sending me two more sets of interrogatories to take for them at the same price. The taking of them was involved with no complications and I netted forty dollars more, thanks to the unruliness of the old Blickensderfer.

About this time, the cottage in which a poor widow with several small children lived, burned; and all she had, except the children, was destroyed. A collection was taken up for her, and Mr. Sam Howard contributed the use of his vacant store next to our law office as a lodging place till she could find another home. The oldest child was a boy about ten years old called "Dees." It was his job to look after the smaller children while his mother was away from home. His easiest method of entertaining them was to bring them into my office and have them watch me write on the Blickensderfer. The little children would sprawl on the floor with their hippings all wet, or toy with the furniture, while Dees would meddle with anything he could get his hands on.

Early one afternoon I said to Dees, "If you will take the children away and not come back in here again today, I will give you a nickel to buy them gum drops with." He quickly accepted the proposition, and went off with the money. In less than an hour he was back with his brood. "Dees," I said, "didn't I give you a nickel on your promise to keep out of here the rest of the day?"

"Yes, sir," he assented, "but I decided that I would rather owe you a nickel than to stay out."

On one occasion when our briefs were due in the Supreme Court in a case of trover and conversion, to use the legal phrase, I was down with malarial fever and too sick to write it out on the typewriter. My father got Miss Henrie Chipstead, who had just taken a business course, to come to his home for me to dictate it to her. She seated herself at my bedside. I gave her the title of the case and began, "This case involves the conversion of a horse."

Henrie did not write it down, but began to look curiously at me. I repeated the statement. She, being church-minded, frowned anxiously and said, "Mr. Arthur, you know a horse cannot be converted."

Early Superior Court met on the first Monday in October; Miller Superior Court met on the third Monday; so that within two weeks from the time I was admitted to the bar, I was in Colquitt. I had joined the circuit-riders.

Being in Colquitt, I naturally thought of my little friend, Annie Wilkin. I had lost sight of her since the time in April when I had seen her on the train at Smithville and she had told me of her father's death. I inquired about her and learned that she was teaching in a log schoolhouse, a short distance off the big road, in Thompsontown district, about four miles from Colquitt.

Knowing that her school would be out at about half past four o'clock, I got the horse and buggy and drove out there and arrived at about that time. I saw her coming through the woods. When I had seen her on the train, she was sitting down. I did not notice then what I saw now, that she had grown considerably taller. She walked erect as usual. Her apparel, though becoming, was simple and inexpensive. She was a very pretty girl. I no longer thought of her as my sweetheart, but as my friend, and (though I did not definitely integrate the thought then), as some one who stood in the relation of a protégée to me.

As she reached the road, I got out of the buggy and greeted her. She seemed glad to see me. But there was about her an air that I then thought was bashfulness, caused by her immaturity, but which I now know was embarrassment at not being as well dressed as formerly. I asked her to ride in the buggy with me to Mr. Thompson's, where she boarded, and after we got there, we sat in the buggy and talked for a while.

She told me that, during the summer, she had taught in Baker County. She had a contract to teach the Thompsontown school during the fall and spring; and she hoped to be able to get the school in the Grimes community, a few miles east of Colquitt, for the next summer. She was trying to make enough money to go to college. She preferred Wesleyan, at Macon, where her sister, Miss Nellie, was graduated in 1884, but felt that going there would prove to be out of the question, and so she hoped to find a school where she could have both normal and academic training.

I tried to tell her how brave she was to endure these hardships, for in those days conditions in the backwoods were primitive and full of hardships; but she would have none of that. So we talked about the boys and girls of Blakely, and other things.

She had too much pride to tell me of the condition in which her father had left his estate, but I learned it from others. Dr. Wilkin had come to Colquitt from New York, a young man with a medical education. He had married a widow, whose family, from time immemorial, had lived in Georgia. He became one of the leading citizens of the county, and was well off in the monetary measures of those days. Mrs. Wilkin was beloved by everyone who knew her, for her fine Christian character and for her universal charity, not only the charity of alms-giving, but also the charity of self-giving to every one in need or distress.

When I read of Ellen O'Hara in *Gone with the Wind*, I thought of Annie's mother. Though Dr. Wilkin himself sat in the back pew at church, where he might easily be reached in the event of emergency calls, he was a member of the church and had a profound respect for it and its influences. Mrs. Wilkin was an active, devoted Christian. Their home was a center of culture and of godliness. So anxious were he and she that their children, the girls as well as the boys, should be well educated, so ready was he to contribute what he had to the needs of others and to the upbuilding of the community, so reluctant was he to press for the payment of bills due him for ministering to the sick, so ill was his health for the last few years of his life, that when he died no money was left. Annie inherited some land, but, being a minor, she could neither sell it nor use it as security to borrow money on it.

Annie's sister Nellie, a few years after her graduation, had married Mr. B. C. Bird, a young man, well-bred, and of better education than most men of that day and time. Mr. Bird and "Miss Nellie," as everyone called her, lived in Colquitt, and after Dr. Wilkin's death, their home was Annie's home. Miss Nellie was her mother over again. Mr. Bird, though he was never very successful financially, felt toward Annie as if she were his own sister or daughter and would have helped her had he been financially able to do so. All this is why the little chicken-feeding princess of my childhood days was teaching in a one-room log schoolhouse set back from the road, surrounded by the wide forests of the tall, soughing yellow pines.

When I thought of her bravery, of her independence, of the pride she had, and of the hardships she was enduring, I almost fell in love with her again, even though she was a mere child— as a matter of fact, she was only sixteen.

16

Riding the Backwoods Circuits

Upon my admission to the bar, i too became a circuit rider. I already knew many of the lawyers of our circuit (the Pataula) and the adjoining circuit (the Albany) and soon knew all of them. Despite the fact that these two circuits were located in the backwoods, in a remote section, their bars were generally reputed to be the two strongest in the State. Some of these lawyers, especially among the older ones, were studious and serious-minded; but many of them were, to put it mildly, picturesque, and smacked strongly of the originality which characterized the general population. Great comaraderie existed among them. In the main, they were very ethical.

One of the most picturesque of this group was James H. Guerry, brilliant, quick-minded—an advocate without a superior —tall and handsome. He was the judge of our superior court at the time I was admitted to the bar. He boasted that he had all the vices of a gentleman. It was told on him that, having become emotionally excited at a Methodist revival, he arose, and after confessing his sins, summed them up in this statement: "As far as I can recollect, I have committed every offense against the Ten Commandments and the Criminal Code of Georgia, except rape and murder."

He had been the solicitor general before he became the judge. I remember that one day, when I was a youngster sitting around and watching cases tried, he was prosecuting several women for keeping a lewd house. They had reserved the right to testify for one another, and one of them on the witness stand had testified on direct examination that she lived in the house and that nothing improper went on there. Judge Guerry took her on cross-examination and asked, "If nothing wrong went on in that house, why were Bob Smith, Tom Jones, Harry Brown [I am not calling the real names] and that bunch of fellows always hanging around there day and night?"

"Why, Mr. Guerry," she answered, "they came there just like you would."

Quick as a flash he replied: "Do you intend that for a plea of guilty?"

A sympathetic jury returned a verdict of not guilty. As he published it, he made a profound bow to the women and said, "Neither do I condemn thee. Go and sin no more."

On one occasion, the paternity of an illegitimate child was in question, and the mother was on the witness stand. Guerry asked her, "What have you named this boy?"

Objection was immediately interposed. Guerry, defending his right to ask the question, made a most brilliant argument along the line that creative love, though misdirected and violative of the conventions, affects the heart and mind of a woman; that every woman, instinctively, and not as a matter of reasoning, expresses an inborn satisfaction when she names her son for the man whom she knows to be his father; hence the naming of the child was an act that corroborated the woman's testimony. Judge Clarke was so impressed that he overruled the objection and directed the woman to answer the question.

Guerry repeated the question, "What did you name him?"

"I named him Guerry," she replied.

Judge Guerry it was who announced a great legal maxim, which has often been cited and quoted, and the soundness of which has never been questioned by the bar of this State. The sheriff had sent word to him while he was in a poker game that it was time to open the Court. "You tell the sheriff," he said to the bailiff who brought the message, "that in this State a judge of the superior court has but damned few privileges, but one of them is to do just as he damn pleases."

Judge Guerry had not been on the bench long before he resigned and announced his candidacy for Congress against the incumbent, Henry G. Turner. When the campaign came, Congress was still in session, and Judge Turner, who was an extremely conscientious man, deemed it his duty to remain in Washington. Guerry was making speeches all over the district. At a caucus of Judge Turner's supporters, it was decided that three of his friends should follow Judge Guerry around the district, and when he finished his speech, should ask the audience to remain a few moments while they said a few words in Judge Turner's behalf. Bill Spence of Camilla, Henry McIntosh of Albany, and John Triplett of Quitman were designated for the purpose.

Judge Guerry came to Blakely and had a big crowd in the courthouse to hear him. In the audience were Spence, McIntosh, and Triplett. After a few preliminary remarks, he said, "Wherever I have spoken in the last few weeks, three fellows have appeared, and after I have finished my speech, have asked the crowd which came to hear me to stay and hear them speak for my opponent.

"They remind me of this story: Once upon a time there was a little boy going to school and the lady teacher was trying to teach him to read the story of the three Hebrew children in the fiery furnace. He got on very well till he got to their names, 'Shadrach, Meshach, and Abednego.' He just could not say them; and she sent him to his seat to study them some more. When he came back he still could not say them. This happened several times. Finally, she took down the switch and said: 'I will give you one more chance; but if the next time you come you can't say them, I am going to give you a dose of this switch.' When he came back again, he read along all right till he got to the names, and then he burst out crying. 'What's the matter?' asked the teacher.

" 'Here's them three damn sons of bitches again,' the boy blurted out.

"Gentlemen," Judge Guerry continued, pointing to where Spence, McIntosh, and Triplett sat, "Here are those three fellows again."

When Judge Guerry resigned from the bench to run for

Congress, James M. Griggs was appointed to the judgeship, and Henry C. Sheffield to the solicitorship.

Judge Griggs did not make what should be called a great judge, because he was young when he went on the bench and had had but little experience in civil law, and his career on the bench was short; but he was intelligent and resourceful, and made a very satisfactory judge. He had not been on the bench long when he was elected to Congress; for a number of years, and until he died, he was a popular and successful congressman.

One of the ablest members of the Pataula Circuit bar, when I was admitted to its ranks, was Judge William D. Kiddoo, of Cuthbert. He was the judge of our superior court when I was born. He was very dignified and very forceful. He prepared and tried his cases without asking quarter, but if a professional courtesy was offered him, he accepted it and repaid it in kind. While he did not enter into the drinking and the poker playing indulged in by so many of our lawyers, and though he rarely told a joke, yet he was very friendly with the whole bar and always an agreeable person to meet; he was one of those who maintained the dignity of our bar.

My father, though a very jovial man, did not drink or gamble with the other lawyers. He was also of those who strove to make the bar a dignified profession.

Another of our lawyers, William C. Worrill, somewhat younger than Judge Kiddoo and my father, was a man of great personal and professional character, ability, and dignity. He was tall and handsome, with piercing eyes and forbidding brows, yet a very kindly man toward his friends. Though he had no thought of being pedantic, his speech was unconsciously somewhat stagey. He had intense physical and moral courage. He prepared his cases well, and tried them well. He knuckled to no man, used none of the arts of the politician, and yet the year I left Blakely, he was elected by the people to be the judge of the superior court—an office he held for many years and until his death. His son is now on that bench.

Friendly and cordial as he was, his dignity was such that there were few who called him Will; we usually called him Mr. Worrill or later Judge Worrill.

He indulged himself in one bad habit—swearing—but his oaths were so picturesque that they did not seem profane. There were some who said that there was a musical quality about them that robbed them of all vulgarity and grossness. He loved to tell of the time when he had his profanity approved by the clergy.

One day when he was sitting in his office at Cuthbert, a gentleman who introduced himself merely as Mr. Wilkerson came in and inquired of him if there was any reason why he could not be employed in a prospective litigation against an Alabama banker with a more or less unsavory reputation; and he replied that there was none. As the client began to outline the details of the fraud the banker had perpetrated upon him, it was not long before Mr. Worrill's indignation was aroused; and, as the recital continued, the indignation increased, and he was punctuating the conversation with one oath after another.

To set down the words he used would not describe his "cussing" at all. I have heard him tell it, words and all, and I can best describe it by resort to a figure of speech—a thunderstorm at night. First came the sheet lightning, flickeringly, illuminating the horizons, and the low muttering of distant thunder. Then came a full flash of lightning and the boom of the thunder. Then flashes zigzagged across and down the skies, and the sound of the thunder was as the roar of cannons. Then one mighty blast, a bifurcated bolt, with its sharp thunderclaps, closed the diapason. He told me that he had never cursed so well before in his whole life, and, as he reached the climax, he grabbed pen and paper and began to write out the bill in equity, which by now he was itching to file.

While he was writing and the client, Mr. Wilkerson, was sitting near by, another gentleman passed the door and, seeing Mr. Wilkerson, spoke to him. "Brother Wilkerson," he said, "will you be at Spring Vale to fill your appointment next Sunday?" "No," Mr. Worrill heard his client reply, "I must be at

Rehoboth; a good old man, who has been a member of my church for twenty years, has just died there, and I am to preach his funeral there next Sunday."

Mr. Worrill said nothing till the stranger left, and then he turned to the client and said, "Sir, I owe you an apology. While I am not a very good church member, and while I am sometimes given to profanity, I would not have used it in your presence, as I have, if I had known that you were a minister of the Gospel, for I have the greatest respect for the clergy."

"Ah, Brother Worrill," the minister-client replied, "considering the subject in respect of which you have used it, and the man you have used it about, I approve every word you have said."

He once gave a definition of the legal phrase, "sustaining general demurrer," that has never been excelled. A man who had attempted to draw his own pleadings in a law suit employed Mr. Worrill to come to his assistance when they were demurred to. Mr. Worrill did the best he could, but his task was hopeless. While he was still on his feet and the judge was making a statement that very clearly indicated he would have to sustain the demurrer, the client, who was seated behind him, began to tug at his coattail and asked, "What is he going to do?"

Now Mr. Worrill did not like to have his coattail tugged, especially when his attention was directed elsewhere, but he whispered back politely, "He is sustaining general demurrer to your pleading."

As he faced the judge again, the client gave another tug at his coattail. "What does that mean?" "It means that he is kicking your whole God-damned case out of court." ·

Old Dick Kennon, of the Fort Gaines bar, was a very interesting character. He was an old man when I first knew him. He was not an educated man; he never knew much law; but he had a fund of anecdotes and a natural power of oratory that enabled him to sway the common people or a jury to a degree that I have seen but few other men attain. So far as I know, he was never in politics for himself, but, on occasions, the National Democratic Committee used him successfully as a campaign orator in doubtful States.

In his later years, he went to Texas and came back to Fort Gaines only a short while before he died. He was then down and out financially, and was in ill health; but the old fire was still in him. He drank heavily. His feet were so swollen that he had to wear bedroom slippers instead of shoes. He wore in court a long linen duster instead of the Prince Albert coat he once had worn. He would sit in the courtroom with his eyes drooping or closed till the battle was on, and then he would pull himself together and would be his old self again.

One day he was trying a case before Judge Griggs and was apparently attempting to kill time, for some reason, by drawing out the examination of a witness to undue lengths, when the Judge spoke from the bench and admonished him. "Mr. Kennon, you must get through with this witness. I have been very patient with you."

Old Dick never raised his voice but in his characteristic drawl, slowly said, "Thank you, Your Honor. I like to see patience in a judge, especially a young judge."

He used to sit around and lecture us young lawyers. "A knowledge of the law," he would say, "is a bad thing for a lawyer. It may be against him and give him less confidence in his case. Study the facts and the jury, and the law will take care of itself."

A quaint member of the old bar was Colonel Eugenius Douglass, of Cuthbert. He was very old and no longer had any practice. He had been reared in the traditions of the Old South, had been a colonel in the Confederate Army, and, despite the infirmities of his extreme age, which bore heavily upon his mind as well as his body, he refused to surrender to them. His attire, in the style of the days gone by, was immaculate; his pride and dignity were untouched; as nearly as his tottering legs could carry him, he walked erect; his manners were those of a gentleman of the old school, punctilious of every convention, brooking no trespass.

Though he had no clients, no cases, no business in the courts, he still "rode the circuit." On the opening day of the superior court of every county, he was always present. At a convenient lull in the proceedings, he would rise, draw himself to his full height and dignity, and address the court, "May it please your Honor, I have pressing matters elsewhere this week, and I am taking the liberty of asking the court for leave of absence for the rest of the term."

The Judge with equal courtesy would reply, "The court will comply with your request, sir. The clerk will enter upon the minutes that Colonel Douglass has been granted leave of absence for the rest of the term."

The old Colonel would eat lunch (or dinner, as we called it) at the lawyers' table in the dining room of the local hotel, and then in the afternoon would return home.

On one occasion a member of the bar, meeting him at the hotel, said to him, "Colonel Douglass, you are looking well."

"Thank you, sir," the Colonel replied. "If it were not impolite for one gentleman to comment upon another's personal appearance in his presence, I would return the compliment."

Once when he was at the lawyers' table in the Livingston House at Blakely, Jim McGreggor, a local wag sitting at an adjoining table, said to him, "Colonel Douglass, what would you say if I should tell you that DuPont Strong here has a hundred pointer dogs? What do you think of that?"

"Sir," he summoned a spark out of the ashes of the old fire that once was in him, to say, "if you should tell me that Mr. DuPont Strong has a hundred pointer dogs, and should demand my opinion, I would have to say that in my opinion either Mr. DuPont Strong is a damned fool or you are a damned liar."

Clarence Wilson was a successful lawyer who did not pretend to any great knowledge of the law, but who did know how to handle facts and the jury. He was a master in getting cases continued when he did not wish to try them.

Judge Sheffield, who had succeeded Judge Griggs, called one of his cases one day. Clarence, not finding any valid reason for continuance, asked the Judge for a few minutes' conference with his client, hoping that while he was conferring the Judge would get engaged in some other case, and that he would get at least a temporary postponement. The Judge granted him ten minutes. He and the client retired to a vacant jury room. When the ten minutes were up, the Judge had him called. He came out from the jury room with a folded handkerchief pressed to his right jaw. "Go ahead with the case, Mr. Wilson," said the Judge.

"Your Honor, I do not believe I can do so, I am in so much pain," and he looked every word of it.

The Judge, in former days, had played poker with Clarence too often not to know his capacity for bluffing; so, after apparently taking the matter under consideration for a moment, he inquired, "What seems to be the trouble?"

Clarence was studying the Judge's face so closely that he had thoughtlessly removed the handkerchief from his jaw. "Your Honor, I think it is jumping toothache."

He put the handkerchief back, but put it to his left jaw.

"It must be," the Judge quickly responded. "It has jumped from one jaw to the other since you have been standing there. Go on with the case and see if you can talk it out of both jaws."

Judge I. A. Bush, of Camilla—"Coup Bush" he was generally called—was an excellent lawyer, especially in land cases, although he had been born in Miller County, before the War Between the States, and had only that modicum of education that was available in the hard times that followed the war.

Many a joke was told on him about the breaks he would make in speaking. I heard one of them as a boy. The famous divorce case in those days was that of Sasser v. Sasser. The young and beautiful Penelope Sasser, née Penelope Douglas, was suing her husband, Bill Sasser, who was not so young but was somewhat well off financially, for a divorce and alimony. The ground for divorce was cruel treatment. Coup Bush was for the plaintiff, and among the acts of cruelty he had had his client tell was this: one time when she was preparing supper and was leaning over into the barrel to get some flour, her old uncle, Gideon Wade, had slipped up behind her and kissed her, and that, when she told her husband about it, he so berated her that she lay awake all night and suffered a nervous breakdown. Coup was addressing the jury:

"Gentlemen of the jury: Consider the fiendishness of this brutal husband—how he heaped abuse and abuse and abuse upon this lovely young bride of his, until it was more than she could bear; till she lay awake all night long in anguish, tears flowing from her lovely eyes, sobbing and throbbing till her nerves were shattered and her health was ruined—and all for what? Just because her old uncle, Gideon Wade, had found her leaning over the flour barrel, preparing supper for her ungrateful husband, and had kissed her"—then suddenly remembering that he had not stressed the element of her not seeing him, added so quickly as to make it a part of the same sentence,—"behind."

Wig (William I.) Geer, of Colquitt, was an oddity. He had a good legal mind and had a fair small-town practice. He was amiable enough with his friends, but he had a tinge of cynicism in him. He could never resist the appeal of the grotesque and the fantastic. I once saw him appear in court wearing a white Prince Albert coat and a white top hat, and he had had the barber shave a gap in his hair across his head from his forehead to his neck, leaving it long on the sides.

He had good grade embossed stationery, but instead of putting his name on it, there was embossed into it the picture of a billy goat (William), of a human eye (I.) and of a set of harness (Gear). His card in the local paper, after giving his name and profession, added, "Practices in all courts, State and Federal, in North and South America, Europe, Asia and Africa, and elsewhere by special contract." He was popular with the people of his county, and represented them in the State legislature.

And then—when he was about sixty—at an early morning hour he walked into a bedroom where two young women were sleeping, and, probably in a fit of jealousy, shot one of them to death with a pistol, and quietly walked out.

He was indicted for murder. He made the mistake of applying for a change of venue and of getting the case tried in another county. In Miller county, he would have been convicted, but the jury would have saved him from death. The jury in the other county convicted him of murder, without recommendation of mercy, and he was sentenced to the electric chair. He was granted a new trial by the Supreme Court, but on the second trial the jury again convicted him and refused mercy and he was again sentenced to the chair. While this appeal was pending, he died in jail. When he was in jail he had two tombstones made, one for himself and one for the girl he had killed, and kept them in the cell with him.

Thus ended an odd but interesting career. His fellow members at the bar, while not condoning his crime, felt great pity for him.

The Bainbridge bar was full of good lawyers. We from the Pataula Circuit came into contact with the lawyers from the Albany Circuit, in which Bainbridge was located, most often at Morgan and at Colquitt. At Colquitt, by common consent, the lawyers from Bainbridge were given leave of absence until Tuesday morning. Bainbridge was twenty miles from Colquitt, and usually the members of the Bainbridge bar drove up after supper and got there about midnight; and several of them usually arrived in a state of inebriation.

One Tuesday morning, in the first case called, one of those who had arrived in that condition the night before was counsel for the plaintiff, and he had not yet fully recovered. As the case was called, he arose, his tongue thick and his legs wobbly, and announced, "Your Honor, I shall have to ask you to continue the case. I am a sick man, a very, very sick man."

"What is the trouble?" inquired the Judge, as if he did not know.

"I think it is locomotor ataxia. There is a regular epidemic of it among us Bainbridge lawyers."

A. L. Hawes, Fayette Hawes, we called him, was in my judgment the best all-around lawyer in the two circuits, but he was one of those Bainbridge lawyers who frequently suffered from this particular type of locomotor ataxia. We used to say that he was a better lawyer drunk than any of the rest of us could hope to be sober. He and Judge Sheffield had been friends since boyhood, and he would take liberties with the Judge, both on and off the bench, that none of the rest of us would have dared to take.

We were at Miller Superior Court, and Hawes was defending a young man for carrying a concealed weapon. It was during the period when Judge Sheffield had become fanatical on the subject of "pistol-toting." Hawes had been slipping off during the trial and taking frequent nips from his pocket flask; yet he made a wonderful argument for his client. Judge Sheffield in his charge to the jury ruined him, not so much by what he said as by the way he said it—that "damned em-*pha*-sis," as Hawes used to say. The noon recess came as the jury retired. The Judge came down from the bench and was passing by where Hawes was collecting his papers, when Hawes said to him, "Henry, if you had not made that concluding argument against me, I would have freed that boy. Why did you treat me that way?"

The Judge indulgently said, "Go on, Fayette, you know I have to charge the jury the law."

"You don't have to do any such thing. The Supreme Court has held in the last year that you do not have to charge the jury the law in a criminal case."

"You would better quit drinking. You are seeing things."

"I'll bet you a dollar I can show it to you."

To humor him, the Judge replied, "I will take the bet."

Hawes staggered to a table, picked up a current volume of the Georgia Reports, turned through the pages, put his finger on a sentence in one of the opinions, put the page up in front of the Judge, and said, "Read that."

The Judge read, "The law requires impossibilities of no man." He laughed and handed Hawes the dollar.

It was customary at the terms of Miller Superior Court to devote one of the evenings to a lying contest between the lawyers of the two circuits. Fishing yarns were opposed to snake stories; alleged feats of skill, against alleged feats of cunning; fictitious personal experience, against other fictitious personal experiences; and so on. One evening, Hawes had led off for the visiting team with some big yarn or other. Clarence Wilson had been selected to lead off for the home team. He began:

"A few years ago I was in Rome, Italy, and, as I came down one of the streets, I saw the most beautiful woman I have ever seen. I inquired, and found she was the Pope's oldest daughter."

"You win," broke in Hawes. "How did you ever think of that lie?"

"But I have not told it," Clarence remonstrated.

"You have told enough," Hawes countered; but it took some time to explain to Clarence how he had won.

Most lawyers of that day and time strove more for oratorical effect than is usual with modern lawyers. Some of these old-timers were real orators and displayed a high quality of forensic skill. Old Dick Kennon, for instance, had much natural power as a public speaker and had also the skill to ridicule the force of an opposing argument out of existence by a resort to whimsical speech. But there were others who affected eloquence without any support for it except a loud voice and sometimes a stagy manner. I recall hearing one of these "falsetto" orators in action one day. He had been employed to prosecute a young Negro for murder and was addressing the jury. There was evidence that the accused had hidden himself with an ax behind the curb of a well where an old Negro was accustomed to come, and that when the old Negro came and was lowering the bucket into the well, the accused split his skull with the ax.

"Gentlemen of the jury," he cried at the top of his voice, "what did this young Negro have in his heart when he hid behind the well curb with that ax?"

He repeated the question—this time more slowly and in a more dramatic tone—"What did this young Negro have in his heart when he hid behind the well curb with that ax?"

He then drew back from the jury, lowering his voice and pointing his finger at them, and uttered in a hoarse whisper, "I will tell you! I will tell you! I will tell you what he had in his heart."

He stopped a moment for a dramatic pause and then roared out, "He had blood in his heart!"

One day I walked into a county court in an adjoining county. The setting inside the bar was such as to reveal the nature of the case. On one side there were an old man, his son in the early twenties, and a lawyer. On the other side was a pregnant woman, with a baby about two years old in her arms, and her lawyer was standing. As I entered the door, the judge made a remark that indicated his doubt that the evidence was sufficient to hold the young man. Whereupon, the woman's lawyer threw himself back into a dramatic pose and roared out, "Why, your Honor, do you mean to say that you would send away from this court without redress this good woman who swears that this man is the father of her child? And she is as honorable, as truthful, as pure and as virtuous as any woman in the county, except, of course (and he lowered his voice) she has one bastard child and is about to have another."

Up in the Southwestern Circuit, just above our circuit, one of these would-be young orators was appointed by the court to defend a Negro charged with hog-stealing. The facts were against him; oratory was his only resort.

"Who was it," he said to the jury, "that was brought from his native lair in Africa to our shores and when sold into slavery, made our farms grow white with cotton and our barns to be filled with corn? The Negro!

"Who was it, when the war clouds, rolling dun, hovered over our Dixie land, and husbands, fathers, and sons were at the front repelling the enemy, stayed at home, tilled our farms, and protected our women and children with a loyalty and a devotion unparalleled in the history of the world? The Negro!

"Who was it, when the war was lost and the Emancipation

Proclamation had stricken the shackles of slavery from him, still stayed on and made the most loyal free labor the world has ever known? The Negro!

"Gentlemen, when you come to consider your verdict, hold these things in mind in favor of my poor client here—the Negro."

The Solicitor General, heavy-set, prosaic, direct-speaking Tom Hudson, arose and slowly said, "Who stole that hog? The Negro," and sat down.

Sam Morton, of Colquitt, was a unique character. He was not a member of the bar, but during all the time I knew him he had some connection with the courts—justice of the peace, county judge, and, I believe, ordinary for a short time. He had plenty of sense, but delighted in posing as a mere blatherskite. One day when he was sitting as judge of the county court of Miller county, a long-winded old gentleman who practiced law on week days and preached on Sunday, argued at great length that under the peculiar language of the Act creating the county court of Miller County, the court had no jurisdiction in civil cases. He talked and talked and Sam did not interrupt him. Finally he appeared to be at an end of his argument and Sam said, "My friend, I know that you know more religion in a minute than I will ever know and that you know more law in a minute than I will ever know; but don't you know that if I were to agree with you and hold that my court has no civil jurisdiction, it would not be a month before some other darn fool would be here arguing that it has no criminal jurisdiction; and if I were to agree with him too, what sort of a hell of a court would it be?"

Here seems to be a good place to throw in as lagniappe the story of Joe McCommack and the court:

In the early days of my practice, my father and I defended Joe McCommack, a character about town, on a misdemeanor charge. While the jury was out, Judge Guerry called us to the bench and told us that he was convinced Joe was not guilty and that, if the jury convicted him, he would set the verdict aside.

The jury found him guilty, and, to complete the record, the judge imposed a light fine. Joe started to the clerk's desk to pay it. My father tried to stop him, by telling him what the judge had said.

"No," Joe said, "I am going to pay it. I believe in being fair. This is the sixth time I have been tried in this court. Three of the times I was guilty and they found me not guilty. This is the third time I was innocent and they found me guilty. That evens it up. I will pay the fine and keep it even."

A few weeks after I was admitted to the bar at Blakely, Sam Bennet was admitted at Quitman, and about the same time, there was admitted one who was soon to join us in a trinity of devoted friendship, Albert Russell, of Bainbridge. Sam moved to Camilla, became the partner of Bill Spence, the solicitor general of the Albany circuit, and handled his civil business. Albert spent a short while after his admission at Bainbridge, and then went to Augusta, where he was a protégé of Judge Joseph R. Lamar, later of the United States Supreme Court. After a year at Augusta, he came back to Bainbridge, and soon became the leading member of that bar.

17

Brother Powell "Eases Along"

M Y RECOLLECTION IS THAT ABOUT THE TIME I WAS ADMITTED
to the bar, the old Blakely Academy was abandoned. The
town council built what was then considered a modern school
building, located above the Methodist Church, on what was
then called Fort Gaines Street and is now called College Street.
They named it the Blakely Institute. I think that Major Lane
taught there the last year he was in Blakely.

This was the year that the question of my dancing career
became acute in the Baptist Church. My relations to the church
had become prominent enough to attract attention. I was probably the church clerk at the time. I did serve as clerk for a year
about then, and I usually went as a delegate from the church to
the Bethel Association, of which it was a member. Brother Hobbs
preferred charges against me for dancing.

Our pastor was Reverend Z. T. Weaver, Cousin Zack we
called him in our family, as he was distantly related to our mother
on the Perry side. Not only was Zack Weaver one of the best
preachers I have ever known, but he was one of the best men.
In both capacities he was full of love for mankind and equally
full of plain common sense. He was almost an Ichabod Crane
in appearance, and had a shrill, piping voice with the semblance
of a drawl in it. He had a keen sense of humor and was a natural-
born diplomat.

When the church conference was called to try me, Brother
Weaver was in the chair. A number of my friends were there,
and we might have outvoted Brother Hobbs; but Cousin Zack
did not want to take that course. He opened the discussion with

this statement, delivered in that shrill, piping, drawling voice of his, and with a twinkle in his eye: "Since these charges were preferred against Arthur, I have had an investigation made; I have found no one willing to say that he has ever danced. They all say that he is just trying to learn how to dance. He cannot learn to dance"—and then with his voice rising to greater shrillness and his eyes twinkling faster, he added, "His feet are too big. My advice is to just let him ease along."

Major Lane, with all his inborn suavity, arose and addressed the chair: "I move that the pastor's suggestion be adopted, and that Brother Powell be allowed to ease along."

The motion was carried unanimously. Subsequent events have proved that the pastor was just about correct in his prophecy as to my ability to learn to dance.

By this time, Blakely was growing; Early County was growing; the whole section was growing; and our practice was growing. I hated to see our beautiful forests of long-leaf yellow pines hacked for turpentining or felled for sawmilling. But these things brought money and many much needed developments, which in our poverty we had been unable to undertake; and they brought practice and fees to the lawyers.

In the fall of 1892, our old friends, Kilpatrick and John Wade, became co-principals of the Blakely Institute, in the place of Major Lane, who had entered the practice of law. They had with them a very attractive coterie of young women teachers, who added much to the social life of the community, and I fell in love with several of them.

I thought of Annie Wilkin occasionally, but for the most part thought of her as a memory of my childhood; and it seemed to me to be an incongruity that she held a first-grade teacher's license at the age of sixteen. I did learn that in the fall of 1892 and in the spring of 1893 she was teaching a piney-woods school in the Union District, west of Colquitt, and later entered the Normal College at Milledgeville.

About this time, Dr. Strong moved from Savannah to Blakely

and opened a drugstore. He brought with him his wife and an attractive family of little girls; but we were told that more was to come; that Mary Lou, the young lady of the family, was off at college and would come to Blakely when she finished there.

One June morning I was returning from Atlanta. Two young ladies came in and took the seat ahead of me. They paid no attention to me. I was just a country yokel. Then there came in a blond youth, with tailored clothes and yellow shoes, and took the seat across from them. I saw them cutting their eyes at him; and the train had hardly gotten under way before he was boldly reciprocating the glances. Conversation across the aisle was bound to follow, and it did, with the girls entering into it at first with the usual maidenly hesitation and giggling, and with the boy getting bolder and bolder every minute. Before they got to Macon he produced a photograph of himself and offered to present it to them in exchange for their names. One of them gave the name, "Gladys Holmes"; I forget what the other said her name was.

He wrote down the names and presented the photograph to them. They received it, giggled and made facetious remarks about it. Just as the train was pulling into Macon, they asked him which of them he intended the photograph for, and he said it was for both of them. Whereupon, they produced a pair of scissors and cut it in two, lengthwise. One of them took one half and the other took the other, and they stowed the halves away in their respective handbags.

I had to change cars at Macon for Blakley. Just before the train left, Miss Gladys Holmes came in and, by coincidence, again took the seat just in front of me. When the conductor came along and punched her ticket, I followed him back and asked him where the ticket was to, and he said, "Blakely." As I came back, she asked me if I knew where we got dinner. I told her Smithville. She had spoken first; so I leaned over the back of the seat and asked her, "South of Macon, do you travel under the name of Gladys Holmes or Mary Lou Strong?"

She gasped, but finally managed to inquire what I knew

about Gladys Holmes. I told her that I sat just back of her all the way from Atlanta. She then broke down and confessed.

When I told her my name, she said that her mother had written her about me and the other boys in my set; and she begged me never to tell them about her escapade, and, most of all, not to tell her mother. I refused to make any promise, but I told her I knew how to keep a secret. I never told it till she was happily married.

In April, 1893, I was selected to make the address on Confederate Memorial Day, quite an honor for a boy of my age. I have recently seen a copy of the address and it is not as sophomoric as some of my previous effusions were. There was liberal quotation from Father Ryan's poems, but that is quite in order on such occasions even to this day. Some of its smoothness of diction may be due to the editing given it by Miss Maggie Bell, one of our teachers, of whom I was very fond. Even then, I was advocating that without detracting one iota from the validity of the "lost cause" or the gallantry of the Southern soldiers, we should seek to allay all the bitterness existing between the North and the South, and to be brothers with every section of the Union.

There always has been a solemn impressiveness about these memorial exercises. Once a gentleman from the North happened to be in my office at Blakely on Memorial Day, and at my invitation he went with me to the church where the exercises were held and to the cemetery where the flowers were placed on the soldiers' graves. He was much impressed and told me that he almost wept when he heard Amzie Davis sing "Lorena." This is the song that Margaret Mitchell mentions in *Gone with the Wind*. It is a song that only a Southern-born woman can sing as it should be sung. I have heard professionals try to sing it on the radio, but they wholly failed to catch the spirit of it. There is a subtlety about it and a nuance in the minor chords that cannot be expressed in a musical score.

Came the fall of 1893: John Wade quit teaching to become the cashier of the newly organized Bank of Blakely; Kil became the sole principal of the Blakely Institute; Annie Wilkin entered as a sophomore at the Georgia Normal and Industrial College at Milledgeville; I had followed my father's advice and was taking every case offered me, often getting little or no compensation, but developing skill as a trial lawyer.

Kil and the lady teachers boarded with Wyatt Alexander's mother, Miss Ella, as we called her. She was a very fine woman, sensible, good, and much interested in all us young folks. Many of my evenings I spent at her home in Kil's room or in the parlor with the young ladies. Kil's mentality was broadening, as well as ours. Miss Ella's home was more than a social center. It was a cultural center.

The bicycle fad had come to Blakely a few years earlier. Even ten years before, Bob Dostor had one of those two-wheeled monstrosities with the high wheel in front and the small wheel in the rear; but after it threw Bob and broke his nose, it lost favor. It was the coming of the safety type that brought the fad to us.

One bright moonlight night several of us, including Kil, decided to ride our bicycles out to Howard's Landing, nine miles away on the Chattahoochee River. Punctures were frequent in those days; so no bicyclist got far from base unless he had along rubber patches, pump, volatile glue, and other appliances. Midway the trip, Kil gave a howl of pain, jumped from his bicycle, and began rapidly disrobing himself, until he stood dancing around almost nude in the middle of the big road.*

"What in the world is the matter with you?" we asked him.

He exclaimed between jumps, "Bees, wasps, hornets, yellow jackets, spiders, something stinging me! My trousers are full of them."

We investigated. He had put into his hip pocket a collapsible tube of glue, containing some very volatile substance to make it dry quickly. In the course of his riding, he had so mashed the

---

*The term "big road" must be a colloquialism; we always used it to describe a public road or highway as distinguished from an alley, a settlement road, a path, or a farm road.

tube that the glue had oozed out and spread upon his buttock, and the evaporation of it was blistering him.

My first bicycle was named "Old Buck." He had the traits of a Mexican mustang pony. He would ride along docilely till I thought I had him gentled, and then he would shy at something and throw me over his head.

John Wade and I were out riding one Sunday afternoon. We passed some girls out strolling just before we came to the footbridge over the Baptist Branch. We decided to show off our skill by riding over the bridge, which consisted of two twelve-inch planks laid side by side for a length of about forty feet. Half way across, Old Buck threw me into a clear pool. The water was less than a foot deep, but he nearly drowned me by jumping in on top of me and cudgeling me with his pedals every time I tried to get up. John was looking back laughing at me when his bicycle pitched him off into a mudhole where a bunch of hogs had been wallowing.

My next bicycle was named "Rhadamanthus." He was of better blood. With him I became quite a skilful rider. I got where I could ride him over footbridges or small ditches, without even putting my hands on the handle bar. Usually, I made eight or ten miles an hour, but one day, with the wind to my back, I rode the twelve miles from Bluffton to Blakely in forty-five minutes. Trips of twenty miles or less I constantly made with him. Once or twice I rode him to Bainbridge, forty miles away. I once made, in a day, a trip of a hundred miles over the sandiest of roads.

I wrote an occasional letter to Annie Wilkin while she was in college at Milledgeville. They were such letters as a kindly old gentleman would write to a young girl in whom he felt a friendly interest. She answered them in a very impersonal way.

I was admitted to the bar of the Supreme Court in 1893, I think it was. That most famous of all Chief Justices of Georgia, Logan E. Bleckley, was in office. His son, Logan Bleckley, was the deputy clerk of the Supreme Court. It was at this time that I met these two men who were so valuable to me in my future years. The present efficient clerk of our Supreme Court is Katharine Bleckley, daughter of Logan Bleckley and granddaughter of Chief Justice Bleckley.

On the day I first saw Judge Bleckley, he was in the clerk's office asking Logan about the twins, a boy and a girl born to him a few days before. Logan said, "Two in time saves nine," and he had no more children. After he was seventy, Judge Bleckley was married again and in due course twin boys arrived at his home.

Soon after the birth of his twins, Judge Bleckley was attending a session of the Georgia Bar Association at Warm Springs. Some friend of his offered a resolution congratulating him on the event. I well remember the unfeigned resentment with which Judge Bleckley arose when the resolution was read, and said:

"Mr. President, I do not believe that this is a matter over which this Association has any jurisdiction; but, if it has, I hope that in the interests of decency and the sparing of my feelings, you will refrain from exercising it."

I argued a case in the Supreme Court a year or so later. Judge Bleckley had resigned, and Judge Thomas J. Simmons had become Chief Justice. Judge Simmons was also a great jurist. More important to me personally, he was from Crawford County, as my father was; and they had long been friends; so he had an interest in me from the time he first saw me. My case was a will case, where the will had been admitted to probate without having been attested by three witnesses as required by the law of Georgia. I had hardly finished my opening statement of the questions involved when Judge Simmons shot this question at me, "Why isn't the judgment of the court of ordinary admitting this instrument to probate as a will conclusive, since the Constitution makes the court of ordinary a court of general jurisdiction over the probate of wills?"

The thought flashed through my mind, "Can it be possible that the Chief Justice does not know that even probate cannot give life to a will that is void for lack of proper attestation?"

I hesitated a moment and then answered, "I think the

answer is that the Constitution gives jurisdiction to that court to probate wills, and an instrument does not become a will until it is lawfully attested."

He smiled with satisfaction and said, "That is the answer. I just wanted to see if you knew it."

Judge Simmons was a rare old gentleman. He was a member of the Hardshell Baptist church, and fully subscribed to its tenet that good liquor never hurt any man. I have seen him mount the bench, and in about an hour, Clayton, the Negro porter of the Court, would open the door back of the bench and in a low tone call him. He would retire to the library, and in a short while he could be seen coming back through the door wiping his lips and mustache. He would lean back in his chair, close his eyes, and in a moment would be snoring and apparently sound asleep. But appearances are sometimes deceitful. Let the lawyer making the argument cite a discredited or overruled case, and, without opening his eyes, the Chief Justice would interrupt him to say, "Yes, and we took it back in Brown v. Smith, in such-and-such a Georgia Report, page so-and-so."

Judge Simmons also had the habit, if a lawyer had stated his point and was merely repeating himself, of stopping his snoring long enough to say, "We have had enough on that point; if you have another point, go ahead and make it." One day he was attending services at one of the Hardshell churches in Crawford County. The minister preached long and tiresomely. Judge Simmons' stentorian snore could be heard all over the room, when he suddenly suppressed the snoring and said aloud, "That will do on that point. If you have any other point, go ahead and make it."

Chief Justice Simmons was succeeded by Judge William H. Fish. There is an old court story of how Judge Dave Roberts, a quaint old judge of the superior court in one of the south Georgia circuits, turned a joke on Chief Justice Fish. It was reported to Judge Fish that Judge Roberts had said Clayton, the Negro porter of the Court, must have written the opinion in an important case in which he had reversed a ruling by Judge

Roberts. A few days later, some one said that Judge Roberts was in the Capitol, and Judge Fish sent one of the secretaries to ask him to come into the library where the Justices were in consultation. When he came in, Judge Fish rang for Clayton, and, as he appeared, said, "Judge Roberts, I wish to have you meet Clayton whom, I understand, you are crediting with having written my opinion in a recent land case from your circuit."

"Clayton, I am glad to meet you," Judge Roberts replied, "and I wish to apologize. I do not believe you wrote that opinion. You look like a right intelligent darkey."

Judge Roberts was the only man I ever saw who could sit cross-legged with both feet touching the floor.

In mercantile failures our courts frequently appointed Tom McDowell as receiver, even when he was a very young man. During his boyhood, he kept books for J. M. & R. W. Wade; so he knew how to keep his records accurately and correctly. Especially in dishonest failures was he particularly valuable in tracing out schemes to defraud and in ferreting out hidden assets. Once a firm of merchants failed at Arlington and, representing the creditors, I filed a bill for a receivership, and the judge appointed Tom Mc. as receiver. The rumor came that just before the failure, one of the partners had filed for record a deed, from himself to a trustee for his children, to a large tract of land in Baker County, and, to give it an honest appearance, had dated it back two years. On the day of the failure, there had come a storm and flood which washed out the bridges on the railroad and on the highways, so that it was impossible for about a week for any of us to get to Newton, the county seat of Baker County, to examine the deed which had been filed for record there. The first day the road was open, Tom went to Newton. He came back jubilant. "The deed is dated back two years," he said, "but it was written with the blue-black ink which I used at Wade's Store, which is blue at first and then turns black, and right now it is in process of turning and will be dead black in less than a month." In my bill, I had charged the dating back of the deed and the defendant's counsel had sent me a copy of the sworn answer he expected to file, denying it. A day or so later, we met at Albany for a hearing before the judge. I gave defendant's counsel a copy of the affidavit which Tom had made, giving a description of the ink and his sworn opinion that the deed was less than a month old.

Defendant's counsel was an honest man. He called his clients outside for a short conference; when he returned to the courtroom, he withdrew the answer and admitted that the deed was less than two weeks old and that it had been dated back, as charged—and the creditors got the land. But the point of the story is yet to come. Tom Mc. was mistaken; the ink on the deed today—forty years later—is just as blue as it was the day it was written.

A few years later Tom Mc. was elected State Senator. He was tall, handsome, intelligent, always well dressed, and genial, so that he was quite popular with his fellow Senators. One evening on the roof garden of the Capital City Club in Atlanta, several Senators, including Tom Mc., were together at a table. I knew all of them and I arose from where I was sitting to go over and speak to them. Having seen Tom earlier in the evening, I spoke to the others first, and one of them undertook to introduce me to "Senator McDowell."

To the astonishment of all the party, except Tom, I replied, "I know Senator McDowell, he once swore to a lie in a case I was in."

They jumped to their feet expecting to have to act as peacemakers, but Tom calmly said, "Sit down, gentlemen, it is true." And then their astonishment was even greater, until we told the episode of the dated-back deed, the blue-black ink, and Tom's affidavit.

18

Judge Henry C. Sheffield

I WISH NOW TO PRESENT MORE FULLY THAN I HAVE PREVIOUSLY done one of the most remarkable characters I have ever known—Henry C. Sheffield. He was born in Miller County, near Colquitt, in the fifties. Even in the days when I first knew that county, it was full of Sheffields. My father used to tell me that if I were in Miller County and met a man I did not know I should say, "Good morning, Mr. Sheffield." If he said he was not a Sheffield, I should say, "Good morning, Mr. Bush." If he protested that he was not a Bush, I should say, "Good morning, I see that you are a stranger here."

I could reconstruct much of Judge Sheffield's early life from things others have told me, but as he himself has told me of it with brutal frankness, I can tell you in his own words that he was the "meanest, sorriest, most no-'count boy in the county." As he came to young manhood he was just as mean, just as worthless. He told me of shooting the cow of some poor woman who depended on it as her only means of living, out of pure wantonness and cruelty—just to see the cow die.

He was admitted to the bar under the slipshod methods of the old days. He made some money and borrowed some wherever he could, but he threw it away and never paid a debt. He drank, he gambled, he ran the whole gamut of the vices. He had respect for neither God nor man. When he was still a young man, he killed one of his cousins in a pistol duel at Colquitt, and fled to Texas to avoid retaliation from the dead man's family, rather than from fear of the law, for by all accounts he shot in self-defense. In Texas, he became a common tramp. After a year or

161

so, when he thought enough time had elapsed for things to cool down, he made his way back to Georgia.

When he could not get food or lodging by begging, he took it by force. As he came through Alabama on his way back, he arrived at the home of an old couple just after nightfall. He asked them for supper and a bed for the night. They told him that they had finished supper, that the only food in the house was a small piece of side meat and two eggs, and that the only bed in the house was the one they slept on. At the point of his pistol, he made them cook the meat and the eggs for him, and made them sleep on a pallet on the floor while he slept on their bed. He went back to Colquitt, stood his trial for murder, was acquitted, and began practicing law again.

It was several years later when I first knew him. He had married a very fine young woman of good family and good breeding, and had moved to Arlington, fourteen miles from Blakely. By then he had managed to acquire an excellent knowledge of the law and had a good practice. He was a very forceful advocate. I have never seen anyone who was more adept than he in dealing with circumstantial evidence.

Though at the time I first knew him he still belonged to the drinking and gambling element of the bar, and usually carried a concealed pistol or a pair of brass knucks, yet he had become a property owner, had paid his debts, and was taking great interest in his family.

A little later, as his children began to grow older, he quit drinking; and when he became a solicitor general he quit gambling. Toward the close of his life he became a prominent member of the Methodist Church and one of the civic leaders of his community.

He became Judge of the Superior Court in 1893 or 1894. He immediately placed himself on the side of law and order. He became a crusader against barrooms, gambling, and the carrying of concealed weapons. He built a large and beautiful residence. He sent his boys and girls to college and began to take a lively interest in the schools and in the churches. He became the model citizen of our section. Before he died he was so militant in the moral cause as to be fanatical.

True repentance implies restoration. This man undertook to make the restoration. He paid old debts, which were outlawed by the statute of limitations—often paid them to the widows or heirs of those to whom they were originally owed. He spent days on a trip through Alabama hunting for the old couple whom he had forced to give him food and lodging at the time he came tramping it back from Texas. He kept on trying to trace them until he found them in direst poverty in a little hut in extreme north Alabama. He figured the food and lodging at three dollars, added compound interest at eight per cent per year, and paid it to them—and gave them a goodwill offering besides.

On the bench he was so fearless, so impartial, so instilled with the principles of justice that his hold on the people of his circuit was tremendous. Justice for high and low alike was an obsession with him. He knew the law, knew the technical as well as the substantive doctrines of the law; but he did not hesitate to violate any and all of them to achieve what he thought to be right and justice. He would say to counsel as he did so, "Oh, I know you can take me to the Supreme Court and reverse me, but this plaintiff is not entitled to recover, and I am not going to allow it if I can help it"; or, "This defendant owes this debt, and he is not going to escape payment if I can help it."

An interesting sidelight is that it was rare for an appeal to be taken from such decisions of his. The lawyer might wish to appeal, but the client would not let him. I do not mean to say that he thus took the bit in his teeth in all cases, or even in most cases, or in any case involving fairly doubtful questions of law or of fact; it was only in a case where right and justice were manifestly with one side of it. Usually, he was the able and impartial jurist, following every legal precept and convention.

One day I saw him apparently in deep thought while the jury was out in the case of a Negro charged with murder. The jury came in with a verdict of guilty. He turned to the foreman and asked if the jury had taken into consideration a certain fact as to which there was no dispute in the evidence. The foreman replied they had never thought of it as having any particular bearing in the case, that counsel for neither side had mentioned it in the arguments. The Judge then began to outline the situation to the jury, and inquired how, if this undisputed fact were true, could the defendant be the man who fired the fatal shot. The foreman responded that he did not believe the Negro was guilty. The other jurors immediately agreed with the foreman. The Judge then inquired of the solicitor general if he had any other evidence. The solicitor general said "No."

"All right, Mr. Foreman, you may put the word, 'not,' before the word 'guilty'; and I will receive your verdict."

While the new courthouse was being built in Blakely, court was held in the opera house. I defended a young Negro woman against the charge of killing another Negro woman in a fight. The testimony of the witnesses who saw the killing, all Negroes, had left the case where I was almost sure to get an acquittal, when at the last moment a white man came to the stand and testified that the defendant had made, in his presence, a statement that greatly incriminated her. This turned the tide and the jury returned a verdict of manslaughter, and the judge sentenced her to one year in prison.

This occurred just before the noon recess. I happened to come back with the Judge, and we arrived at the opera house a few minutes before the time for the court to convene. Instead of going around to the entrance, we came up the back way and entered the main room by coming through the stage scenery. As we came into one of the wings, we heard a low, crooning voice and we stopped to listen. The sheriff, instead of taking to jail the woman who had just been convicted, had left her sitting just below the stage. She had a baby about a year old and was nursing it and talking to it. We heard her say, "Baby, white folks swear a lie on your mamma. Your mamma got to go 'way and leave you for a year. But your mamma won't forget you. She will come back to you."

Neither of us said anything for a moment, but, after we had

come into the main auditorium, the Judge asked me if I intended to file a motion for a new trial. I told him that I did not see any ground on which to hope to get one; that, if the white man had told the truth, my client had gotten off as light as I could hope for.

He knew the white witness, knew him better than I did. "What is back of his testimony? I am sure that there is something that has not come out," he said.

I told him that I suspected the witness's motive, but had no proof to justify my suspicion.

All the afternoon, I saw the Judge calling to the bench and talking to one man after another from the community in which the witness lived.

Finally, he spoke up and said, "Mr. Solicitor, in regard to the case of the Negro woman sitting back there—the one the jury convicted for manslaughter this morning, I am reliably informed that the dead woman carried a policy of insurance in one of the Negro lodges, agreeing to pay two hundred dollars if she was killed in a fight and the person killing her is convicted for the homicide, and that the relatives of the dead woman have agreed to give Tom Thomas [as I will call him] half of the money to help them convict this woman. Have the witness come to the front."

The Judge put Tom through a searching cross-examination. He stuck to his story as to the statement which he had said the accused had made, but finally broke down and admitted he had been promised half of the insurance money to testify in the case.

"Mr. Solicitor, have you any additional testimony?"

"No, sir, Your Honor."

"Fill in a skeleton motion for a new trial, Mr. Powell, with an order granting it."

It took me but a moment to do so.

"Call twelve jurors into the box," he ordered. "Hand the indictment to the jury. Gentlemen, have one of your members, as foreman, enter a verdict of not guilty on the indictment."

When the verdict was signed and published, he turned to all

in the courtroom and said, "Our courts must be kept as places of truth and justice."

Any lawyer acquainted with criminal procedure knows what a cutting through of form and technicality was involved in the summary way in which Judge Sheffield dealt with the two situations I have just described.

He had a keen sense of humor; and the form of speech and the mental attitude of the Negroes interested and amused him. Usually when the time for the call of the criminal docket arrived, the prisoners, mostly Negroes, were brought from the jail and were seated just inside the bar rail, on what was colloquially called the "mourners' bench."

The first thing in order was to question them, so that those who wished to plead guilty could do so without delay and so that counsel could be assigned to those who were not able to employ counsel. I can see him now interrogating the prisoners:

"You little short nigger at the end, stand up. What's your name?"

"My name's Tommy Smith, but dey calls me 'Gator.' "

"What have they got you for?" and he would begin looking up the name on the docket.

"Sumpen bout er hawg, Jedge."

"Got a lawyer?"

"Naw sir; ain't able to hire none."

"I appoint you, Mr. Oliver. You kinky-headed nigger next to him, stand up. What's you name?"

"Bozy Reddick."

"What have you been doing?"

"Dey caught me skinnin' " (skin is a Negro card game) "An' I pleads guilty."

"All right, sit down. I will attend to you later. You next one there, with the toothpick behind your ear, stand up. What's your name?"

"Bum Mulligan."

"What have you been doing, Bum?"

"I hain't been doin' nuthin', Jedge. 'Fore God I hain't."

The Judge had caught his name on the docket and the charge against him. "I suppose you are pleading guilty, too. You are charged with vagrancy."

Bum got busy at once. "No, sir, Jedge, I hain't guilty. 'Fore God I hain't. An' I needs er lawyer, an' I hain't got no money to hire arry one, but I chooses Mr. Jubose."

"All right, Mr. DuBose, I assign him to you."

During the short time I served as county judge, a series of "whitecappings," directed against Negroes, occurred in the lower part of the county. It had been impossible to identify the offenders, as they wore disguises. One night a sixteen-year-old boy, an orphan who lived with his uncle, an orderly and respectable citizen, was caught red-handed, though the older men who had persuaded him to join them escaped. The boy was put in jail, under a warrant returnable to the county court. His uncle had a confidential talk with me and told me that the boy was thoroughly repentant and wanted to turn state's evidence, but he was afraid of losing his life if he did so. I knew how much more Judge Sheffield's word stood for than mine did in such a situation; so I told the uncle that I would talk to Judge Sheffield about it and would advise him further in a few days.

I did talk with Judge Sheffield, and he talked with the sheriff and told him to pick a dozen or so men that he could rely on, quietly swear them in as deputy sheriffs and have them in the courtroom when I took up the boy's case. I conferred again with the boy's uncle and told him confidentially what had been done and said he could assure the boy that if he turned state's evidence he would have ample protection.

When the day came for the boy to appear in court, there was a big crowd present, many of them the very men we suspected of being the whitecappers. Howard Sheffield, the county solicitor, whom I had also taken into confidence in the matter, had a number of warrants filled out except as to names and signatures.

As the first step in the proceedings he called the boy to the witness stand and administered the oath to him. I turned to the boy and advised him as to his constitutional privileges. He broke in with, "I would tell everything I know, if I were sure I would be protected."

I spoke slowly and earnestly, "You will be protected. Trust me for that."

The county solicitor said, "Give me the names of those who participated in the whitecapping," on the occasion he specified; and the boy began to give them. The whitecappers in the room began to rush out. As the boy called a name, the sheriff would point to a deputy who would go after his man. Nearly a dozen were caught and imprisoned. I paroled the boy into the custody of his uncle.

As the cases were misdemeanors, I could have tried them in the county court, but I thought it more expedient to let them be tried in the superior court, which met in a few days. When that court met, indictments were promptly returned, and the cases were set for trial on Wednesday of the following week at two o'clock in the afternoon. That day came, and with it came the rumor that the whitecappers were going to plead guilty, and that, if Judge Sheffield sentenced them to the chaingang instead of letting them off with fines, their sympathizers were going to storm the courtroom and rescue them.

Two o'clock came. The jail doors opened, and out came the procession, the sheriff in front, and behind him the ten prisoners, each guarded by a heavily armed deputy sheriff. The prisoners were placed on the "mourners' bench." Their sympathizers flocked into the courtroom.

As soon as the crowd was seated, Judge Sheffield announced to the sheriff, "I have been informed that there have come to this court today a number of armed men, who have come with the purpose that if the result of certain cases does not suit them they will attempt to thwart the judgment of the court by violence. It is unthinkable that any court should be compelled to function in the presence of such threats. Therefore, I am about to order you and your deputies to search all persons in the room to see if they have concealed weapons upon them. Now there are many persons who dislike to be searched, even though they may have nothing to conceal. Therefore, before I order the search to begin, I shall allow three minutes for those who prefer not to be searched to retire from the room."

A minute passed; no one moved. Then Britt Davis, the court reporter, suddenly jumped up and said, "I left my note-books downstairs and I must go get them."

"Any person is at liberty to go out who feels that he should go for any reason," replied the Judge.

Another minute passed. Charlie Bush, the leading lawyer from Colquitt, rose. "I have a long way to go this afternoon; so I expect I would better be going."

"There is no reflection on anyone who wishes for any reason to leave," replied the Judge, as the audience smiled.

Thirty more seconds passed. "Half a minute more," the Judge announced.

A thin fellow on one of the raised seats in the rear of the courtroom arose and made for the door. He walked with a peculiar stride as if he were trying to narrow his rear in order to keep the print of the pistol in his hip pocket from showing through his coattail; but as he went out the door he hastened his pace. This was the signal for the break. The "pistol-toters" could not get out fast enough. They created a jam at the door. They were afraid the time would expire before they could get out.

The Judge announced, "Give them another minute, Mr. Sheriff. Everyone will have a fair chance to get out."

Soon the room was cleared. "Shut the door, Mr. Sheriff. I think we can now call off the search, as all the pistols seem to be gone. Proceed with the cases set for the afternoon, Mr. Solicitor."

The defendants pleaded guilty and were sentenced to terms in the chaingang, where a corps of deputies delivered them next morning.

Judge Sheffield loved to tease his friends. Though it was not the custom to open our courts with any greater formality than for the Judge to announce, "Be in order; the court is now in session," yet, at the session of the court which immediately followed the election of Bill Hodges, a popular but bashful young countryman, as sheriff of Early County, the Judge mounted the bench and said, "Mr. Sheriff, open the court in due and ancient style."

"How's that, Judge," said Bill.

With every appearance of seriousness, the Judge said, "You will proceed, sir, to the crier's balcony, overlooking the public square, and there announce in a loud voice, "Oyez! Oyez! Oyez! The Superior Court of Early County is now in session. God save the United States of America, the State of Georgia, and this Honorable Court."

Bill proceeded to the balcony. "Oh, yes; oh, yes," he began; then faltered and started over again, "Oh, yes; oh, yes," hesitated again and then blurted out, "Big court is now in session, God save Early County."

I was once trying an important land case in Cuthbert, and was opposed by three of the ablest lawyers in the State, Judge Kiddoo, Judge Worrill, and Arthur Hood. The trial was hardly under way before the people of the town began to come into the courtroom, mostly out of curiosity. When the seats outside the bar rail were filled, the crowd began to intrude upon the space inside it. At the noon recess, the Judge told the sheriff to put a bailiff at the gate when the court reconvened, with instructions not to let anyone inside the rail except court officials, the jury, the parties, the lawyers, and the witnesses.

The Judge and I left the courtroom together. He remarked on the number of spectators, and said, "Quite a crowd have come to see you perform."

I replied that if they came out to see me perform, it was quite a compliment to me.

To tease me he said, "You remember about Dr. Johnson's dog, do you not? Dr. Johnson had a dog that danced, and the people came for miles around to see him perform; not that the dog danced so well, but that the dog could dance at all."

As I came back to court that afternoon I went by the record

room downstairs. I heard the clock strike. I grabbed my papers and hurried to the courtroom. When I got there the Judge was already on the bench. As I started to go through the gate, a wooden-legged old bailiff stationed there caught hold of me and shoved me back into the aisle, saying, "You can't go in there, Sonny."

Judge Sheffield spoke up quickly and told the bailiff to let me in.

When the Judge and I started from the courtroom at the adjournment for the day, the old bailiff came up to the Judge to apologize for his action. "Judge, you will have to excuse me for not letting that boy go by the gate; but you know that if you had put me at the foot of the stairs with a gun and told me to shoot every lawyer that come by, he could have gone right on by and I wouldn't even have cocked my gun." I may add that though most of the audience thought I won my case, I lost it.

Judge Sheffield, toward the close of his career, after his zeal for morality became fanatical, never lost an opportunity to denounce liquor and "pistol-toting." It was impossible for him to be impartial in a prosecution for the carrying of concealed weapons. Indeed, before the close, it became definite that he was suffering from a mental breakdown. There would be times when, for a short while, his mind would seem to be as clear and his mental grasp as strong as ever. Sometimes on such occasions, he would seem to be even more brilliant than was normal with him. I have seen an electric bulb flare up in an intensity of illumination just before it burned out. So with him, except that with him, the light did not go out all at once, as with the lamp bulb. In the midst of what he was saying or doing, one could sense the change. Those noticing him would realize, almost as plainly as they would if they were looking upon some outwardly visible phenomenon, that he was struggling to retain his grasp upon his mentality, but that it was fading away like a firelight slowly dying down. Then he had to quit and be put to bed in a state of practical imbecility. He realized his condition and was tractable in it.

I witnessed his last appearance on the bench, and I shall never forget it. It was in Blakely at the fall term of the Early Superior Court. He had asked Judge Moses Wright, of Rome, to hold the court for him, but Judge Wright could not get there before Thursday. So it was arranged that Judge Sheffield should organize the court on Monday morning and should recess it till Thursday.

He seemed to be feeling unusually well that morning. He organized the court, gave the grand jury a short but clear charge, and asked if there was anything else needing attention. The solicitor general remarked that, while it was not criminal week, the witnesses in a case against a little Negro, who was in jail charged with carrying a concealed pistol, had come to the court that morning by mistake, that it was a short case and that he and the defendant's counsel would be glad if the Judge would try it, so that the witnesses would not lose another day in coming back later. The Judge consented to try it.

The defendant was a coal-black, undersized, scrawny little darkey, apparently about twenty years old. The evidence of his guilt was overwhelming. The only thing to the contrary was his unsworn statement, or, to use the phrase of our law, "the bare statement not under oath," which, under the Georgia Code, the prisoner is allowed to make in his own behalf, and to which the jury may give just the credence to which they think it is entitled. He admitted having the pistol, but denied that it was concealed. The jury was out but a minute or so, before it was back with a verdict of guilty.

While they were out, Sanders Walker, one of our best citizens, went up to the Judge's desk and told him that he had no interest in the case, but thought he ought to tell him that he had known the prisoner for a number of years, and that while he was not so idiotic as not to know the difference between right and wrong, still he was only a harmless half-wit.

The verdict having been published, the Judge told the little Negro to stand up, and proceeded to lecture him:

"The jurors have found you guilty. Under the evidence they

were obliged to do so; but one of your white friends has been to me and has told me that you are not very bright." He looked down and saw how black the boy was and added, "Certainly you are not very bright in color."

The Judge's next remark was not so much an inquiry of the prisoner as it was a rhetorical question addressed to the audience at large, "Tell me what in the world you wanted with that pistol?"

But the boy thought the Judge desired an answer from him, and he proceeded to give it: "I wuz wukin' at de hardwood mill, an' late ever ev'nin', I had to go home through Beaver Ruin Swamp, an' dey tole me dere wuz er bear in dat swamp, an' I was afeared I might meet dat bear in de road and have nuthin' to defen' myself wid."

"Bear! Bear!" broke in the Judge, "Who ever heard of such a thing as that?"

He looked down where I was sitting, and saw a smile of amusement on my face. "You are thinking about something mischievous. What is it?" he asked.

"Why, your Honor, just a few moments ago this prisoner heard you say to the jury that he had a right to make a bare statement in his own defense."

"I certainly did," laughed the Judge, "but this is the first real bear statement I ever heard made by a prisoner."

He became solemn again and turned to the prisoner. "No, people do not shoot bears with pistols."

Then he looked up to the gallery and saw it full of Negroes, and he began addressing his remarks to them: "I want to tell all of you Negroes up there, as well as all these white people down here, that pistols are not manufactured, sold, bought, or carried to kill bears with, or lions, or tigers, or wild cats, or to shoot birds, or any other game." His voice was getting high and impetuous now. "They are manufactured, sold, bought, and carried with but one purpose only, and that is to kill human beings with. Every man who carries a pistol is a potential murderer."

He followed this strain at some length till he had reached a very high pitch. Then he stopped in the middle of a sentence, turned his eyes to the ceiling, and began in a subdued, tranquil voice: "Very soon I shall have to go on trial before a Judge that sitteth on a throne and judgeth justly. He sees all things and knows all things, even the innermost secrets of a man's heart. When I stand before him, what plea will I have? My excuses, even those excuses with which I have often justified my conduct to myself, when seen in that clear light will seem flimsier than the excuses this poor ignorant Negro has made here today. No, there is but one plea that I can make with any degree of assurance, and that is a plea for mercy; and if I would make that plea with any degree of consistency, I must show mercy here."

His mind was fading away and was about to elude his grasp. Men all over the courtroom were wiping tears from their eyes. He put his elbow on the desk, leaned down, held his forehead in the hollow of his hand, and rested thus a moment. Then in a low quiet voice, he said, "You can pay a fine of one dollar and be discharged. The court is in recess until Thursday morning."

These were the last judicial words of this remarkable man.

In the County Court

SOON AFTER I BECAME TWENTY-ONE, I SERVED ABOUT TWO AND A half years as judge of the county court, which has jurisdiction in misdemeanor cases. Nearly every Saturday night between midnight and day, I would be awakened by Negroes coming to swear out warrants against others for some offense, usually assault and battery, which had taken place at one of those "mullet suppers," of which country Negroes are so fond. These prosecutions usually came to naught, as the Negroes would make up their differences before the court convened; and when one Negro does not wish to testify against another, it is futile to try to make him do so.

One Saturday night, a Negro "church festival" was held at "Sugar Tit," about halfway between Blakely and Arlington. Shortly after midnight, some of the church officials were knocking on my door to get warrants against "de Teott boys an' de Reddick boys, for fightin' at de festibule, and skeerin' de crowd away."

The county court met during the next week and the case was put on trial before the participants in the riot and the prosecutors could make up. As his first witness, Howard Sheffield, the county solicitor, called a big, fat, bland, soft-speaking old Negro woman.

"Aunt Hattie," he began, "were you at the church festival at Sugar Tit, in this county, on last Saturday night?"

"Yazsuh."

"Did you see the fight that occurred there between the Teott boys and the Reddick boys you see here on trial?"

"No, suh, I didn't zackly see de fight."

"Will you tell us what you did see?"

She spoke softly with an air of disinterestedness: "I wuz a-settin' over on one side de room, sellin' de fried fish and de ginger cakes, and on de udder side de room, one er de Teott boys had er stan', sellin' sody water in bottles. De oldes' Reddick boy, he come up ter de stan', an' dere wuz two bottles of sody water settin' dere; an', while de Teott boy wuz waitin' on anudder customer, de Reddick boy, he tuk one er de bottles er sody water an' drunk it, an' put down de nickel fer it; an' anudder boy from over on de Peru place drunk up de udder bottle, an' he don' put down no nickel. When de Teott boy look roun' an' see two bottles empty an' only one nickel, he say to de Reddick boy, 'You owes me er dime 'stid uv er nickel, yer drunk two bottles.'

"De Reddick boy, he say, 'You tells a dam lie.'

"De Teott boy, he say, 'Don' yer call me no dam lie,' an' wid dat he up and hit de Reddick boy on de haid wid de empty sody water bottle; an' de Reddick boy, he juck out he razor an' cut at de Teott boy, but he miss 'im an' cut he clo'es.

"Den de Teott boy, he juck a laig off er de table, and commence a-hittin' de Reddick boy wid it, an' de Reddick boy, he keep on tryin' ter cut 'im wid de razor; an' erbout dat time, de udder Reddick boys run up an' start shootin' wid dey pistols, and de udder Teott boys run up an' start shootin' wid dey pistols; an' by dat time, I seed dere wuz gwine ter be er fight, an' I lef'."

The proneness of Negroes to prosecute and then to make up is shown in a story, told and vouched for by my friend, Judge Ira Hutcheson, of Panama City, Florida. He is full of jokes and good stories, and a few years ago he told me this one:

A Negro man and his wife had a fight, and she called the police and had him arrested. The case came on a few days later in the Mayor's court, but not until after reconciliation had been effected. Mayor Frank Nelson asked the woman to tell him what had happened.

"Oh, Bill an' me jus' had er little spat, an' hit don' mount ter nothin'."

"Did he hit you?"

"Yas'r, he hit me a light lick on de haid."

"What did he hit you with?"

"He hit me wid er stick."

"Take off your hat and let me see."

She took off her hat and there was a large, open scalp wound.

"That's too serious a lick for me to pass it off," the Mayor stated. "Bill, I will have to fine you ten dollars."

Between Bill and his wife they got up the ten dollars and paid the fine. Judge Hutchinson says he overheard Bill, as they got out into the hallway, lecturing his wife thus:

"Now, Nancy, yer see whut yer done callin' dem perlices. Here it is Crismus nex' week, an' we had ter gib 'em de ten dollars we'se bin savin' fer Crismus. I'se tellin' yer now, de nex' time we rows an' I hits yer, I ain't gwine ter hit yer wid no stick. I'se gwine ter hit yer wid er boa'd, an' I'se gwine ter hit yer whar you ain't gwine ter show it ter no jedge."

At one of the sessions of the county court, I called a case in which it developed that the accused was a ten- or twelve-year-old grandson of Aunt Tildy's, the old Negro woman who lived in the rear of my premises. Before letting a case against so young an offender go to trial, I asked the sheriff to tell me what the boy was accused of. He told me that a merchant had sworn out a warrant against him for stealing two or three apples off a fruit stand in front of his store. He added that when Aunt Tildy heard about it she gave the boy a good thrashing. In open court, the merchant told of the boy's "snitching the apples" while his back was turned, and running off with them. I saw Aunt Tildy in the room and asked her what she had done about it. She replied that she had cut her a bunch of good switches and had "warmed up dat young un's britches till he'd know better nex' time." I remarked that Aunt Tildy had administered better punishment than I could, and dismissed the case.

When the next case was called, there came forward a slatternly Negro girl with a scowl on her face that spoke more of desperation and resentment against fate than of maliciousness. She was charged with vagrancy, and pleaded guilty. I inquired of the sheriff and he told me that two or three times previously she had been sent to the chaingang, but that they would not keep her there; that she had served the rest of her sentence in the county jail; that, when she was released, instead of seeking work, she had attempted to live by prostitution, but that she had a venereal disease and had to resort to begging.

I told her to stand up and said to her, "I do not know what to do with you. The chaingangs will not take you. You cannot pay a fine. To put you in jail merely means an expense to the county. I wish you had an old grandmother like Aunt Tildy to give you a good whipping and teach you some sense."

Her face brightened, the scowl left it, and she broke in with "I'd heap ruther Aint Tildy give me er whuppin' then ter go ter jail."

"All right, Mr. Sheriff," I said, "I have no power to sentence this girl to be whipped, but if, at the noon recess, she will voluntarily go with you to Aunt Tildy's, and when court opens in the afternoon, you report that she has had a good whipping, I do not intend to sentence her to jail."

Aunt Tildy was still in the courtroom. I turned and said to her, "Now I do not wish this girl beaten up, but if she asks you to whip her, give her a whipping that she will feel and make her remember to be a good girl." I told the sheriff privately to go along and see that Aunt Tildy did not inflict any cruelty on her.

On the reconvening of the court, the sheriff told me that Aunt Tildy had complied with the girl's request. I made some suggestions to her as to how she could find work on a farm where she could get food and shelter, and could be cured of her malady and make on honest living, and dismissed her. She thanked me and went out. Later, I learned that she was at work on a farm, behaving herself well and leading the carefree life of a Negro farmhand.

About a month later, a friend mailed me a marked copy of the New York World. He wrote me that a woman from New England, who was berating the Southerners for their viciousness toward the Negroes, had given it to him as proof of her assertion.

I think I can quote almost literally the marked article. It ran thus: "Arthur Gray Powell, a rural county judge, residing in Blakely, Early County, Georgia, is in jail on a charge of assault with intent to murder, with the sheriff and a corps of deputies guarding him against being lynched by irate citizens. A few days ago, this judge was presiding in the county court, and a young Negro girl pleaded guilty to some misdemeanor before him. He sentenced her to be whipped, took her to the rear of his premises, and was so severely beating her that the sheriff, attracted by her cries, intervened just in time to keep her from being beaten to death. The sheriff arrested Powell and lodged him in jail."

Perhaps I should have been indignant; but instead I was amused.

20

Down the River and Harry Floyd

TOWARD THE END OF THE NINETEENTH AND THE BEGINNING OF the twentieth century the steamboats still used to ply the Chattahoochee and Apalachicola rivers between Columbus, Georgia, and Apalachicola, Florida. Fares were cheap, and occasionally we would treat ourselves to a trip down the rivers and back, with a stop-over between boats at Apalachicola.

It was a special pleasure to us if we found on the boat Old Captain Wingate, who had been running the river as a pilot for about fifty years. When off duty, he regaled the passengers with his experiences. One of his stories I still remember.

He said that once when he was on duty in the pilot-house, he saw a man fall overboard. The man was struggling in a rather swift current, calling loudly for help, and was about to drown. Captain Wingate yelled to him, "Put your feet down! Stand up!" The man did so. He was over a sandbar, and the water was not waist deep.

Soon after I was admitted to the bar I made one of these trips down the river and met at Apalachicola a very interesting character—a young lawyer named Harry Floyd. He usually spent about half of each year in a hospital for the insane, and for the other half was a brilliant lawyer and politician. He was well educated and well read.

He was the only person I ever knew who liked to discuss his own insanity or could laugh at his own irrational experiences. He once said to me that he knew of no experience more pleasurable than the ecstasy of an insane delusion. He told me that he once escaped from the sanitarium and got as far away as Cincinnati; imagining that he was a duck, he was swimming around in the pool of a fountain, perfectly happy, when a policeman came and took him away. Even the arrest did not make him unhappy, because it made him glad to see that the policemen in Cincinnati noticed ducks.

He served a term in the Florida legislature. He opened his maiden speech with, "Mr. Speaker and fellow maniacs, chiefly klepto-." When I next saw him I asked him how he got elected, and he answered, "Without opposition." He then explained that two years before, soon after he had paid his entrance fee in the primary election, he had been stricken with one of his attacks and sent to the sanitarium, but he escaped by a ruse and got back to Apalachicola the afternoon before the election. That night all the candidates were to speak to the voters at the armory, and he claimed the right to be put on the program as he had paid his entrance fee.

"I got up," he said, "and used my twenty minutes to drag all the skeletons out of the closets. I repeated all the scandals, old and new, that had been whispered about the opposing candidates. I did not get elected then, but when the election was about to come on this time, I went to each person I thought might probably be a candidate and asked him if he were going to run.

" 'I don't know. Why are you asking?' the might-be candidate would say.

"Because I am thinking of running, myself. You know that if I kept my right mind I would not say anything unkind about you, but if I went crazy as I did at the last election I might get up in public and tell that old scandal about you and that woman on Depot Creek, and I wouldn't like to do that."

" 'No, Harry,' each and all would reply, 'I do not intend to run this time.' "

When Harry was in the legislature he got into a heated controversy with another member. "Mr. Speaker," he said, "if I were a telephone pole and the gentleman from blank county were a cur dog, I would not let him even greet me as a dog greets a telephone pole."

His opponent was offended and demanded an apology. Friends intervened, and next day Harry agreed to apologize.

He arose: "Mr. Speaker, I wish to apologize for certain un-parliamentary language I used on the floor of the House yesterday. I said that if I were a telephone pole and the gentleman from blank county were a cur dog, I would deny him the usual courtesies that exist between telephone poles and dogs. I now retract the statement. I make full amends. I now say that if I were a telephone pole and the gentleman from blank county were any kind of a dog, he could use me just as dogs have used telephone poles from the beginning of time."

Harry's legislative experience reminds me that in the Georgia legislature a number of years ago the representative from one of the small counties in north Georgia became known as the "watchdog of the treasury" because he fought every increase in the annual appropriations. A bill was up to increase the appropriation for the lunatic asylum, as our State Sanitarium was then called, and this representative was advocating it. "This," he said, "is not giving away our money to strangers nor to some favored few. These unfortunates in this asylum are flesh of our flesh and blood of our blood. We owe them the duty of care and attention. Sirs, from my little county of Forsyth there are now twenty of our own people being treated and cared for in this institution."

The representative from a larger county, who was given to teasing, interrupted him. "Mr. Speaker, will the gentleman yield for a question?"

Assent was given and the question asked: "Why is it that there are twenty there from your county, and only half that many from my county, which is twice as large?"

"Sir," he replied, "I believe the answer to be that when a man from my county goes crazy we send him to the lunatic asylum, while if one in your county goes crazy they send him to the legislature."

21

South Georgia Traits

THE JOKES AND STORIES WHICH THE PEOPLE OF A SECTION MAKE up and tell are a part of the lives of that people. Georgia, for example, for many purposes may be considered as if it were three states—north Georgia, middle Georgia, and south Georgia. This is true as to the jokes and stories from these sections. The genuine north Georgia story is Rabelaisian in type, involving action of almost any sort couched in lewd or vulgar language. The middle Georgia joke or story involves no action, but depends for its point on the *double entendre* or some element of verbal surprise. The south Georgia type involves both action and the element of surprise; and every south Georgia story has a name—"The Story of the Man with the One-Eyed Wife and the Double-Barreled Shot Gun"; "The Story of the Wooden-Legged Woman on the Georgia, Southern & Florida Local Sleeper"; "The Story of the Boy Who Stole His Grandma's False Teeth and Wore Them to the Party"; "The Story of the Fat Girl Who Ate the Green Persimmon"; plus and so on, as the mathematicians say when they start something they cannot finish.

Many of these jokes and anecdotes are off-color, but today one may hear on the radio programs or see in the joke books some of these old stories of fifty years ago, so dressed up as to avoid some of their grossness.

Fifty years and more ago, there came from Miller County "The Story of the Time Uncle Bill Fudge Went to Sleep on the Banks of Spring Creek, and the Moccasin Snake Tried to Swallow His Big Toe." The element of surprise occurs in what Uncle

183

Bill said, as he "give a big jump and flang the snake clean across the creek"; but for the life of me, I cannot remember the words now.

Buck Murphy's story of the Negro woman who "shouted" so at camp meeting that she fell into a trance, and some fanned her and some poured water on her, and some said, "Get a doctor," and some did this and some did that, until the preacher cried out, "Stand back, bretheren; stand back sisteren; let Sister Riah lay where Jesus flang her"—that story could have originated in southwest Georgia; but it would have been embellished with more details and given a name.

This characteristic of calling things by descriptive names extended to cases in the justices' courts. It was not at all uncommon for a case in one of these courts to be called by the subject-matter of the controversy; for example, the "Red Ox Case," or "The Case about Not Digging the Well," or the "Cow-Killing Case," instead of the names of the parties.

Soon after I was admitted to the bar, I was employed in a case between two Negroes in the justice's court at Cedar Springs, involving the ownership of a boar alleged to be a wild hog caught in the swamps of the Chattahoochee River. It was called "The Wild Hog Case." Howard Sheffield, whose parental home was at Cedar Springs, represented the plaintiff, and I represented the defendant; and each of us had been promised by his client the wild hog for his fee. It was tried several times, with mistrials, appeals, and new trials. Adam Moulton, the local constable, had custody of the hog pending the litigation. Each court day, he would bring it to the court ground in a stout, slatted wooden crate, built upon a one-horse wagon. If anyone approached the wagon, the hog would rush to the side of the crate, push his snout and tushes through the cracks, and snort viciously. Finally, Howard's client won; and Howard told the bailiff to take the hog to his father's barn and fasten him securely in a horse stall there. Just at that time, Bill Hodges, one of the leading citizens of that district, came up and was looking at the hog. In sticking its snout and tushes at Bill, the boar also exposed enough of one ear for him to see that it was marked with a swallow-fork.

"Wild hog, nothing!" said Bill. "That's my hog."

The boar was pinned into a corner, and the other ear was examined. It was marked with an underbit. Bill's mark was underbit in one ear and swallow-fork in the other. Bill took the hog home with him, and that ended the famous "Wild Hog Case."

As a boy and young man I heard many words and phrases I have never encountered anywhere else, not even in the dictionary. For example, if one of our country folks spoke of going diagonally across a tract of land, he said that he went "catabias" across it. A straight diagonal land line was spoken of as running "catabiased". We also used the words "catawampous" and "cata-cornered", which the dictionaries take cognizance of, but with us a line or a route had to be crooked or meandering before we called it "catawampous." For certain purposes the helve of an ax was a measure of width with us. One would speak of "a fat old woman, ax-helve and a half broad at the keel."

There were phrases we used as the Greeks used certain of their particles—just to make the statement approach the feeling of the speaker. One of our boys, Jim Fort, encountering such a combination of Greek particles, translated it "also, whether, and, both or not" and said it helped the sense considerably. He often used the phrase in his personal speech. One day Frank Pickle brought in the election returns from the Cuba district, and it was discovered by the consolidating board that the other managers in the precinct had not signed them. Frank argued for the inclusion of them in the consolidated returns, and when he saw that his argument was of no avail and that the board was not going to receive them, he blurted out, "If you are going to throw them out verbatim whether or no, just go ahead and do it." While the phrase "verbatim whether or no" had no exact meaning, it was a phrase of emphatic opprobrium almost equivalent to our other phrase, "nolus bolus."

If someone were late for a morning appointment, the one he was to meet would say "You must have had fish for breakfast, and it took you a long time to pick the bones out of your teeth." Occasionally, I have heard this in other sections, but nowadays I rarely hear it.

The expression, "short horse, soon curried," to describe a slight task quickly performed, was in general use among us, but I do not think it was necessarily a localism of ours.

If one farmer looked into another's corncrib and saw that it was nearly empty and asked "What are you going to do for corn till the new crop comes in?" the reply was almost sure to be "Do like they do in Alabama—do without." Our people seemed to have a notion that "over in Alabama" the people had nothing of any kind. It is true that there was not much there then, but there is plenty there now.

Another localism of ours in those days grew out of the Victorian prudery which affected us in speech, as well as in many other things. We were not allowed to say Devil or Hell; for the one we said "bad man," and for the other, "bad place." Dothan, Alabama, which is now one of the most important of all the thriving small cities in that whole section, was then in its growing pains and was a wicked little place. If one of us boys at Blakely wanted to tell another to go to Hell, he said "Go to Dothan," and it answered the purpose. One could say that he was in "a Dothan of a fix" and his meaning would be understood.

One of the girls who was taught to respect the pruderies of speech became our telegraph operator. At Albany one day, where a diamond shirt stud was being raffled off, a drummer who had taken several chances on it had to leave for Blakely before the drawing took place, and he asked a friend to telegraph him the result. The next morning his friend telegraphed him "You have won the stud," but the drummer was in a state of puzzlement when the telegram was delivered to him, for it read, "You have won the horse."

In court at Colquitt one day I heard Mel Middleton, a jolly and substantial farmer, use a striking phrase. I do not know whether he coined it for the occasion, or whether it has a place in the speech of Miller County. A case was on trial in which he had been sued for the price of a parlor organ and in which he had pleaded a total failure of consideration. After he had testified to the worthlessness of the organ, he was asked, on cross-examination, why, if it was as bad as all that, he had not complained to the seller.

"I did complain," he said, "and they sent two fellows out to my house to fix it. They tore it all to pieces and then tried to put it back together again, and when they got through they had two tubfuls of organ guts left over."

One of Mel Middleton's sons is now a prominent citizen of Blakely—Dr. Charles S. Middleton. He was educated in medicine and soon had a very respectable practice; suddenly he quit and went into commercial pursuits. When asked why he had done so, he replied, "I found that the phrase 'practicing medicine' was too literally true—I was just practicing on my patients."

One day after he had retired from practice, Dr. Middleton was driving along a country road just out of Blakely, when he heard an old darkey, who had been a former patient of his, calling to him. He stopped and inquired what was the trouble.

"The little boy, he done broke he laig, and we uns wants you to set it."

"I have quit practicing, you know. Send and get Dr. Z. to come and set it."

"Dat's de trouble. We sont fer Dr. Z., and he done come, but de little boy's so bow-laiged he done sot de wrong laig."

In those days meals were not served in courses, either in the homes or in the hotels; all the food would be placed upon the table, except replenishments of hot coffee and biscuit, and each one helped himself from the nearest dish and passed it around. In the country homes the etiquette was that if a guest was present, as soon as the blessing was said, the host or the hostess would say to the guest, "Make a long arm and help yourself." The conventional reply was, "I don't care if I do," usually pronounced "Doan keer fidoo." Sometimes the dessert was served as a second course. In that case, it was the custom of the host to inquire of the hostess at the appropriate time, "Is there a Second Epistle?"

All over south Georgia in those days there were a number of what were called long-talking women. The reference was to their method of speech—they drawled out their words so slowly that it took them a long time to deliver the simplest utterance; for instance, "Wo-ont yeer ha-ave er bi-is-cuit?"

A client and I set out from Blakely one day to catch a raft of timber, which certain other persons were trying to get out of Georgia and into Florida before we could seize it with legal process. We located it in the Chattahoochee River, just above the Florida line and hastened off to the home of the justice of the peace to take out the necessary papers and get them into the hands of the constable. By the time the papers were fixed it was three or four o'clock in the afternoon. We had eaten breakfast at daylight that morning and had had nothing since then, and the prospects of getting supper were small. The justice of the peace discovered this in asking us about our trip. He discussed the situation with his wife, and told us that while they had no cooked food in the house, they did have plenty of cold corn-bread and clabber.

His wife brought in a five-gallon dishpan full of clabber topped by a thick layer of fresh rich cream, and large goblets to eat it from. She was one of those long-talking old women. Her voice was cushioned to a gentle softness which enhanced her drawl.

"Mi-is-ter Pow-ow-ell," she would say, "Le-et me gi-ive ye-er so-ome er the-er cla-a-ber," and she would hand me a gobletful.

After a while she said, "Mi-is-ter Pow-ow-ell, ha-ave so-ome mo-o-er cla-a-ber."

"No thank you," I replied. "I have had quite enough."

"Why," she said, "si-ix gob-er-lets-full hain't mu-uch to er per-er-son as lo-oves it li-ike ye-er sa-ay yoo-oo doo-oo."

I do wish that somehow or somewhere I could get a pone of cold cornbread and six gobletfuls of clabber which would taste as good as what I got that day way down there in the southwest corner of southwest Georgia.

Originality in Verdicts

OUR JURIES WERE NOT ALWAYS CONSISTENT IN THEIR VERDICTS. A reputable white man had sold an old Negro a mule. The buyer made no down payment, but gave his note for the price of sixty dollars. As he was taking the mule home with him later on the same day, the mule ran into a railroad train, and lost some hair and hide as a result of the collision, but was not crippled or killed. That fall I sued the old Negro on the mule dealer's note, which he had failed to pay, and he defended on the ground that the mule was wholly worthless at the time he bought it. The jury found in favor of the defendant on this plea. The next case called was a suit the old Negro had brought against the railroad for the injuries received by the mule in his collision with the train, on the day he bought him. I defended the case for the railroad; and, by consent of counsel, we tried it before the same jury. They found a verdict awarding the old Negro sixty dollars.

Verdicts were sometimes tinged with a conscious sense of humor. My father told me of an instance that occurred about the time I was born. Under our law, upon a proceeding to commit a person to the sanitarium for the insane, the jury is required to find as to which, if any, of the following classes the alleged incompetent belongs, "Idiots, lunatics, insane persons, habitual drunkards, and persons imbecile from old age or other causes." The verdict was: "We the jury find that the alleged incompetent is not an idiot, and that he is not a lunatic, and that he is not an insane person, and that he is not a habitual drunkard, and that he is not imbecile from any cause, but that he is just a natural born damn fool."

In my experience as local counsel for the railway company, I met with some unexpected verdicts. For instance, there was the case in the justice's court in the Rock Hill district, where the company was sued for killing a yearling in the cut just below Hilton Station. I first put up as a witness Jule Skinner, who was the engineer on our passenger train for so many years that when the train whistle blew the Negroes would say, "Yonder comes the Jule." He testified that it was impossible to prevent the killing; that the yearling jumped down from the shoulder of the cut so close to the cowcatcher that he could not stop the engine before hitting it.

I next called Will Fitts, the fireman. He testified to the same thing. I then remembered that I had not shown the time of the day and the condition of the oil-burning headlight. In reply to my question as to the time, he stated that it was about seven-thirty P.M., and when I added, "And your headlight was burning as usual?" he answered:

"No, sir, that old lamp was smoking so badly you could not see fifty yards in front of you. I got off at every station and wiped it off, but we could not go a quarter of a mile before it was all smoked up again."

I waived my argument to the jury, being sure that I had lost the case, but soon the jury was back with a verdict for the defendant.

"But the defendant is the railroad," the justice blurted out when the verdict was read.

"Yes," the foreman of the jury explained, "we know that; but when that young fellow there told about that lamp, it was the first time we had ever heard a railroad witness tell the truth in court, and we decided to reward him."

Tom Jay had a case in the superior court, in which he sued the railroad company for killing a cow and a hog. Judge Bower was presiding and he charged the jury, paraphrasing the language of Chief Justice Bleckley, that "An animal and a railroad train each has a right to be on a railroad track, provided that both do not attempt to occupy the same spot at the same time. If they do, and damage results, it becomes a question of which was at fault; and unless the railroad company was guilty of negligence, it would not be liable."

The verdict of the jury was, "We, the jury, find the hog guilty and the cow not guilty."

Usually, in our section, if a damage suit was to be tried, the public generally made up its mind ahead of the trial as to the amount of damages the plaintiff should have if he recovered at all. The juries generally respected this consensus of community opinion and expressed it in their verdicts. Some forty years ago I brought a suit, in the superior court of Calhoun county, for a boy who had received severe injuries in a mill at Arlington. The case was defended by John Little, of Atlanta, who later became my law partner. After a hard fight, I got to the jury, and John knew it was just a case of how much; and I knew that the consensus of the community was that, if I got to the jury, I was to have a verdict of five thousand dollars.

I was opening my argument, when John, who was a Chesterfield if there ever was one, interrupted and asked me to suspend a moment. He told the judge that he had been taken ill the night before and that the physician had just advised him that he should return to the hotel and go to bed, but that he was unwilling to ask for a mistrial in a case which had taken so much time to try; that he had to obey the physician's orders, but that he consented for the trial to proceed in his absence; that he would waive his right to address the jury, but that he wanted the jurors to know why.

The verdict was for three thousand, five hundred dollars. Later I talked with Bill Ragan, the foreman of the jury, and asked him how they had arrived at the amount of thirty-five hundred dollars.

"Well," he explained, "when we got into the room we all agreed on five thousand, but, just as I was about to write it out, one of the jurors said, 'Mr. Little is a mighty nice man, and it is a pity that he got sick and could not make his speech. If he had made his speech, he might have got us to take some off the verdict'; so we agreed to give him fifteen hundred off for not being able to make the speech."

The Ranch—A Fight

IT WAS JANUARY 1, 1895. SOME TIME BEFORE THAT, THE NEW school building had been completed and the property of the old Blakely Academy abandoned. The Academy lot, consisting of three acres shaded with large beautiful oaks, on Main Street, about two blocks from the courthouse square, belonged to an unincorporated society. The court had taken custody of it through a suit in equity and ordered it sold that day at public outcry, for distribution of the proceeds to the members of the society.

I was standing by when the sheriff offered the property to the highest bidder. I had no intention of buying it. I had supposed it would bring somewhere between a thousand and fifteen hundred dollars, but just to start the bidding off, I said, "Five hundred dollars." No other bid was offered, and the sheriff knocked it off to me.

Not having five hundred dollars, I went to the bank and asked John Wade, who was then the cashier, if he would lend me that amount with a mortgage on the old school lot as security. "Certainly," he answered. "It is worth more than twice that amount." Thus I became the owner of the old schoolhouse and lot, which were closely associated with many of the pleasant memories of my childhood.

Labor, lumber, and other building materials were cheaper that winter than I have ever known them to be at any other time; and so I decided to build a residence on the lot I had bought. My youngest brother, Perry Powell, though only fifteen years old, had considerable skill as an amateur architect and builder;

and I put him in charge of the work, with the result that before the year was out, we had replaced the old buildings with a neat seven-room cottage, at a cost of less than $1,000. (The next year it was rated for fire insurance at $3,500.) I used one of the rooms as a bedroom, and we boys used another as a club room. Across the hall were three rooms with folding doors between them, that could be turned into one large room, which we called the ballroom. We had our dances there. The boys named it "the Ranch."

This dancing got me into trouble again with the Baptist Church. Brother Zack Weaver had gone, and the new pastor was a narrow-minded fellow whom I did not like. And he did not like me. I could not dance, at least not enough to count, but I was accessory to the dancing of others. For this I was charged with being an immoral influence upon the young people.

I was given notice that charges would be preferred against me, but, instead of attending the conference, I went off to see Evie Layton or Cliff Hightower, or on some other such mission. They turned me out of the church. Two weeks later, I was there, and the conference rescinded its action. From then on for several months, every time I was absent, they would turn me out again, and as soon as I got back, they would turn me in again. This kept up till one of the boys, probably Bob Dostor, said that the place where I had gone in and out of the Baptist Church so much had gotten to be as slick as where an old sow goes in and out under a rail fence.

Finally, I became disgusted with the row and when they turned me out, I refused to be turned back. Several years went by, an intelligent man was in our pulpit, and I was willing to go back into the church, but there was an obstacle in the way. In those days, to get back into the church one had to agree to quit doing something sinful. I had never learned to dance, and long since had stopped trying to; so I could not quit that. But we hit on this device. I was one of the commissioners of a public liquor dispensary; I agreed to resign that position, and for this I was restored to fellowship. Hence, I was turned out of the church for something I had never done—dancing, and was turned back into it upon my promise to quit doing something I had never done—selling liquor.

Before I built a permanent paling around the Ranch, I put up a rough fence, partly of boards and partly of fence rails. Gertie Jones, now Mrs. James Boyd McCampbell, of San Antonio, Texas, will smile if she remembers, as I am sure she still does, the night I made her climb the rail fence.

The girls were giving a masquerade party and Gertie honored me by asking to be my escort. It was arranged that the girls would call for the boys, and Gertie came to the Ranch for me. There was a gate in the corner of the front yard, but she did not see it; so when she got to the fence, she halloed. I had arranged to go as the Devil, and had on a tight-fitting red suit with a forked tail and carried a pitchfork. As I came to the fence, she spoke to me, but I pretended not to be able to talk and put on a lot of foolish mummery. In sign language I told her I could not climb the rail fence, but that she would have to climb it. She protested, but finally climbed the fence. I took her arm and escorted her to the gate. She was much too amused to be angry, but she gave me a good-natured lambasting.

Gertie it was who once told me that the other boys and girls made a "hominy pot" out of me. People do not have hominy pots these days. They buy their lye hominy, or big hominy, as it is also called, already prepared, in cans from the grocery store. In the old days, the grains of corn were cooked in lye—not lye from a can, but lye leached from an ash hopper—in a big pot till the husks were eaten off the grains. When the pot was not being used for cooking hominy, it sat near the kitchen door and into it were thrown bits of useless meats, bones, gristle, and things of that kind, not good enough to be cooked, but too valuable to be thrown away. Our scouring soap was homemade in those days, and the contents of the hominy pot were valuable for that purpose. Gertie, who was always my friend, complained that the other boys were constantly putting off on me some girl that nobody wanted to go with, but for some reason had to be taken to the party—that they "made a regular old hominy pot of me."

During my term as county judge, I performed two marriage ceremonies. The first was performed at the Ranch. One evening we boys were going there to arrange for a dance. At the gate an old darkey hailed me. "Jedge, yer kin marry folks, kaint yer?"

I think this was the first time it had ever occurred to me, though I knew it in a general way, that this was one of the functions of my office.

"Who is the couple?" I asked.

"John Daniel and ole Si's Louisa."

I inquired as to ages, and found that they were both over twenty-one and had the license. So I invited them in. Wilk Wade proposed that we should have a regular wedding with attendants, and he gave a few hasty instructions. The eight boys who were with me marched in as attendants and arranged themselves on each side of the arch of one of the folding doors. The groom was without a best man, but Wilk made him stand under the arch; and the old darkey brought in the would-be blushing bride, and placed her next to him. It was then up to me to perform the ceremony.

I had neither form book nor ritual. I had seen a few marriages performed but had paid very little attention to the words of the officiating minister or magistrate. However, I knew that no special form is required; so it was up to me to improvise.

"John," I began, "do you take Louisa to be your lawfully wedded wife; do you promise to love her and to honor her; and to make for her the best husband you can; to quit running around with other women; to work hard, and make a good living for her, and to support her and the children, when they come, to the best of your ability?"

At Wilk Wade's prompting, he answered, "I will."

"Louisa," I continued, "do you take John to be your lawfully wedded husband; do you promise to love, honor, and obey him; to quit running around with other men; to make a good wife for him; to look after the house, and do the washing and the cooking, and to take care of the children when they come, and help him all you can?"

She replied in the affirmative. Then I announced: "I pronounce you husband and wife. If I catch either of you violating the promises you have made me, I will have you up in the county court and give you twelve months in the chaingang. The attendants will now have the choice of saluting the bride, or of chipping in a quarter apiece as a present for the bride and the groom."

The wedding present was two dollars. They went away happy; and I suppose they lived happily ever after, for at the end of ten years, I heard they were still together and had ten children.

About this time I had a fight with Jim Bush, a good friend of mine, in court at Colquitt. Just before the noon recess of Miller Court, I said something which offended Jim. He called me a liar. I struck at him, and he struck back at me, and we were going at it like two old fighting Dominique roosters, neither doing the other much hurt, when my father, who, though he did not know why I was fighting, had a way of hitting first and investigating later, struck Jim a smart blow on the face. Charlie Bush, who was a friend of us all, tried to get between us and was asking us to desist. My father had left his crutches lying on the "mourner's bench," and was supporting himself by resting the stump of his short leg on a table. Like a flash out of the sky, something struck me on the top of the head, and I fell to the floor stunned.

By long standing custom in Miller County, when a fight starts, everyone is invited to attend and participate. When, after a few seconds, I came to my senses and got up, I saw that the courtroom was in an uproar. Men were rushing inside the bar rail, drawing pistols. Judge Sheffield was standing wildly gesticulating and calling to the sheriff and to the crowd. His judicial calm was gone. I heard him say, "Mr. Sheriff, get busy; get men to help you, and stop this God damned riot." He pointed toward those trying to rush in, "Stop, stop, God damn you! Stop right where you are! If you move hand or foot, I will give you the limit of the law." People were rushing toward the courtroom from the courthouse square. The Judge shouted: "Shut those doors and let no one in or out!" I was bleeding profusely; so he let me go out to see a doctor, and made every one else sit down, and thus restored order.

At the reconvening of the court after the noon recess, he had the grand jury come into the courtroom, and proceeded to hold in their presence an investigation of the fracas. The facts were undisputed: Jim Bush called me a liar, I struck him, and we began fighting with our bare hands; my father intervened in my behalf and struck Jim a blow in the face with his fist; Charlie Bush was trying to separate us; Drew Glass, an ignorant country-man, picked up one of my father's crutches and frailed down on us all. The brass ferrule at the end of the crutch struck the top of my head, cutting a gash in the scalp, and glanced off and hit my father on the side of his head, inflicting a bruise. The crutch split and the splinters cut two gashes in Jim's cheek. There was some question as to whether Glass had made one lick or two, but, at any rate, Charlie Bush's arm was broken.

The Judge said to Glass, "What did you have to do with it?"

"Nothing," he replied, "I was just separating the fighters."

The Judge fined us for contempt of court; then he gave the grand jury in charge the law of affray—"the fighting of any two or more persons in any public place." He also instructed them that since their foreman (Jim Bush) was one of the participants, they should elect a foreman pro tem, if they had not done so already, and proceed with their investigation.

The grand jury had already elected Sam Morton foreman pro tem and when they got back to the jury room, Sam said (so I was told), "Gentlemen, you have heard the evidence. It seems to have been a fair fight. If we took the time to investigate all the fair fights that occur in this county, we would have no time to attend to any important business. Mr. Roberts, you are sitting near the door, tell the bailiff to tell Jim Bush to come on back in here, and let's get down to something worth fooling with." That ended the investigation.

Jim and I made friends. I had a scalp wound that took some time to heal, but ever thereafter I was recognized as a member of the Miller County brotherhood, and was honored as we honor the veterans of our wars; so there were compensations for my injuries.

24

The Rocky Road to Matrimony

A MAN WITH A HOME OF HIS OWN IS LIKELY TO BEGIN TO THINK of marriage. I did think of it, and the more I thought of it, the less attractive the idea seemed to me. The comfort and the freedom of my bachelor's quarters at the Ranch appealed to me.

I kept up a more or less desultory correspondence with my little girl friend, Annie Wilkin, during the time she was in college. I saw her a few times during this period, and, though I did not have any real chance to talk with her, I did notice that she was no longer a pretty little child, but that she had grown to be a beautiful young woman. In the fall of 1895, I found from Annie's letters that she was greatly interested in her course in literature. I told her that I would be glad to send her from time to time such books as I had been reading. As a Christmas present, I had sent her a few years before a fancy-bound copy of *Lucile*. She expressed appreciation, but no special enthusiasm. This time, I sent her some other book. I wish I could remember what it was, but I cannot be sure. It may have been Lew Wallace's *The Fair God*, as I had recently been on a trip with the Georgia Press Association to Mexico City, and had found Wallace's book, the action of which is laid in Mexico, to be especially entertaining. Whatever book it was, I was very much surprised to receive in a few days a letter from her, full of charm and versatility, reviewing the book with a literary skill far beyond what I had ever supposed she had.

I do not see how I could have been such an egregious ass as to do what I did. I should have had sense enough to see that I was riding for a fall. I sat down and wrote her in a big-I-little-you vein, congratulating her on what a fine letter she had written me. That was bad enough, but then I undertook to compare this letter with her previous letters, and to criticize the earlier ones for their stiffness and primness.

Among other things, I wrote: "The main thing I had to say to you is, that your letter is an exceedingly good letter. Social letters to be interesting or praiseworthy should be informal, original and spicy. So was yours.

"You apologized for the undignified style. Dignity spoils a social letter. If people had to have dignity to keep out of jail, I'd be where my clients are.

"I remember that we used to write to each other a long time ago when we were little. You used to be just as dignified in your letters as if you had copied them out of a 'Patent, Practical Letter Writer,' under the head of 'A Letter Written by a Prim Young Lady of Boston to her Aged Maiden Aunt.'

"People ought generally to cultivate dignity, but in your case it was like the little boy whom Charlie Lane tells about. 'Once upon a time there was a little boy who was very fond of battercakes. His mother decided that she would see that he had as many as he wanted for one time. So she had a dishpanful made. The little boy just kept eating and eating until at last they passed him another plateful, and he broke out crying. His mother inquired what was the matter, and asked him if he didn't want some more. The little fellow shook his head and sobbed 'I don't want them I already is got.'

"So it was with your dignity. You had just a little too much."

In a short while I received her reply. I wish I had that letter now. I kept it for years, but it was recently accidentally lost or destroyed. Oh, how she laid it on, smiling at me, even grinning at me, between the lines, as she wrote! She had kept the old letters I had written her when I was at Mercer.

"How," she asked, "could an ignorant country girl from the little town of Colquitt be expected to reply in kind to a letter from a distinguished college man living in the midst of the bright lights of the city—to a letter beginning even with beautiful poetry, such as,

> 'Oft in the stilly night
> Ere slumber's chain has bound me,
> Fond memory brings the light
> Of other days around me.' "

She quoted from another enthusiastic letter I had written her about Major Lane's graduation speech delivered at the opera house "when the band played Dixie and the house went wild."

She continued: "And there I was, a little country girl from the small town of Colquitt which had only one hundred inhabitants, while your town of Blakely had the enormous number of two hundred inhabitants; and as for that great city of Macon where that famous Mercer University was located—why, Macon must have had a million inhabitants—but there I was, never having seen an electric light, nor a street car, nor a playing fountain, and never having heard a band play Dixie, attempting to write a letter to a sophisticated young genius who was accustomed to such brilliant surroundings."

"How," she went on to say, "could the almost-child teacher of school children in the little log school houses of Miller County, know how to reply to letters written by that prominent lawyer and society young man, 'Colonel Powell,' who wrote so excitingly of his many successes with the law and the ladies.

"How, even when she got to Milledgeville, and daily saw but little outside the college walls, could she be expected to write of much except to tell about her roommates, her classmates and her teachers, in reply to the high-sounding phrases with which this brilliant young man bedecked his letters telling of his continued successes."

Why say more? I had been a conceited ass, and she did not spare me. It would have done me good if I could have carried that letter constantly with me all the rest of my life, could have read it, from time to time, as a brake upon my natural egotism.

Wounded as I was, I was not wholly slain. One thing I did

realize was that the little child-princess of the chicken yard at Colquitt was no more; that the little "school marm," trudging through sunshine and rain, heat and cold, over paths through the tall pine woods, where the pine straw gave softly to her tread, was no more. I realized I was dealing with, and henceforth must deal with a beautiful, intelligent young woman, who still held her head high, who still was "biggity," but sweet.

I licked my wounds for a while till the pain somewhat subsided, and then I undertook to reply. There was nothing to do but plead guilty, and pray forgiveness. I have the letter I wrote her. I will quote parts of it:

"In one of Shakespeare's plays somewhere he speaks of a poor fellow who was 'whipped with wire, stewed in brine, smarting in a lingering pickle.' That's me. . . . Your letter was an indictment, verdict of guilty, sentence of the court, and the execution of poor me. What defense can be made against the terrible arraignment of your letter? You are certainly ahead of me one time, and I am very badly left at my own game. I never would have jumped on the studied dignity of your letters if I had once dreamed that you remembered any of the contents of any of mine."

I admitted the writing of all the florid stuff she had charged me with. I quote again:

"If you had called me a verdant youth, I could bear it patiently, but you touch me up with 'that deeply learned college student.' You know too well that the self-conceit within me is one of my weak points. You know I flinch when accused of the 'big head,' and yet you spared me not."

I put in a page or two about the good old times we had together at Blakely under Professor Fitzpatrick, and then said:

"To recur to the former theme, let me say that while those little old letters of yours were prim, precise, and dignified, they were not unappreciated, for I thought then that they were the choicest pieces of literature in all the world.

"And now that each of us has had a turn at the other and each of us has passed unbiased criticism on the former letters of the other, let us make up and join in mutual congratulations that your letters are no longer stiff, prim and dignified, but are sharp, witty, sparkling and versatile and that I am no longer 'a deeply learned college student' dealing in flourishes of rhetoric and pyrotechnics of high sounding words, but am simply plain, every-day Arthur."

She graciously accepted my apologies.

At Christmas that year, I sent her a copy of Ruskin's *Crown of Wild Olive*, which she had said she would like to read. In spring of 1896, she sent me her copy of Browning's poems with the marginal notes she had made in the classroom. Without the cues I got from those notes, I would never have been able to make a start toward an understanding of Browning's poems. Browning is still my favorite poet of his era.

Somehow the notion began to form in my mind that Annie was the girl I really loved after all, that she was more than a mere friend to me. Several letters passed between us that spring. I began to want to know how she really felt toward me. Our letters were in no sense love letters; but mine began to inch up in that direction. Her replies came back cordial enough, but always evasive of my suggestions of more than friendship.

She received her diploma in June and came back to Colquitt. She wrote me that she was going back to Milledgeville in September as college librarian, and would be associated in a minor capacity with Miss Bacon, who held the chair of English.

I wanted to see her and talk with her; yet, somehow, I was afraid to see her. I debated in my mind all summer long the matter of visiting her at Colquitt. I found that she would be returning to Milledgeville on a day early in September. As there was no railroad at Colquitt then, she would have to make a trip of twenty miles, either to Blakely or to Arlington, to catch a train. So I wrote her that I would go to Colquitt and bring her back with me to Blakely on the day before she was to leave.

I drove down there that morning expecting to explore her mind and perhaps her heart on the way back. When the time came to leave that afternoon, she told me that her little nephew,

Wilkin Bird (Wilkin was about eight years old) wanted to go
to Blakely, and asked if I would mind if he went with us, that
she had promised him before hearing from me that she would
take him to Blakely with her when she went up to take the train
for Milledgeville, and hated to disappoint him. I wondered if
she really thought we needed a chaperone, but, of course, I
consented.

At the time, it was a trip of three and a half hours from Colquitt to Blakely. We had hardly gotten over the turnpike at
Spring Creek, on the edge of Colquitt, before she produced a
copy of Tennyson, and began to read to me "Oenone" and one
or two others of his poems. We chatted pleasantly along during
the trip, but when I put her out at the Stewart home in Blakely
late that afternoon, I knew more of her intellectuality, but no
more of her heart, than I had known before.

I became afraid that she was all brains and no heart. I said
as much to her in one of my letters during the fall. I kept on
trying to put just a suggestion of lovemaking into my letters.
Her replies were tantalizing; they were just as cordial as before,
but they ignored my sallies into the frontiers of stronger affection.

In those days, the legislature elected the judges of the superior
court. Bill Spence, the partner of my friend Sam Bennet, had
announced his candidacy for the judgeship of the Albany Circuit. Sam had allowed himself to be elected to the legislature
to be of help in the campaign. I volunteered my services also,
and went to Atlanta for the election. I wrote Annie that I might
be able to go by Milledgeville on the return trip.

Judge Spence was elected on Thursday, and I telegraphed
Annie that I would be in Milledgeville Friday afternoon. She
was staying in one of the dormitories, Atkinson Hall. When I
arrived, she greeted me cordially, and introduced me to some of
the girls and to some of the members of the faculty. I had on
the top of my head the scalp wound I had received in the fight
in court at Colquitt two or three weeks previously. The dressing
on it had the general shape and appearance of a sunflower; and

I learned later that the girls had dubbed me "Miss Wilkin's beau with the sunflower on his head," or, more briefly, "the sunflower man."

Dr. Chappell, the president of the college, and Mr. Bullard, the secretary, were very kind to me. My being a county judge and prima facie of some potential influence may have had something to do with it. Both were very fond of Annie. They told me that they had chartered a special train to take the girls to Atlanta on the next morning to attend the inauguration of Governor Atkinson for his second term, and invited me to go along as their guest. I accepted; especially as Annie had said she was going.

We went to Atlanta on the special train next morning. There were several hundred of the girls on it, wearing their college uniforms of white shirtwaists, brown skirts, and jackets and mortarboard caps. Annie also wore the college uniform, though she was not under strict college rules as the other girls were; she could leave the party without a chaperone.

She wanted to do some shopping in Atlanta before the inaugural ceremonies began; so it had been arranged that she and I would leave the rest of the party on arrival in Atlanta and would join them later. As the train came into Atlanta, three of the girls came to Annie and said they wanted to go shopping and that Dr. Chappell had said they could go if she would chaperone them. She consented, much to my disappointment.

When the train stopped at the old Union Station, or the old car-shed, as it was commonly called, the girls were lined up under the eyes of the various members of the faculty. The train had been met by a number of young men, each of whom had probably come to see some girl in the party; but they were not allowed to come within speaking distance of them. I took Annie and the three other girls and started out. As I passed the gates where the boys were huddled, I heard one of the boys say: "Look at that damned hog. He has got four girls, and I can't get one." I felt like a damned hog, though a very unwilling one.

Late that afternoon, the girls were assembled on the mezzanine floor of the old Kimball House. There had been a football game between two college teams and the boys were crowded into the lobby, giving their college yells and displaying the general hilarity of such an occasion. The girls would lean over the railings of the mezzanine corridors and throw chrysanthemums down into the lobby to see the boys scramble for them. It was a very gay and colorful scene.

I was called away for a moment and when I came back, Annie was standing near the rail talking animatedly with a handsome young fellow, who, I later learned, had been admitted to the sanctum of the mezzanine floor because he was the brother of one of the girls. I did not like it at all. I did not want that young fellow there talking with Annie. I wanted to hit him, kill him, blow him up with dynamite, do anything to get him away. I had always looked upon jealousy as a most disgusting human emotion, but I was jealous, and I realized it.

I could see Annie looking, from time to time, in my general direction, looking toward me in a sort of abstract way, as if she were looking beyond me. I was sure that she saw an unusual look on my face and was pleased with it.

I came home from Milledgeville realizing that I had had no opportunity for the private, personal talk I had desired and had intended to have with Annie. However, I had become certain of one thing, I did love Annie and I wanted to marry her just as quickly as possible, provided only that I could be assured that she could love me. I was conceited enough to believe that if she could love any man she could love me. My doubt was whether she could love any man. This was late October.

During November, my letters to her became more frequent; they began to take on the tone of love letters; not that I said, "I love you," but that I said a great deal on the subject of what a beautiful thing love is. I gave her every chance to say that she could love a man, if she were sure he loved her, but she did not say it.

Early in December I determined to have it out with her. I

wrote her that I was going to Milledgeville on the following weekend, and wished to have a confidential talk with her. She wrote me that she would be glad to see me.

I got there Friday, but did not have much chance to talk to her that evening. I lay awake that night and planned my campaign. On Saturday morning, I went to Dr. Chappell's office and told him I expected to marry Annie if she would have me, and that I had come to resign her position as college librarian, to take effect at the end of that school term, which was a few days off. He assured me of his fullest coöperation. I remember that he said that he knew of but one thing better for a woman than a good education, and that was a good husband.

I left word for Annie at Atkinson Hall that I would call for her in the early afternoon to take her for a ride. I went to the livery stable, and told the proprietor that I wanted the best horse and the best buggy he had. He promised it to me. So at the appointed time I drove up to Atkinson Hall with a beautiful horse and a neat new rubber-tired buggy.

I proposed that we first drive out to the State Sanitarium for the Insane, and a little later drive across the river. My idea was that out at the Sanitarium she could see the effect of a man going crazy, as I realized that I rapidly was doing. Then I would drive across the Oconee River, and come slowly back over the red old hills of Georgia facing an Indian-summer sunset—an ideal setting for a declaration of love.

In those days, a steam dummy line ran down the street in Milledgeville that leads to the State Sanitarium. The horse I had hired was trotting beautifully along, when suddenly there emerged over the brow of a little rise in the street the small locomotive that pulled the dummy train. The horse snorted and tried to make a break, but I held a tight rein on him, so tight, indeed, that he reared up on his hind legs and pranced around on them for a few seconds and then fell over on the shafts of the buggy and lay there trembling.

Two boys from the military school near by were passing. I called to them, "Will one of you young gentlemen please come and hold this horse till I can get the young lady out of the buggy?"

"No," one of them replied, "but we'll be glad to hold the young lady while you get the horse out of the buggy." But they repented and came to my assistance.

We unloosed the horse. The shafts were broken. So I left Annie in the buggy, and led the horse to the livery stable, which was near the place where the contretemps had occurred, and was soon back with another buggy and a less fiery horse.

We spent a short while at the Sanitarium. I then drove across the river a distance of four or five miles into the country, and turned back. The time had come. I relaxed the reins, and the horse fell into a slow gait. Red old hills, Indian summer, and the setting sun did their full part. I began my pleading.

"You did not answer my letters in which I asked you if you could love a man, and by a man, I meant me." She turned her head to the roadside and made no reply.

"I must know. My whole life, my whole career depends on it." I was already speaking in broken accents. She looked solemn, but kept her face turned away and made no reply. I said everything that I could think of to say except the one thing I should have said, the thing I did not say because I thought she and everyone else knew it, namely, "I love you." She still sat silent and solemn. She did not even look at the setting sun, as I had hoped she would.

Later, I learned that the reason she did not look toward me or the setting sun was that she had a "sniffly" cold, and, in her excitement in leaving the dormitory, had brought only one handkerchief and had accidentally dropped it when she got in the buggy at the Sanitarium.

I had been invited for supper at Atkinson Hall, and had been told that the girls would dance in the study hall that evening; that the music would be furnished partly by a large music box which a young jeweler who had been saying nice things to Annie, so I heard, was going to bring with him. I told Annie that I wanted to talk to her before the dancing began, and we went into one of the parlors.

I began: "You would just as well answer my question and answer it now. I am due in court at Morgan on next Monday morning, and if I am to stay here longer than tonight, I must telegraph someone to go in my place. I do not propose to leave here till you give me an answer."

I went on: "Here I am half crazy. I have been loving you from the first day I ever saw you. I love you with all my mind, heart, and soul, and I want to marry you at the earliest possible moment, provided only you love me, or believe you can learn to love me. Tell me! Do you love me; can you love me?"

She said softly, "I will tell you in two weeks."

"Why wait two weeks? Don't you see that I can't leave here without an answer. I will be crazy in two weeks, if I have to wait that long." I was pacing the floor, half crazy already.

She said demurely, "It does seem that you could wait two weeks to find out from me what I have been waiting for ten years to find out from you."

That is the time I ought to have grabbed her and kissed her. It was not fear of her that kept me from it. I was no longer afraid of her. The simple truth is that I was so happy, so impetuously anxious to marry her, that I did not think about kissing her.

I said with relief, "You have answered. You can go dance now; I am no longer afraid of the man with the music box."

I did detain her long enough to tell her that I was going back and arrange for us to get married before the year was out.

"But if I were going to marry you, it certainly could not be before next June. I have a contract here with the college that does not expire until then," she interrupted.

"You are wrong," I replied. "I resigned for you this morning, and your resignation has been accepted." I told her of my interview with Dr. Chappell.

I told her that I would like for us to get married just as soon as she came home for the Christmas holidays, but that I wanted time to go to Macon and buy some furnishings and furniture for the house. She said that if she were going to marry me, she would have to have time to get ready after she got home. I told her that I had no intention of putting her sister Nellie and Mr. Bird to

the trouble and expense of a wedding, that the simpler the ceremony, the better it would suit me. She assented to that; but when
I proposed that we drive over to Arlington and have my good
friend, Judge Sheffield, perform the ceremony, she said that she
preferred a minister. She suggested that at Bainbridge there was
a young Methodist minister, Rev. W. N. Ainsworth (later Bishop
Ainsworth), whom she and her family knew and thought a
great deal of; and, as he was a fraternity mate of mine, I promptly
accepted her suggestion.

I suggested December the thirtieth as the day, but she said,
"If I were to marry you, I could not get ready by then."

I replied that I was willing to a reasonable postponement,
"just so we get married this year"; so I said, "December thirty-
first."

She didn't say "Yes"; but she didn't say "No." The truth is
that, except for the wedding ceremony, she has never promised
to marry me to this day.

We went then to the study hall where the girls were dancing.
I did not dance, but my eyes danced; my heart danced.

I rushed away to get to court at Morgan. When I got to
Albany, I learned that the court had been postponed; so I went
on home. In those days I slept at the "Ranch," but I ate at my
father's. That evening at supper, my father asked me where I
had been for the weekend. I told him that I had been to Milledge
ville to see Annie Wilkin. As I was leaving that evening, I overheard him say to my mother, "I do wish Arthur would marry
Annie Wilkin." I wanted to tell them; but I had promised Annie
to keep it secret till she came home. Annie told me in later years
that once while I was at Mercer my mother had met her on the
street and kissed her twice and remarked, "I kissed you once for
myself and once for Arthur." My father and mother both loved
Annie, and no one else I could have married would have pleased
them half so well.

I went to Macon and with the assistance of Gus Jones and
the girl he was engaged to, Nettie Watkins, whom I had to let
into the secret, selected such furniture and furnishings as I felt
able to buy and had them shipped to Blakely.

The day Annie left Milledgeville for Colquitt, I went up on the train and met her where the "up" train and the "down" train passed, and came back as far as Arlington with her, and told her I would spend the day with her at Colquitt on the following Sunday.

We sometimes have bad weather in south Georgia in late December, but that year, the Indian summer lasted into January. I went to Colquitt on Sunday as I had promised. It was a lovely day in more ways than one.

Annie said something about not seeing how she could get ready by the next Thursday. I told her that unless she wanted to break up a wedding with the minister and all the witnesses there, she would better be ready at noon on the next Thursday. A woman will go to a lot of inconvenience before she will break up a wedding.

Early Thursday morning, December thirty-first, 1896, I set out for Colquitt. Along with me came my father and my brother Dick, Kil, Wilk Wade, Bob Dostor, and Tom Mc. Many of Annie's friends and relatives were there also.

Just before noon, I took my friend Ainsworth aside and said to him, "When you perform the ceremony, do not say to Annie 'Will you take this man,' but say 'Do you take,' and so forth. Marry us in the present tense; for every time I have asked her to marry me, she has either said 'No,' or tried to put it off." He promised.

As twelve o'clock came, the family and friends gathered in the parlor. Annie took my arm, and we came down the stairs together, and stood in front of the minister. He followed the ritual till he got to the part where he was to put the question to Annie. He began as I had asked him, "Do you," but right in the middle of the question, forgetting himself, he commenced asking "Will you," and so forth. It dawned on me that she could not answer the question either "I will" or "I do." I wondered what she would say. She said "Yes."

It was not a stylish marriage. It was the simple and un-ostentatious attestation of the plighted troth of a young man of twenty-three and a young woman of twenty-one, who looked too seriously upon this consummation of their heart's desires to wish it made a public spectacle. As the minister spoke the words "I pronounce you man and wife," I had full realization of the fact that my first sweetheart had become my last and only sweetheart; that despite the several little love affairs which I had had from time to time with other girls, I was now able to see clearly that there had been but one girl for me; and that now she was wholly mine.

We had a most sumptuous midday dinner at Miss Nellie's following the ceremony. Miss Nellie had Milus, the old darkey who was porter, headwaiter, and general factotum at the Hunter Hotel, to assist in serving. I recall that Milus gave Miss Nellie and Annie much embarrassment by his praising of the food as he passed it. "Have some of this turkey, nice turkey, nice turkey. Have some of this gravy, nice gravy, nice gravy. Have some of this cake, nice cake, nice cake," and so on.

I have never seen a lovelier day than December 31, 1896; and it was under the clear skies and soft sunshine of that afternoon that I took my bride from Colquitt to Blakely. As the carriage bore us along the old road over which each of us had so often come and gone, Annie had on her face the expression of one whose dream has come true but who is afraid to be buoyant lest it prove to be still a dream; I was never happier in my life, and I think my face showed it.

We arrived at our home soon after sunset. We were invited into our own dining room to an excellent supper which had been prepared under the direction of my mother, Miss Ella, and other intimate friends of Annie's and mine.

In the hallway sat my trusted steed, my bicycle, old Rhadamanthus, and by his side was his bride, a new, shining, ladybicycle. In the ensuing months, the two brides and the two grooms had many pleasant rides together.

25

Home, Sweet Home

WITH THE COMING OF THE NEW YEAR, THE RANCH LOST ITS
status as the Ranch, and became our home. It was no
longer the rendezvous of the Villainy Club, as such, though the
members were often there as our guests. It was no longer a place
where dancing was allowed; not because Annie objected to
dancing, but because she knew it would wound Miss Nellie, who
was faithful to all the traditions and rules of the Methodist
Church.

Jeff Robinson, a tall, black young Negro, had been the man
of all work around our home when I was a child. We boys loved
him as only Southern boys can love the Negro man of the family,
and his fealty to us was natural with him. Shortly before the time
of our marriage, Jeff had married Adaline, a bright, intelligent,
chocolate-colored girl, and it was in accordance with the tradi-
tional order of things that she should do the cooking and house-
work for us.

Toward the rear of the old school lot was a small but substantially built house that had been called "the music room." I
moved this around to front on the alley that ran beside the lot, and
converted it into a servant house. However, Jeff and Adaline
had their own home; so I rented it temporarily to Aunt Tildy,
a fat, good-natured old Negro woman.

It was Jeff Robinson who had secretly taught me and my
brothers those things a boy ought to know about life, including,
among other things, hoodoos and superstitions; how to have
good luck, how to avoid bad luck; that it was bad luck to start
off and turn back, but that you could avoid the bad luck by

making with your foot a cross-mark in the road and spitting in it; that to hear the doleful tremolo of a screech owl in the night meant death in the family, but that you could avoid it by turning your pocket wrong side out; and dozens of other like things.

To this very day, if a cat, a rabbit, or a squirrel crosses the road in front of me, I remember Jeff's admonition and turn my hat around. Several years ago, I was making the trip through the Utah Parks, and as we entered the Kaibab Forest the mule deer began to run across the road. Jeff had not instructed me about deer, but, to be on the safe side, I began turning my hat around, and, before the trip was finished, so many of them had crossed the road that I almost wore out my hat.

At Christmas, or with any other good excuse, Jeff and Adaline expected a present, usually a half dollar apiece, even after they were no longer working for me. After I left Blakely, if I went back there for any purpose and met Jeff or Adaline, it cost me a dollar. Their loyalty to me was such that either of them, I believe, would have laid down his life for me or mine; and they knew, without the word ever being spoken, that I stood as a protection against imposition upon them by any white man.

Now back to Annie and me in our home in the old Academy grove. Before our marriage I had put a neat picket paling around the front yard. Soon after I was married, I was enabled to make further improvements when a Negro carpenter whom my father and I had saved from the gallows or a life term in the penitentiary by successfully defending him against a charge of arson, asked to be allowed to pay our fee by working it out. He built fences around the back of the lot and around a vegetable garden; he also built a small barn with stables for the cow and the horse. My father had given Annie a beautiful young Jersey cow when we were married (the horse came later), and we had the garden planted with sugar cane and vegetables.

With milk from the cow and vegetables from the garden, and the back yard full of young chickens, which Adaline proudly raised and tended, we lived that year on the five hundred dollars

I drew for my salary as county judge. I do not remember to have lived better or more comfortably in any other years of my life. But it must be remembered that food was cheap, clothing was cheap, servants were cheap, everything was cheap, and we lived simply.

While I was building fences and barns, Annie was erecting a small but enduring edifice not made with hands or visible to the public eye, a necessary adjunct to every successful marriage—a doghouse, it is called. No man makes a happy or successful husband till he becomes hen-pecked. (I can see the women rising up in protest; but they know it is true, and their husbands know it is true.) And nothing else so quickly and so effectively produces the requisite state of hen-pecking as the doghouse.

I have been told that when a Seminole Indian chief sentences one of his tribe to death, he merely stands before the condemned man in a magnificent silence, looking him straight in the eye, unblinking, and finally raises his hand and points in the direction in which the condemned man is to go to meet his punishment at the hands of his executioners hidden in the forest.

The silence of the Indian chief is not more magnificent than Annie's silence when she condemns me and figuratively points to the doghouse. She condemns without hearing, is deaf to every demurrer, motion for specification of facts, plea, answer, alibi, or excuse. She merely ignores her cowering victim and tantalizes him with a silence more caustic than any words could be. It is an eloquent silence, a silence so exquisite that it thunders. In other words, she knows all the tricks of the matrimonial trade which every other normal loving wife knows.

But there is a silver lining to the cloud. Bob Dostor used to tell of the little boy he saw hitting his finger with a hammer, and when he asked, "What are you doing that for?" the boy replied, "It feels so good when I stop." Of course, it feels good merely to be let out of the doghouse; but, best of all, after one of these spells, Annie becomes so sweet and so gentle with me that she surpasses even her normal sweetness and gentleness. Why are we strong men so afraid of these little women?

A few years ago at a session of the American Bar Association, at Kansas City, the members from Georgia and their wives got together at a breakfast. I was at the head of the table and Annie was at the foot. Smythe Gambrell, counsel for the Eastern Airlines, was urging me to fly back to Atlanta with him on the plane, and I was saying, "No."

"Why not," he asked.

"I am afraid of airplanes," I answered.

"They are not dangerous."

"I know that."

"You ride sixty miles an hour in an automobile, and that is much more dangerous."

"I know that."

"Well, if you know they are not dangerous, why are you afraid of them?"

"See," I said, "that lady at the foot of the table? She is not dangerous, but I am as scared as hell of her."

A man has no such fear of a woman unless he loves her and believes she loves him. It is that kind of fear which is meant in the text from Ecclesiastes, "Fear God and keep His commandments."

26

A Son Is Born

THE FALL OF 1897 WAS FULL OF ANTICIPATION IN OUR HOME; a coming event was casting its shadows before.

The morning of Tuesday, November thirtieth, was clear, crisp, and cold. At about four o'clock certain omens we had been told to watch for became presageful that the time was at hand. There were no telephones, no automobiles, no trained nurses. I rapidly dressed and walked out into the clear night, just as the break of day was beginning to dim the stars. I half ran, partly walked, the quarter of a mile to awaken Dr. Dostor, and another mile to get the Negro woman who served as a practical nurse in such cases. My father was in Colquitt at an adjourned term of court there; so I did not awaken my mother then, but sent for her later in the day.

The labor was very slow, and all through the day the pains kept coming slowly and somewhat mildly at first, but more frequently and more severely as the afternoon wore along.

In those days, childbirth, especially for a primipara, was a terrific ordeal. Obstetrical practices in the last forty years have made great advances. It is no easy thing that the about-to-be mother faces now, but it is almost nothing as compared to what it was then. It is true that among some country women and among most Negro women it was comparatively easy. Mr. Jim Hobbs's cook went to the well to get a bucket of water, and, a minute or so later, came back with the baby in the bucket. But civilization, especially as it had impressed itself upon the rearing and activities of the *jeunes filles bien élevées* of that day and time, made young women of the better classes ill-fitted for their natural function of child-bearing.

Dr. Dostor, for his day and time, was an excellent physician of the old school. Following the obstetrical teaching of that time, he considered the administrations of anodynes inadvisable, on the theory that they would slow down the labor. He did, at my insistence, use a little chloroform in the last stages.

I have been at the birth of every child and every grandchild but two in my family, except that I was not present in the operating room at the actual time of delivery of my grand-children, as they were born in a hospital; and I think that every man should be required to be with his wife throughout this ordeal.

After supper, the pains became constant and severe. Annie was put to bed. Dr. Dostor stood on one side of the bed; I stood on the other with the chloroform in an improvised cone. My mother stood at the foot, and the Negro nurse puttered about the room. As a paroxysm would strike, Dr. Dostor would give me the nod, and I would place the cone impregnated with the chloroform in front of Annie's nose and hold it there until the doctor gave me the signal to remove it.

At about ten o'clock, came the final paroxysm. The doctor caught in his hands and held up a small body of naked pink flesh which gave a cry, the typical cry of the newborn babe. Annie lay there all exhausted, holding to my hand. At that little cry, she opened her tired eyes and smiled an endearing smile. As the Doctor said, "It's a fine boy," she pressed my hand again.

We knew his name already. If it were a girl, we had not been able to agree. If it were a boy, it was to take my first name, "Arthur," and Annie's family name, "Wilkin." So this new-comer was Arthur Wilkin Powell.

The doctor and the nurse were engaged in performing for the baby the usual services required by the newborn. I was standing by Annie, and my mother was standing near by. I felt Annie's hand twitch convulsively. I saw the general spasm come on; her eyes rolled back and I heard her murmuring: "I am going—I am going—going." Dread puerperal eclampsia! I was badly frightened, but tried not to show it. I motioned to my mother and she touched the doctor. He came quickly and gave her a hypodermic. The convulsion subsided, and she fell into a deep sleep.

This would not have happened if she had had proper prenatal care; but this was a thing of which the doctors knew little in those days. When we saw that she was awake next morning, we brought the baby to her. She looked toward it and put out her hands to take it; but she could not see it. Annie was blind!

In my horror at discovering that Annie could not see, I went quickly for Dr. Dostor. He told me that such a complication was to be expected, that it was not likely to be permanent, that usually it lasted for only about three days. He was right. On the third day her sight returned; and she was able to see the baby for the first time. From then on, she recuperated rapidly.

Despite the protest of all young mothers to the contrary, I still insist that it takes the exercise of a great deal of imagination for anyone to see in a newborn baby any resemblance to anything, unless it be a piece of beefsteak—or Winston Churchill. They were discussing whom the baby looked like, and they asked me what I thought. A fad in those days was a squat, comical, quizzical figure of a little old man, called "Billiken." So I replied that to me he looked more like a Billiken than anything else I could think of. The nickname stuck, and later became contracted to Billy; and to this day he is more generally called Billy than by his real name.

A mutual admiration grew up between Billy and my father. My father had grown quite heavy; he weighed, with one leg gone, about 225 pounds; so any great amount of walking on his crutches irked him. He got himself a gentle family horse and a buggy cut low in front, so that he could get in and out easily; and he used that to get about in. From the time Billy was able to sit alone, he was constantly on the buggy seat with my father.

First Trip to Saint Andrews Bay

THE NEXT SUMMER, WHEN THE REGULAR JUNE SESSION OF
the county court convened, there was nothing to try. I
adjourned the court and sat in the courtroom talking with two
young lawyers, Joe Sherman and Perryman DuBose. They were
complaining that law practice had dried up for the summer.
Some one made the suggestion, "Let's go on a camping trip to
Saint Andrews Bay."

None of us had seen this blissful spot, but we had heard of
it. Those who had been there came back to report that the Bay
was the most beautiful body of water in all the land, that the
Gulf beaches and waters were marvelous, that the fishing was
the finest in the world, and so on until they gave out of super-
latives. It lay on the Gulf of Mexico, only about a hundred miles
away; but the only way to get there was in a wagon—a big,
covered wagon if one were so fortunate as to be able to acquire
one—or to go down the Chattahoochee River on a steamboat to
Apalachicola, and from there travel seventy-five miles on the
Gulf in a sailboat, if one could not catch the Tarpon, an old
steamboat that made the trip occasionally.

The difficulty of the trip by wagon was that while there
were long sandy roads for the first fifty miles, as far as Marianna,
Florida, the roads gave out there, and the rest of the trip had to
be made over unmarked trails through pine woods, primeval and
practically uninhabited except by a few isolated squatters.

Nevertheless, the proposal of the trip met with a hearty
response, till some one asked "Where will we get enough money

to go on?" None of the lawyers had made a dollar at that term of court.

Someone suggested, "Let's go *in forma pauperis*," having reference to the oath a poor person is allowed to make in lieu of paying the costs to appeal a case. Someone else said he knew where he could borrow a one-horse wagon. Another said he thought Mr. Ed Fryer would be glad to let us have old "Big John" for his feed. Old "Big John" was a large horse that had seen better days, but was then too old for livery service, though he could still pull a wagon—at a slow pace. Among us we had two bicycles.

To shorten the story: Joe Sherman, Perryman DuBose, and I borrowed "Big John" and the one-horse wagon. My brother Perry joined us; also a twelve-year-old Negro boy volunteered to go along with us as helper without pay. We got together a frying pan, a coffee pot, and a couple of quilts apiece. We had no cover for the wagon and no tent. We had lard, sugar, coffee, salt, meal, a piece of bacon, and some canned goods; and, for "Big John," a bundle of hay and some oats. We must have had matches, but I do not remember about soap. Thus, the five of us set out to be gone for from three weeks to a month. I had been in the woods enough to believe that I had sufficient trapper's instinct to pilot the party through the trails below Marianna. I sent Annie and the baby to Colquitt to stay with Miss Nellie and Mr. Bird while we were gone.

The plan was that two of us would ride ahead on the bicycles to find suitable camping places, and that the three in the wagon would follow the bicycle tracks, which was easy to do in the sandy roads. We alternated in riding the bicycles. As it was too hot to travel in the middle of the day, the bicyclists would set out about daylight and try to find a suitable camping place that Big John could reach by ten o'clock in the morning, and about three o'clock in the afternoon to find a suitable place for the night. Thus we could make about twenty miles a day.

We lived mostly on canned goods, soda crackers, and coffee for the first three days, by which time we had passed the final outposts of civilization below Marianna. On the third night we slept in the silence of the untamed forest; and it was the most complete silence I have ever known—no sound except that of our own voices and of Big John muzzling in his feed.

Most of the country through which we passed after we left Marianna was a vast sandy area covered with a rather thin growth of yellow pines and scraggy scrub oaks. To avoid the chance of being unable to ford the large creeks, we usually went around them, by following the watershed; though occasionally, by following the trail of a wagon, we would find a crossing on a bridge which had been made by putting two large logs across the creek and laying on them a flooring of poles. Some of the creeks had but little or no swampland adjoining them, but many of the streams ran through thick growths of gum, titi, and other swamp trees and jungle bushes. There was a marked absence of all animal life—wild or domestic. The squatters' cabins, usually with a few acres cultivated around them, were miles apart. The water in all the streams was clear and drinkable, though some of it tasted slightly of sulphur.

One day we passed a one-roomed cabin with a few acres of corn around it; and the corn was just ripe enough to make good tender roasting ears. The owner was absent but we bought a half-dozen of the roasting ears, by taking them and leaving a dime on the door step. At our next camping place, when we had fried our bacon, we cut and scraped the grains of corn from the cobs into the bacon grease in the frying pan, and fried it. The resulting mess was black and greasy, but I give you my word that I have never eaten anything that tasted better. We were all sorry that we had not taken a dozen ears.

We had fishing poles and rude tackle with us, and worms for bait. At noon on the fourth day we stopped beside a stream and Joe Sherman put hook and line on a pole, baited the hook and cast it out into the water. In a moment he was wrestling with a fish, which, when landed, proved to be an enormous shell-cracker, an excellent fresh-water food fish. Soon we had a dozen. Fried fish just out of the water; cornbread; coffee in a tin cup— what a feast we had!

We had been told that as we got toward the Bay we would have to cross Bear Creek on a bridge. There were two points at which there were bridges—the Nixon bridge, near where the highway and the railway now cross this creek, and McAlister's bridge farther west, near the place where the creek enters the Bay. As we found a pretty clear trail leading to McAlister's bridge, we took that route. In the middle of the afternoon we came to the bridge; and there we saw old man McAlister, a quaint, weather-beaten but wiry old fellow with gray hair and beard. Beside this creek, which is as deep and wide as a river there, he had a two-story house, painted white once upon a time, with glass windows in it, and to the side and rear of it a vegetable garden and a small orchard containing ill-kept grape vines and fruit trees. Evidently he and the house had seen better days.

He heard us coming and rushed out to meet us and to welcome us. Visitors from the outside world did not come that way often. He invited us to spend the night in his house, but we told him that we preferred to camp under a large wide-spreading live oak which stood on the creek bank near his barn and wagon shed. He took us into his yard and showed us his prize possession—an artesian well which flowed a sulphur water; according to him this water was a panacea for human ills and he said he had refused an offer of seventy thousand dollars for the well. Just before nightfall he led us to a spot a few hundred yards away where in a very short time we caught a number of the largest bream I ever saw. He persuaded us to stay over next day and go fishing with him down the creek. The fishing was pretty good, but when he tried to get us to stay longer, Joe Sherman protested—Joe got mad with the old fellow because he laughed so heartily when Joe fell out of the boat and got a good ducking.

While we were there, two native youngsters, about nineteen or twenty years old, came along walking. Mr. McAlister tried to detain them, and they did stop long enough to get a drink of water, but insisted that they were anxious to get to town. In response to our question, they said that they lived at the "Deadening" up on Econfina Creek, which from circumstantial evidence we identified as being about ten miles away; that they had never before been as far away from home as they then were; that all their lives they had heard of the town and had decided to go there and see it. It turned out that the town was Bayhead, about three miles further on, consisting of a store, a residence, and a dock running out into the bay, at which a number of small boats were usually moored.

The sand under the big live oak at McAlister's was the best soil I ever slept on. When the bedding was laid upon it, it had a way of snuggling softly up against ribs and joints, and cuddling one off to sleep. When one has had a strenuous day in the open and has topped it off with a hearty supper of big fat bream just caught out of deep, clear water and fried brown in deep fat before they had hardly quit flapping, with a hoe-cake of cornbread and strong hot coffee in a tin cup, a bed like that is a bed indeed.

We reached Saint Andrews on July 3, 1898. Here was a store where we could replenish our supplies. Here was a post-office where we could send and receive mail. Mr. Lambert Ware, the big man of the community, who owned the store and whose sister was the postmistress, had built through the woods a telephone line to Chipley, Florida, and over this telegrams could be sent. Here was a fine grove we could camp in, with water near by.

The thing we craved most was syrup. We had failed to bring any with us, and we had been eating fish. Fish soon palls the appetite unless there is something sweet to go along with it. Mr. Ware sold us the syrup, but we also wanted bread to eat with it, and he told us his entire supply of bread had been sent across the Bay to the West Peninsula, where a Fourth-of-July celebration was to be held next day. We showed such manifest disappointment that his sister, then Mrs. Parker, later Mrs. Gwathney, went to her home and brought us all the bread she had—half a loaf.

We poured our tin plates full of syrup, divided the bread into five parts, not forgetting our little Negro, and proceeded to sop up the syrup with the bread. The bread was soon gone, and we were so hungry for the sweet that we licked the syrup from the plates with our tongues.

At Saint Andrews we found a large pen full of those land tortoises which we called "gophers." It is the burrowing land tortoise, which often attains more than a foot in length and a width of say ten inches, that we called the gopher; but the small burrowing rodent about the size of a rat and looking like a chipmunk with his ears clipped off, which others call the gopher, we called the salamander. There were few or no gophers or salamanders north of Blakely, but a great many of them south of Blakely, all the way to the Gulf of Mexico. We saw the gophers oftenest when they were ambling around in the woods in search of food, but they lived in winding burrows which went down about six feet into the ground. Often a rattlesnake would occupy a gopher hole with the gopher, and the two would dwell there in amity. Occasionally a frightened rabbit would escape into a gopher hole. That was a poor refuge for the rabbit, for, if a rattlesnake did not get him first, the hunter would cut a long switch, run it down into the hole, catch it into the fur of the rabbit, twist it until a good hold upon his pelt was obtained, and then pull him out.

At Apalachicola, Saint Andrews, and other ports of call for the schooners that plied the gulf coast of northwest Florida, there were those who bought gophers and sold them to the schooners. Ships carried them in those days, as fresh meat, to prevent scurvy among the members of the crew. All over the piney woods the natives would catch the gophers and take them in carts or in sacks to Saint Andrews and sell them or barter them at Ware's store there. Mr. Justice Rivers Buford, of the Supreme Court of Florida, who was born in that country, is authority for the statement that in the old days gophers were legal tender there; that one could pay for an article with a big gopher and get back one or two little gophers in change.

We stayed in Saint Andrews about two weeks. We found excellent salt-water fishing in the Bay and in the bayous, and the best fresh-water fishing I ever saw over on the West Peninsula in the lake which was destroyed when the Government, a few years ago, built the ship canal from the Bay to the Gulf.

When we were about ready to start home, I got a message from one of my regular clients, John Callahan, a large turpentine operator living about sixteen miles south of Blakely, asking me to come back as soon as possible to attend to a matter for him. So we left at once. We had encountered no rain thus far, but that afternoon it began to cloud up. We remembered that in the midst of the forest, about thirty miles from Saint Andrews, we had noticed on the way down a little log church, beside a small stream of clear, clean water, and we decided to stop there that night. Knowing that it would be after dark before Big John could make it there with the wagon, Perryman DuBose and I were sent ahead on the bicycles to build a large fire as a beacon to those in the wagon after it got too dark for them to follow the tracks of the bicycles.

As we approached the church, just about sundown, we saw a fire already burning in front of it, with a man, a woman, and a dozen children of various ages around it. The man asked us where we were going, and we told him, and mentioned that we had thought of camping in the church that night, in view of the impending rainfall; but that we supposed we would have to go somewhere else, as he and his family were using the church. The church did not look as if it could accommodate more than the dozen he had with him, but he assured us he would not think of having us go, that there was plenty of room for all. So we agreed to stay.

The church was less than twenty feet wide. We moved to one side the seats, which were made of pine slabs with auger holes in them, into which peg legs were inserted. The family spread their pallets on one side, we spread ours on the other, and we put the little Negro to sleep in the pulpit. It did rain, but it cleared off during the night.

We learned that the small stream was Sweetwater Creek and that the church was the Sweetwater Hardshell Baptist Church. Little did I think then that some day I would be the pastor of that church.

The native who camped with us said he often came there with his family to sleep; that he was cutting some timber in the woods near by, and that he brought his family up there because it was so far for him to have to go home every night. We asked him how far it was to his home. He said it was three miles. Some two years later, I passed his house and looked in, and saw that his family had just as many of the comforts of life in the church as they had in the home.

I mentioned to another of the natives, whom I met later, my experience of having met this man and his family at the church and expressed surprise that a man so young as he should have so many children.

He replied, "She had all but two of 'em when he married her."

"Oh, he married a widow," I said.

"She weren't no widow," he answered laconically.

Early the next morning, I bade my fellow campers goodbye, mounted Rhadamanthus, and rode away. I was at Callahan's still, eighty miles from Sweetwater, that afternoon, and after seeing Mr. Callahan and agreeing to meet him in Blakely next morning, rode on twenty miles further to Colquitt. I spent the night there with Annie and the baby and rode to Blakely next morning in time to catch the nine o'clock train. I had made my century on a bicycle—quite a feat, considering that it was over fisherman's trails and sandy roads.

A Birth and a Death

IN THE SPRING OF 1899 A BABY GIRL CAME TO US. ANNIE GOT through the accouchement this time somewhat more easily than she did before. We had difficulty in deciding on a name, but finally agreed on "Frances."

It was in this year that Bob Dostor died. He had an instinct for medicine, and his reputation as a physician was growing rapidly. Mrs. Wade, the mother of John, Wilk, and Pearl, became very ill. Bob, though he himself was suffering from acute appendicitis, stayed by her bedside, night and day, fighting to the end a battle that no one could win.

As soon as Mrs. Wade had been buried, Bob, accompanied by his father, went to Dr. Holmes's Sanitarium in Atlanta for an operation. Dr. Holmes was a pioneer in the surgical treatment of appendicitis; and all such surgery in those days was extremely dangerous. The operation was too late; the appendix had ruptured, and peritonitis set in. Bob knew only too well what the end would be.

My father was in Atlanta and telegraphed me of his death. The remains arrived in Blakely next morning. Bob's was the first embalmed body any of us in Blakely had ever seen. The undertaker had done his work well and had robbed death of much of the physical grossness that naturally attends it. As he lay in his casket, there was a loveliness of manly beauty about him that none of us will ever forget. Bob's death was the first in our set.

Our Colored Friends

IT WAS IN 1898 OR 1899 THAT ALLEN ALEXANDER TOOK THE place in our menage which Adaline had formerly filled. Allen was about eighteen years old when he became our servant, and he remained constantly in my employ, with the exception of a brief absence which I will later mention, until the time of his death in 1928—about thirty years. He was of medium height, thickset, and of a dark gingercake color.

Allen did not pose as a saint, but he was honest; he did not drink or steal, and his loyalty and fidelity to me and my family were unbounded. For practically the whole time he was with us, he would, of his own initiative, serve breakfast to Annie and me in bed every morning; and as the children came along and became of school age, he would give them their breakfasts and get them off to school. My children were devoted to him. If one of them was disobedient toward Annie or me, a word from Allen was all that was needed to get immediate obedience. He knew that Annie and I, as well as our children, had a real affection for him; and he never abused it. He lived in the house on the alley at the rear of our premises—the one formerly occupied by Aunt Tildy. After two or three years he married a young Negro woman, Jennie Bell, who worked elsewhere in the town.

The Sunday regimen in our household was that Allen would serve breakfast, and, while Annie and I were at church, he would prepare the midday meal and set the table; then he would have the rest of the day to spend as he pleased, except that he was expected to come back late in the afternoon, feed the chickens, the horse, and the cow, and do the milking.

A few months after his marriage he came to me and told me that a Negro from Fort Gaines, who said that Jennie Bell was his wife, had come to claim her and take her back with him, and that Jennie Bell did not want to go. I told him that he would have to give her up; otherwise he would be guilty of bigamy; that Jennie Bell did not have to go back to her husband, but that he (Allen) must not let her live with him unless and until she got a divorce, which would take several months. Jennie Bell refused to go.

The next Sunday morning Allen served breakfast as usual. When we got back from church the table was set and the meal prepared, but by nightfall Allen had not come to do the evening chores. Inquiry among the other Negroes developed the information that he was so perturbed by Jennie Bell's attitude that he had run away from her and had gone to Albany. In another context I shall tell of his return to Blakely.

Two or three years later he married a woman several years older than he, named Jennie Robinson. They had a child named Buster. They came to Atlanta with us at the end of 1906, and lived in the rear of the house we occupied on Gordon Street. When we moved across the city to Columbia Avenue, Allen occupied the servant house there, but Jennie refused to come with him, and he divorced her. When we moved to where we are now living on Peachtree Street, he had his room over our garage, and claimed to be a single man, until shortly before his death when he married a high-headed woman who gave him and us a great deal of trouble. How many common-law wives he had, I do not know.

I was at Blakely just before he married the last time, and an old friend of his, a colored boy named Willis, saw me and asked, "Mr. Arthur, how is Allen getting on in Atlanta?"

"Fine," I said.

"How many wives has he got up there?"

"I only know of Jennie Robinson, whom he brought with him; and he divorced her. I do not know how many he has on the sly; but he now claims to be a single man," I replied. I then asked, "How many wives did he have down here?"

"Just them two what he resigned from," Willis solemnly declared.

For a year or two before he died, Allen's heart began to give him a great deal of trouble. I still paid him his regular wages, hired others to do his work, and furnished him with medical care. He objected to going to the hospital, but finally his condition got so bad that he had to go. He showed improvement under hospitalization, but in July, 1928, while Annie and I were at Seattle at a meeting of the American Bar Association, we got a telegram from our children saying that he had died suddenly. We telegraphed back to them to see that he was properly buried and to have all the family attend his funeral services, and they did so.

The Southern Negro has made much advancement in intelligence, in morals, in education, and in culture. No right-minded Southerner begrudges this progress. The day may come when the Negro will attain many equalities, and these will be accorded to him as he merits them; but social segregation is a very different thing.

The Negro himself generally respects this status. All my life I have lived among Negroes. I have never had a word of insolence from one of them yet—except once in Washington; and it so surprised me that the fellow, seeing the expression of shock on my face, took to his heels before I had time to think what I should do about it.

There is an old saying among our people that no white man can conceal his mind from a Negro, and that no white man ever knows what is in a Negro's mind. I do not know what degree of success attends the efforts of the Negroes to read the minds of one another, but I do recall an amusing incident in which one Negro misinterpreted another's words. A Negro employed me to secure his release from jail, where he had been lodged under a peace warrant charging him with having threatened to kill another Negro. He insisted that he did not know the Negro who had sworn out the warrant, had never heard of him before, and certainly had never threatened him in any way. I demanded and got a hearing before the magistrate. The prosecutor swore that at a mullet supper, on the Saturday night before, the defendant had drawn his pistol and threatened to kill him.

I cross-examined him. He admitted that he did not know the defendant, had never seen him prior to the night in question, and had never had any quarrel with him. I then asked him to tell me just what the defendant said and did.

"I was out in de yard by de fire wid some udder boys when dis nigger come out on de front porch and swung his pistol 'round in de air and yelled out, 'Look at me, boys and gals! I'se gwine to kill me a God damn black son of a bitch befo' dis night is over.' "

"He did not point his pistol at you or look at you, did he?" I asked.

"No suh, but when he say dat about a God damn black son of a bitch, I jus' knowed dat he must er meant me."

The Negro is a natural born opportunist. I recall that when I was a boy a mule dealer brought a drove of mules to Blakely, and from day to day conducted an auction of them. There was one old mule no one would bid on. Finally, the dealer announced, "Tomorrow I am going to sell this mule to the highest bidder regardless of price. I will require no cash payment down, but will sell on two years' time, with only a mortgage on the mule as security."

The next day, when the old mule was offered for sale and the terms stated, the bidding among the Negroes was brisk. Two Negroes, one of them, Old Uncle Henry Powell, kept running the price up until it was finally knocked off to him on his bid of two thousand dollars.

"You must have thought a good deal of that old mule to bid that much for him," some one said to Uncle Henry.

"I didn't care so much for de mule," he replied, "but dem terms suttinly did suit me."

I thought that with the coming of education and better opportunity for the Negroes they would learn to take thought for the morrow, but it seems not so. We had a man of all work about our home in Atlanta, whom I recently told that I was going to increase his weekly wages, but that because of the increase I would have to report his wages to the government and that he would have to pay income tax on it.

"How much is income tax?" he asked.

With apparent seriousness, I said, "Lots of times I have to pay over a thousand dollars."

"I'd better not take the raise, then," he said.

"You do not have to pay it till next year and you can pay it in four instalments," I told him.

"Oh, that's all right," he said. "If I have till next year to pay the tax, I will take the raise."

Throughout that part of Georgia in which I was born about sixty per cent of the population is colored. Yet, except for a short while during Reconstruction, there has never been any "Negro problem" there. I know of no word in our language that applies accurately to the feeling that exists between the two races, though it is a form of affection. It must be lived and experienced to be understood. It involves an inborn spirit of noblesse oblige on the part of the whites and the frank acceptance of the status on the part of the blacks. In many respects the mind and conduct of the ordinary Negro are the mind and conduct of a child. He needs and expects from the white man understanding and protection, especially against himself.

Yes, there is a problem; but it is not a Negro problem. It is the low-down-white-man problem. High-mindedness is no more universal in the South than it is in any other part of our country. A sorry white man, seeing a Negro tilling the field that he would like to rent and use as a center of his loafing, or doing some job he would like to be employed at, hates the Negro, and, unless prevented by the better class of whites, inflicts injury and injustice upon him.

The lynching problem is not a Negro problem, especially in so far as it relates to assaults upon women. When rape is involved, the color of the man, be it white, black, red, yellow, blue, or green, is immaterial. A white rapist stands in practically as much danger from the fury of the mob as a black one. I have seen and know what I am talking about. I will not stop to discuss that now, but will offer corroboration later.

While the average Negro is prone to commit misdemeanors and minor infractions of the law, and, against other Negroes, often commits even more serious crimes, the white man of the better class is quite tolerant of him as to offenses of this nature. Occasionally a Negro goes berserk, and when he does he is a wild beast apparently without human instincts. Then his vicious-mindedness extends indifferently toward whites and blacks, and he is usually hunted down by both races and is often put to death in the attempt to arrest him, as it is difficult to take him alive.

"White supremacy" is a phrase of possible transiency. Supremacy will naturally depend on which race develops the higher culture, intelligence, and ruling qualities. But that will depend on broad categories and not on individual cases. What I mean is that white supremacy is not a thing which exists in and of itself. Like any other supremacy, it ultimately depends upon what proves itself to be supreme. The white race is supreme today, because up to date it has so proved itself.

Social equality is another loose and transient phrase. It is merely a matter of individual taste and thinking. According to my way of thinking, the Negro is not my social equal; nor are some white people. It is up to me to maintain my status if I can, but I have sense enough to know that if I and those I deem my social equals do not maintain our assumed status by social worth, it eventually will go for naught. We shall never sustain it by denying to the Negro his constitutional rights of life, liberty, or property. But it must be remembered that no constitutional clause guarantees the social status of anyone.

Physical separation of whites and blacks upon streetcars, trains, and other public conveyances to which the Negro has, by law, the equal right of access is merely to promote the peace and well-being of both races. I would not in any wise deprive him of any constitutional right in this respect. If there be but one vacant seat in a streetcar and half of that is occupied by a Negro, I stand rather than sit by him, but I do not ask him to get up. If a sick or crippled Negro enters a streetcar and cannot get another seat, I give him mine. That is the duty of any gentleman.

The social segregation of the races is the important thing to both races—in that lies the preservation of both races. There is no disagreement on this point between the self-respecting white man of the South and the self-respecting Negro. I do not invite Negroes into my home as guests; nor do the Negroes invite me into theirs. The Negroes want their own churches, their own schools, their own hotels, their own eating places, their own lodges and social institutions. If I were to offer for membership in the biggest Negro Baptist Church in Atlanta, there would be as many blackballs against me as there would be against a Negro if he applied for membership in the First Baptist Church, of which I am a member. If the Pecksniffs and fanatics from other sections, who are trying to force blacks and whites to enter into free social association, will let us alone, we will work out our situation satisfactorily to all of us. The only effect of their activities is to retard the advancement of the Negroes and to stir up strife, which will injure the Negroes more than it will the whites.

Whoever can understand this story will be able to understand, somewhat at least, the thing I have been talking about: Soon after Booker T. Washington, the great Negro leader for whom we all had the highest respect, dined with President Theodore Roosevelt at the White House, he spoke to a large audience at Macon. Among those who heard him was a white farmer. At the conclusion of the address, he rushed up, caught the speaker by the hand, and said with fervor, "Booker, that is the greatest speech I ever heard. I believe that you are the smartest man in America."

"I appreciate your compliment," Booker replied, "but of course, I cannot take you seriously when you say that I am the smartest man in America. There is President Roosevelt, for instance—"

"Who? That ——?" the farmer broke in. "I have less respect for him than I have for a suck-egg hound dog—he eats with Negroes."

30

Other Trips to the Bay

I HAVE MENTIONED GOING TO SAINT ANDREWS BAY IN 1898. FOR the next eight years, it was an annual event. In 1899 my mother, Annie, our two babies, a colored nurse and her small child made the trip with me. I rented for a month the Doty cottage on the bluff above the Bay, and arranged with Ed Hand to meet us with his sailboat at Apalachicola and take us to Saint Andrews.

I had hardly been at the Bay a week when I got a message from my father that a matter had arisen requiring my attention. My quickest way to get home was to go on the mail launch to Wetapo at the head of East Bay and go from there with the man who carried the mail to Wewahitchka on the Dead Lake, get someone to carry me in a bateau across the lake to Iola, on the Apalachicola River, and catch the steamboat there.

Early the next morning, I set out, expecting to get to Wetapo at noon, and to Wewahitchka late in the afternoon. The launch gave out of breath just before we got to Parker's, about five miles from Saint Andrews, and we did not get away from there till late afternoon. We got to Wetapo after nightfall. The mailman had become tired of waiting and had gone home, but the postmaster told me that, if I would walk about two miles through the woods along the path he showed me, I would see a light, and that would be the mailman's home. I followed instructions, and the man I was seeking drove me to Wewahitchka, and we reached there shortly after midnight. He went to a small cottage, woke a man up, and told him that he had a passenger who wanted to be rowed across the lake.

When the old fellow came out, I was sure that it was old

Charon himself. He was tall, gaunt, gray-headed, and hollow-eyed. He had a long, slender bateau paddle in his hand. He gave no greeting, but pointed his paddle toward the lake, and in a deep sepulchral voice said, "Let's go."

The Dead Lake was formed about a hundred years ago when the Chipola River broke through its banks and overflowed the adjacent swamps; and the waters have never receded.

That night the moon was full, and the five or six miles through which old Charon rowed me was a ghostland. In the lake's dark waters, the trunks and limbs of cypresses long since dead stood stark in the moonlight, draped in gray Spanish moss, like phantom brides shrouded in the gossamers of their wedding finery. Occasionally a large moccasin would slither from a dead limb and fall with a thud into the water. The slow, soft beat of wings told that roosting nightbirds were easing themselves away from our approach. Through this ghostland, old Charon paddled his bateau the whole distance, without speaking a word, not even in reply to an occasional question from me. At last, as he shoved the boat ashore, I asked him the way to Iola Landing. He merely pointed with his paddle.

I trudged along a wagon road deep-rutted in the sand, till I came to the river bank and saw a warehouse, indicating the location of the landing. Day was breaking across the river. I had not been there over five minutes when I heard the whistle of the steamboat.

As I finished the work I had come home to attend to, I came down with an acute attack of malarial fever. I had to let Annie know why I was not returning; so I wrote her that I had a slight attack of malaria and would be delayed for a few days. The morning she got my letter, she telegraphed me, "Leaving for home by Ed Hand's boat and river steamboat."

The next morning I saw in the Atlanta Constitution a dispatch from Pensacola saying that, in the early afternoon before, the gulf coast of northwest Florida had been swept by a storm. I never saw a man get over a spell of malarial fever as quickly as I did when I saw that news item. Out of bed I came, and to the telegraph office I went. I sent a telegram to Mr. Ware at Saint Andrews, asking if my family had left there, and to a friend at Apalachicola asking if they had reached there. In a short while I got a telegram from Mr. Ware stating that they had left there in Ed Hand's boat at about ten o'clock in the morning. In the afternoon came a reply from my friend in Apalachicola saying they were not there. That night I caught a steamboat going toward Apalachicola.

I told the captain of the steamboat whom I was looking for; and he told me that we would pass the upcoming boat at about noon next day. Sure enough, we had just finished lunch when we heard its whistle. As it loomed up around the bend, the first person I saw was Billy, standing with his nurse at the deck rail. I transferred from one boat to the other in midstream.

Ed Hand had seen the storm coming just as he was approaching Ladseen's Point, at the entrance to Apalachicola Bay, and had run the boat in as close as he could and anchored it just as the storm struck. He carried his passengers ashore, wading through the waves with them in his arms. The Negro woman had deserted our two children and was holding on to her child. My mother was perfectly calm in her usual implicit faith in everybody and everything, and in the protection of an ever present Providence. Storms have always frightened Annie. She put my letter into her bosom, grasped the two children, one in each arm, and, thus prepared to meet her God, stepped from the rocking boat into Ed Hand's arms.

They had to spend the night in a fisherman's shack, and made it into Apalachicola just in time to catch the outgoing boat; and that was why my friend there had not seen them.

For the next seven years we spent a part of every summer at the Bay. After the first two trips, quite a party of our friends would go with us. Frequently we had two large covered wagons and two or three buggies—a real caravan. When we went thus we usually had with us our wives and children and two or three unmarried couples. On one or two occasions my mother went along. We had tents, and had the wagons arranged so that berths could be made down in them; yet after the first night we all slept by choice in the open air on pallets spread on the ground. No one ever got sick. Annie gave me a scolding one night because I made down our pallets under a large live oak with very thick foliage. "It is too stuffy," she complained, "and I cannot see the stars."

My daughter Frances was recently telling her five-year-old son, "Teenie," of these trips through the woods and of camping out. "Mother," he asked, "was your father an Indian?"

"He certainly was, and still is," Frances replied.

I remember these trips best for the quietude of the unbroken forests of scraggy pines and scrub oaks through which we had to travel for the last sixty miles. Many woods give forth a soft murmur or echo the chirping of birds. In these, there was only dead silence—no, not the silence of the dead, but of the yet unborn.

It was an impressive quietude, an infectious stillness. We approached the forest talking, laughing, and singing. Soon, a silence descended upon us all, as if to sing or to speak aloud would be a sacrilege. The groaning of the sand, as the iron of the tires of the wagon wheels crunched into it, became a fortissimo, in contrast with the hush of the wilderness.

The young people we took along on the trip usually fell in love before it was over and got married before the next trip came around. So often did this happen, that we had applications from several old maids to join the caravan, but we told them we were not running a home for incurables.

During this period I made a special trip to the Bay, in a buggy, to buy for a client some timber from Jack Gay, who lived on the Bay, but who owned lands in Early County. I took Clarence Alexander along with me for company. I bought the timber, and we were returning when we got to the site of Sweetwater Hardshell Baptist Church about noon. We had noticed as we went down that the church had been burned. We built a

fire and were warming some lunch, when I saw one of the natives
coming along the trail in a jog trot with his old musket across
his shoulders. As he saw us, he halted and then came up to us.

Knowing how shy and reticent these squatters are, and yet
being anxious to know how the church had been burned, I restrained myself and let him begin the conversation. I was stirring
something in the frying pan and I did not stop what I was doing
until he said, "Howdy"; then I looked up and said "Howdy."
Nothing was said for a minute or so, and then he asked which way
I had come from, and I said "from the Bay." He waited again,
and then asked if I had passed Old Man Bennett's place—a small
clearing a mile or two away. I said "Yes," and no more. He then
asked if Bennett had any boards stacked in the woods, and I told
him yes and opened up enough to tell him where they were across
Cull branch; and then, upon his further inquiry, I expressed the
opinion that two of the stacks were pretty good, but that one of
the stacks had a lot of warped boards in it.

Seeing that I was not unfriendly and not inquisitive, he relaxed
a little and began to talk. Upon my suggestion that perhaps he
had lived there all his life, he said that he was born just across the
line in Georgia, but about the time he became grown the country
began to settle up too thickly, so he moved away to where he
could get "more freedom"; he even went so far as to say that the
reason he was inquiring as to the boards was that a man had
started a settlement only a little more than a mile from where he
lived, and that he didn't like to live that close to anybody, so he
was thinking of moving and starting in a new place, and needed
the boards to build his new house. I then broached the question
of how the church was burned.

"We had er preacher," he finally confided to me, "who lived
in Blountstown and preached here on the third Sunday ever
month; and we had church conference ever Saddy 'fore the third
Sunday. We got up a church row at the conference on the Saddy
'fore the third Sunday in Augus', and we talked all day and
couldn' settle it; and it come up agin at the conference on the
Saddy 'fore the third Sunday in September, and we talked all

day and couldn' settle it; and we took it up agin at the conference on the Saddy 'fore the third Sunday in October, and we
talked nearly all day and couldn' settle it. Late in the evenin',
Brother Horn, from over on Econfina, moved a move that we
set fire to the damned old church and burn her up and end of
the row; and the move carried, and we put light'd knots under
her and set 'em afire and burnt her up and ended of the row."

My friend, Ira Hutcheson, the circuit judge at Panama city,
that thriving port city which has sprung up on Saint Andrews
Bay since the old days of which I have been speaking, is the
keeper of the traditions of that section. He tells the story of the
burning of the Sweetwater Church differently. He says that I
passed there a few days after the church was burned and saw the
congregation standing around the ashes disconsolately. To my
inquiries they replied that when the church burned the pastor
resigned. The deacons had gone to Vernon, the county seat, to
get a permit to make communion wine (they made it of distilled
corn and molasses, so the tradition goes) and the county judge
had told them that if they had either a churchhouse or a pastor, he
could issue them a permit, but, since they had neither, he could
not do so. He says that I came forward with an immediate solution—that they should elect me pastor and I would sign the application for the permit. So I became pastor, and have never resigned; hence I am still the pastor, and they still make the wine
under the permit.

Judge Hutcheson's word is better than mine at Panama City;
so I have had to accept his version. At any rate, if one should
ask almost anybody there who is the pastor of the Sweetwater
Hardshell Baptist Church he will get the reply, "Judge Powell."
The pastors of the other churches there extend me all the courtesies due a clergyman. I even have to preach a sermon occasionally
in one of the hotels to an appreciative congregation. I have a
choir with a rum basso and a whiskey tenor in it; and so many
of the prominent citizens, including Judge Hutcheson, have professed belief in the doctrines of my church and have openly declared that they have so felt the little wheels of love a-turning in

their hearts that they moan like Noah's dove (one of the tests of extreme piety, and a qualification for a deacon) that I have a large and prominent board of deacons.

The sermon they like best is the one I preach from the text, "These eight sons did Milcah bear." I begin with telling them that this text shows how difficult it was for the saints of old to get a little milk. They had to milk bears, for they had no kine cows. Seven of them had to hold the bear down while the other one milked her.

The exegesis continues with a description of the kinds of bears there are, including a sidebar reference to Bear Creek, on the banks of which the members of the old congregation are still supposed to distill the communion wine. The climax comes with the peroration, wherein I describe the visit of the Queen of Shebears to King Solomon and tell how she exclaimed, "O, King, the half has never been told," and he replied, "Yes, and if I hear of you telling that half, I will break your fool neck."

31

My Father's Passing

FOR A LITTLE MORE THAN EIGHT YEARS MY FATHER AND I HAD practiced together. He was not an old man—not quite sixty—but he had led a hard life and was breaking rapidly. I was trying to take more and more of the work off him. I did nearly all of the office work and tried most of the cases in the justices' and county courts. We usually were together in the superior courts, but occasionally one of us went alone, especially when there were two courts meeting in the same week.

In December, 1899, he and I were together at the first week of Calhoun Superior Court at Morgan. We drove home over the weekend, and on Sunday afternoon I went to his home to arrange for us to go back for the second week of the court, but found him in bed. He told me that he was suffering considerably from a boil on the back of his neck, and was not feeling at all well; so I went to the court without him. When, toward the latter part of the week I came home again, I found him quite ill —the boil on the back of his neck had developed into a virulent carbuncle. Dr. Dostor frankly told me that he had developed diabetes, and that the prognosis was unfavorable. It was before the days of insulin.

Though some local anesthetics, such as cocaine, had been discovered, the physicians used them sparingly, and were afraid to use them in the face of constitutional complications. My father submitted to the lancing of the carbuncle with much of his old fortitude, but you could see that he was wincing under the pain and was very greatly weakened by it.

Just after Christmas, he called me to him and told me that

he would not survive his illness, and that he wished me to draw a will for him, leaving all he owned to me, but with a direction that I use it for the support of my mother, my brother Perry, who was in school at Auburn, Alabama, and my sister Kittie Lee, who was then a young schoolgirl. The other two boys had already finished school. I delayed taking it to him for fear that when he signed it he would resign himself to the end and would thus give up some of the vital power which so often had sustained him.

However, on Saturday morning, December thirtieth, the doctor told me that we would better have the will executed. I asked three of my friends of whom he was very fond to go with me to act as witnesses. He greeted them with his usual cordiality and expressed his appreciation of their being there. One of them read the will to him, and he signed it.

He thanked the young men and they went out. I was left alone by his bedside. He took my hand in his and said: "My boy, you have never disappointed me. I have trusted you and you have never failed me. I am not leaving enough to provide for your mother and your sister, but you will not shirk the burden." He clasped my hand in a stronger grasp and added, "It's all up to you now."

His grasp relaxed. He immediately fell into a deep coma from which he never awakened. The final breath came about three o'clock that afternoon. There was no gasping, no struggle, just a cessation of breathing and of life.

The Sabbath which followed his death and on which we buried him was a cold, dreary, wintry day with occasional drizzles of sleet. That afternoon, as the last day of the year was wearing itself away into sunset and evening and into the dark of night that ever comes and goes, after a short service at the church, we took the body which in life he had worn and laid it away in the family plot in the Blakely Cemetery. Beside his grave was left space for my mother; she would be the first person of all whom he would wish to see on the morn of the Resurrection.

New Year's Day, 1900, was an important day in my life. New responsibilities were upon me. My father, who was also my friend, my partner, my brother, my mentor, my guide, my inspiration, and the main ballast to my career, was gone. I was left to fight alone; but the resolution to carry on effectively was strengthened by a realization of the fact.

I was a little more than twenty-six years old; but I had had over eight years' active experience at the bar, under the most excellent tutorship of my father, and had the reputation of having attained some skill in the trial of cases. We had built up a good clientele, and I believed that I could retain it.

The Environment Broadens

D URING THE NEXT FEW YEARS MY LAW PRACTICE GREW. IT WAS not long before I was being employed or associated in many of the important cases of our circuit and in near-by circuits. Before the next seven years had gone by, I was attending courts pretty regularly in about fifteen counties.

It was in 1901, I think, that I was in Vienna, Georgia, and Judge Henderson introduced me to a young man named Walter George, who was studying for admission to the bar and who, he said, was going to make a great lawyer. Judge Henderson was right; for this is the same Walter George, who, a few years later, became solicitor general of the circuit, and then, in rapid succession, Judge of the Superior Court, Judge of the Court of Appeals, a Justice of the Supreme Court, and United States Senator from Georgia.

This is the same Walter George, who, but recently, having refused to obey the commands of a popular President, was to be purged by that President. The word was passed that his denunciation was to occur at the time when the President was to speak at the stadium in Barnesville, Georgia, and was to turn the switch which was to set that part of middle Georgia alight through a newly completed rural electrification system. That day the stadium was thronged. Walter sat upon the platform and heard the President denounce him. As the President ended his speech, Walter arose. The President extended his hand. Walter took it, and looking straight into his eyes, said, "Mr. President, I accept your challenge."

The President blurted out, "God bless you, Walter," and

was so excited that he rushed off to his special train and forgot to turn the switch which was to set the countryside ablaze. But he set Georgia ablaze.

I do not vouch for the actuality of the following story, but it was told at the time, and it pretty well expresses the reaction of the majority of Georgians to the President's speech. They say that among the thousands who came to hear him speak was an old coon hunter, a Talmadgeite from the Towalagi District; and he brought his favorite hound, Old Tige, with him. He managed to get his dog into the stadium unnoticed, but when the band began to play, the dog began to howl. The members of the Georgia State Patrol are very efficient and polite. One of them came to the old fellow and said, "Old friend, I am very sorry to have to take your dog out, but I must do so, as he might disturb the President. Don't worry about him. We will take good care of him, and, when you go out, you will find him in the back room of the filling station, just across the street from the entrance."

When the speaking was over and the old fellow was going out, the patrolman met him and said to him, "You will find your dog safe and sound at the filling station. I am sorry I had to take him out."

"Mister," the old coon hunter replied, "I'm certainly much obleeged to yer fer takin' that dawg out. He's er fine dawg, and I wouldn't er had him a-heered that speech fer er thousan' dollars."

Walter wasn't purged. His recent services, as Chairman of the Foreign Relations Committee and as Chairman of the Finance Committee of the Senate, have given him national and international renown. He and the President now are good friends and are working together to save our nation.

One day shortly after the turn of the century, I received a letter from Mr. Donalson, of Bainbridge, the General Counsel of the G.F. & A.R.R., which runs from Richland, Georgia, to Carabelle, Florida, and is now a part of the Seaboard System. He

stated that Mr. Williams, President of the road, had asked him to
see if he could employ me as trial counsel for the company and
requested me to submit a contract embodying the terms on which
I would be willing to be employed. There were reasons why I
did not specially care to accept the offer, but I liked Mr. Donalson and could not afford to ignore his request. So I prepared a
contract setting out the terms, and in it stated a salary higher than
I thought Mr. Williams would be willing to pay. I put into it
another term as to which I thought there would be no objection,
namely, annual passes for my wife and for me.

He promptly replied, stating that all the terms were satisfactory except the one relating to the passes; that it was against the
policy of the company to issue annuals to the wives of officers or
employees; that his own wife did not have one. I wrote back
saying that it was largely to gratify my wife's desire to have the
pass that I had agreed to accept the contract and that we would
call the matter off.

A few days later he wrote me that Mr. Williams was having
the contract executed as I had proposed, and that Mrs. Powell's
pass would accompany it. The passes came from the General
Manager of the company, Mr. Legg, and he wrote: "It is the
custom of this company to insert in every annual pass the title
of the person in whose favor it is issued. When I was instructed
to issue the pass in favor of Mrs. Powell, I was at a loss as to
what title I should use; but, after seeing the correspondence between you and Mr. Donalson, I have hit upon one which I deem
appropriate and which you will find on the face of her pass."

Annie's pass was enclosed, and the title written into it was,
"Manager of the Legal Department."

Throughout all the time from my earliest childhood until I
left Blakely at the end of the year 1906, there had been constant
progress throughout all Southwest Georgia in culture and in
wealth. By the beginning of the present century Blakely had
a population of over twenty-five hundred. The shoddy buildings
that stood around the Square in my boyhood had given place to

brick structures. We had an excellent system of water works. People did not wait until Saturday nights to take baths. Electricity had largely superseded kerosene. Our streets were lighted, and hogs and cattle no longer roamed them. Paved highways had not yet come, but we had many improved and passable roads. Our railroad was put into good shape and we had two passenger trains, each way, a day. Our boys and girls were going off to college. The little thirty-acre patches with cabins on them were rapidly giving way to fertile farms with commodious residences and out-houses. New and better churches and new and better school buildings were the order of the day.

Our people were coming into contact with the outside world. I thought nothing of catching a train in the early evening and of being in Atlanta the next morning. We all loved to go to Atlanta, and began to acquire friends there. One of the disadvantages of living in Atlanta is that you can not go to Atlanta; there is a difference between coming to Atlanta and going to Atlanta.

In those days the Supreme Court called its dockets by circuits. At least twice every year, when the dockets from our section of the State were called, there would be a gathering in Atlanta of the lawyers from the Pataula and the adjoining circuits. There is a spirit of camaraderie among lawyers that makes such gettings together very enjoyable.

During the last ten years of my life at Blakely my environment was broadening rapidly. I had a number of business houses in Albany, Columbus, and Bainbridge on regular retainer, and was frequently trying cases in all those cities. Maurice Tift, one of Albany's leading wholesale merchants, who once was young, as I was, and who now is old, as I am, still occasionally comes to Atlanta to ask me if advice I gave him nearly forty years ago still holds good. Sam Bennet and Albert Russell were having a like experience. The old lawyers who were the leaders of the bar when we were admitted to it were dying or retiring from the active practice and we were taking their places.

In 1905, Logan Bleckley told me that Bob Pottle, who was law clerk to Mr. Justice Cobb of the Supreme Court, wished to get into the active practice, and was an excellent lawyer. He suggested that I take him in with me at Blakely. We formed a partnership under the name of Powell and Pottle, which continued until I went on the bench. Bob had had no courthouse experience; but he soon acquired it and became a great lawyer. He succeeded me on the bench, and later resigned to become division counsel for the Central of Georgia Railway Company at Albany.

Conductor Smith

A MONG THE CONDUCTORS WHO RAN ON OUR RAILROAD WAS LIN-wood Smith. Outwardly there was nothing about him to suggest that depth of appreciation and of self-sacrifice which he possessed and which I saw him display. He seemed to be merely the run-of-the-mine young conductor, who called the "all aboard" for the train to start, collected and punched the tickets, and passed a few pleasant words of chatting with the passengers he knew. There were some who knew that he was not a well man—that he was, at the time of which I shall presently speak, suffering from a kidney trouble that caused his death before he was forty years old.

There are so many of those who ride upon trains and who ask of the conductors unreasonable things and display anger or irritation when their requests are refused that most conductors do appreciate kind words and kind services, but I have never seen anyone else go as far in this respect as Linwood Smith did.

One morning in 1903 I received from him an urgent message to meet him at the station on the arrival of the nine-thirty train from Albany. I got on my bicycle and rode to the station. As soon as Linwood saw me, he told me to get aboard the train and go to the end of the road with him. Without prolonging the preliminaries, it is sufficient to say that I got on the train and went to the baggage car and found there several men with Mauser rifles. Linwood soon entered and explained:

"Last night going toward Albany, we were running late and trying to make up time. At Arlington, a tall yellow Negro man, a short black Negro man, and a Negro woman got on with tickets to Williamsburg (a flag station in a Negro settlement seven miles beyond Arlington.) As the train was approaching Williamsburg and I was signalling the engineer for the stop, the flagman reported to me that the short black Negro and the Negro woman had been engaged in a gross impropriety in the colored car. The three Negroes were already on the platform between the colored car and the baggage car, and the train was stopping. I spoke to the couple and said, 'I ought to arrest both of you and send you to jail; but get off and don't ever let me hear of your doing such a thing on a train again.'

"The yellow Negro had gotten off first. As I was pulling the cord to start the train, he called out, 'If you don't like it, we will shoot it out,' and, with that, he drew his pistol. My baggage-master, who is an expert rifle shot, was standing by his desk on which a pistol lay, and, when he saw the yellow man reach for his weapon, he immediately grabbed the pistol and fired at him; but just as he was in the act of doing so, the start of the train caused a jerk that threw him off balance, and he missed his mark. The yellow Negro fired several shots, all of which missed me but went into the side of the cars.

"I made no report of the matter, because I feared it might get the baggagemaster into trouble, and because I thought the incident was closed. This morning before I left Albany, I got a message that I had killed the little black Negro, and that a mob of Negroes was congregating at Williamsburg to take me off the train and kill me. It seems that, though the baggagemaster missed the man he shot at, he hit the other Negro.

"You are the only person except the baggagemaster and me who knows that it was he and not I who killed the Negro. In so far as everyone else is concerned, I want them to think so. He was acting to save my life. He is my friend. He has a wife and several children, and if he were to be discharged, he would have no way to support them. I have only a wife, and I have laid aside enough to support her even if I were to lose my job.

"These men you see back there with the rifles are friends of mine that I asked to come with me today to protect me against the Negroes at Williamsburg. However, when we got to Williamsburg, we found that the Negroes had gone to Morgan to swear out a warrant against me, and I am afraid the sheriff will attempt to arrest me and take me off the train tonight.

"To complicate the matter, when I got to Arlington, I received a wire from Mr. Hall, the superintendent, asking why I had failed to report the killing of a Negro at Williamsburg last night. I will probably be discharged for failing to report it. That's the situation."

I thought quickly. "Give me some telegraph blanks," I said.

I first telegraphed my old friend, Hub Davis, the sheriff of Calhoun county:

"If any warrant sworn out against Conductor Smith for killing Negro Williamsburg last night do not arrest him but notify me."

I next telegraphed Superintendent Hall:

"I am investigating killing of Negro at Williamsburg last night. As counsel for Conductor Smith and for the company have advised him to make no report or statement of any kind to anyone until I can investigate. A sufficient reason for this precaution is that any statement he might make to you could be used in court against him and against the company. On the other hand, any statement that he makes to me as his attorney, or that I make you as my client, is privileged and cannot be used either against him or against the company. The investigation, so far, seems to exonerate fully both him and the company. I will complete it as promptly as possible."

Soon I had a telegram from Sheriff Davis:

"Will not arrest Smith. Will notify you if necessary."

Next day, I forwarded to Superintendent Hall statements from the baggagemaster and from Conductor Smith, giving the facts as they were, except that instead of saying that the baggagemaster fired the shot, I merely said, "At that instant the shot was fired." I corroborated what they said as to the Negro firing shots at the conductor and into the side of the train by statements from several of the passengers and by the fact that the marks where the bullets hit were still on the car.

I got a letter from Superintendent Hall thanking me for my

thoughtfulness in handling the matter as I did. Linwood Smith got a letter from him congratulating him upon his narrow escape, and adding, "I would rather see a dozen such outlaws killed than to lose one brave and faithful conductor such as you are."

The local magistrates refused to issue warrants; the grand jury refused to indict.

In fiction, and perhaps in history, there are numerous instances recounted where one man has died or offered to die for another, or where to shield a son, a brother, a father, or a sweetheart, some father, son, brother, or lover has confessed to a murder that the other committed, but I have never seen any other instance in which one man, from a pure sense of gratitude and an altruistic spirit, has taken upon himself a homicide committed by another.

I sacredly observed, so long as he and the baggagemaster lived, his request that I should never tell that it was the baggagemaster and not he who had fired the fatal shot.

Not only was he grateful to me for what I had done for him, but he told other conductors of it and they too appreciated it. A few years later I was making a trip with Annie, and in requesting and obtaining passes for her, one of them, by inadvertence, named the wrong destination. It was the custom on the train we were using for the sleeping-car porter to take up the transportation as the passengers came on board the train, and to deliver it to the conductor who came aboard later. As I handed the passes to the porter, I told him that my wife's trip pass was improperly routed and that I would have to pay fare for her part of the way, and gave him a ten-dollar bill out of which to pay what was necessary in that respect. Next morning when we were about to arrive at our destination, the porter handed me back the ten dollars and said, "The conductor would not take the money. He said to tell you that he had heard what you did for Mr. Smith and that you could not pay any fare on any train he was on." I asked the porter who the conductor was and he could not, or would not, tell me.

As we shall presently see, it was not long till Linwood himself did me a great personal service.

In Time of Grief

I N NOVEMBER, 1903, OUR SECOND BOY WAS BORN. WE NAMED
him Albert Henry—Albert for Albert Russell and Henry
for Judge Sheffield.

Little Albert was a bright, sunny child. Even in his younger
months, he was full of laughter and good will for everyone. He
was a handsome little fellow with light hair and blue eyes. He
was unusually strong and active.

One day in May, just as he was turning his first half year,
illness came upon him with that suddenness with which it often
comes upon a child. It was cholera infantum, as it was then
called—the dysentery of childhood. Doctor Dostor was dead;
Bob Dostor was dead; but Wyatt Alexander made a brave fight
for him. The medical profession did not know as much about
that disease then as they do now; and, despite all we could do
for him, he grew worse and worse.

About sunrise one morning, we saw that his condition was
extremely critical. The ablest physician in our entire section was
Dr. Hilsman at Albany, fifty miles away. The train left Albany
a little after seven o'clock and the telegraph office was not yet
open. I got Mr. Perry, the station agent, to call the agent at
Albany over the railroad wire and to ask him to get a message to
Dr. Hilsman to come to Blakely on the morning train—that my
child was desperately ill, and that if he could not get to the
station in time to catch the train there, we would ask the conductor to pick him up at the crossing where the railroad passed
near his home. I did not know what conductor was in charge of
the train, but I asked the agent to tell him to be sure to pick up

Dr. Hilsman at the crossing, if he failed to get him at the station.

Very soon the answer from the agent came, saying that Dr. Hilsman would catch the train. Then came a message signed by Linwood Smith:

"This train will never leave Albany without Dr. Hilsman on it unless over my dead body."

When the train arrived, I drove with Dr. Hilsman at breakneck speed to my home. It was too late. As we walked into the room, Annie was holding our little fellow to her breast, and even before the doctor could examine him, his life gently flickered out.

No good can come from prolonging the anguish of that hour. Let me merely say that deep as was my grief I recognized that it was not comparable to Annie's. She was never a person to parade her emotions, and she met this disaster with outward calm. Time has done much to lessen the poignancy of her grief; but she has never forgotten and will never forget little Albert and her love for him.

The people of our section may have been rough in some of their ways, but when sorrow came to a home their sympathy and kindness were heartfelt and without limit. We shall never forget the gentleness and loving kindness of our friends and neighbors in our bereavement. Instead of the pine coffin made by local carpenters, in which we would have had to bury our baby a few years before, we were able to get a small white casket lined with white satin; and, when the time came to go to the cemetery, two of our friends got into a buggy and, placing the casket across their laps, carried it there. One of them, a young friend of ours, had a baby son of about the age of ours, and for several weeks his child had been at the point of death but was getting well. As he and the other friend placed the casket in the grave, I could see the tears in his eyes and could mark the struggle he was making to restrain them. There are some things one does not forget.

In an earlier context, I told of our colored boy Allen, who went away without notice, and I promised to tell of his return.

During the morning on which our baby died, I walked into the kitchen, and there was Allen preparing the noonday meal.

I said, "Good morning, Allen," and he said, "Good morning, Mr. Arthur." That was the only explanation asked or given as to why he had gone away or why he had come back. I did not want to embarrass him by asking him questions, but I knew I could find out about it from old Hattie, who had taken his place when he went away, and from some of his other Negro friends.

Here is the story as I patched it together from what they told me: When Allen went to Albany to avoid the row with Jennie Bell, he got himself a job of sorts there. He happened to be at the station when Dr. Hilsman came driving up. Allen knew the doctor's driver and asked where the doctor was going. The driver told him that the doctor had received a telegram to come to Blakely on that train, that my baby was very sick. Allen never hesitated; he boarded the train as it pulled out. His words to another Negro he told about it were, "I just couldn't stay away when I heard my folks were in trouble."

He never left us again to the day of his death.

The ashes of little Albert rest with those of his grandparents and of his great-grandparents and little Harry Lee, my infant brother, in the burial plot in the cemetery at Blakely. I hope that somewhere in the spirit world Allen is with him; for, in many respects, Allen was as a little child, of that such of which is the Kingdom of Heaven.

A Country Law Practice

ONE OF THE CHIEF CHARMS OF A LAW PRACTICE, ESPECIALLY a country law practice, one of the things that keep it constantly interesting, is that the lawyer never knows where the next case is coming from or when he is going to win some case in a bigger way than he ever hoped for. Of course we all have lost cases we expected to win—and perhaps ought to have won; but that itself gives poignancy to the joy of winning, when we do win.

In every trial lawyer's experiences, many interesting and amusing things occur; and this is a good thing, for a lawyer sees so much of the sad and sordid side of life that he would likely grow cynical or pessimistic or callous if it were not for the lighter and brighter side.

Two or three years after my father died, I tried a case in the City Court of Bainbridge before Judge Bower, in which I gained some reputation and also unexpectedly made the largest fee I had ever made up to that time.

Mr. Stevens, an old friend of my father's and mine, came into my office one day and told me that his son had been struck and almost killed by a locomotive of the Alabama Midland Railroad (now a part of the Atlantic Coast Line) at Donaldsonville. It occurred about four o'clock in the morning; there were no immediate witnesses except the train crew; and the boy had never recovered his mind to the point that he knew anything about how it had happened.

I told Mr. Stevens that I saw no basis for an expectation of a recovery and advised him to see if the claim agent of the railway company would not pay some small amount in settlement. He said that he had already seen the claim agent, and that he had said flatly he "wouldn't pay a damn cent." Mr. Stevens begged me to bring the suit and agreed to give me half of anything I could get by way of suit or settlement.

I filed the suit and went to Donaldsonville to investigate. There I met my old friend Key Knight, who was always extremely grateful to me for having successfully defended his son for shooting a man a few years before. He was an old, one-legged Confederate soldier, just a plain countryman, but he had a greater faculty of discovering facts than any other man I ever knew. He was a natural-born detective, and he had already ferreted out several important facts as to this case.

He told me that the boy lodged in a room in a livery stable just across the track from where the injury occurred, and that he had been put to bed the night before in a spell of unconsciousness. He had had such spells before, and when he had them he would walk in his sleep. The assumption was that he was doing so when he was struck by the train. He was knocked or carried by the locomotive over ninety feet, because his lantern and his shoes were found beside the track that distance back from where he was found injured and where a pool of blood could be seen next day. There was an ordinance in Donaldsonville limiting the speed of trains to ten miles per hour.

I saw that the operation and effectiveness of air brakes would be involved in the case, and I got my old friend, Jule Skinner, to take me on his engine for several trips and teach me the practical operation of the brakes. He also procured for me a copy of *Westinghouse's Instruction Book on the Operation of the Triple-Valve Air Brake*, and I made a careful study of it.

When the case came on for trial, counsel for the company treated it with considerable nonchalance, notwithstanding I had associated with me Albert Russell, who was a lawyer of unquestioned skill and ability. The defendant in its answer had admitted the striking of the boy by the locomotive; so it had the burden of proof as to lack of negligence.

The engineer was called to the witness stand. He testified that he had reduced the speed of his train as he entered the limits of the town and was running about six miles per hour when the boy suddenly stepped in front of the engine; that he instantly applied his air brakes in full emergency, but could not prevent striking him.

When I took him for cross-examination, I put on the appearance of a simple ignoramus. By muddling along I finally got him to admit that he ran at least ninety feet after he first saw the boy.

I then asked, "When you first saw him did you put on them brakes just as hard as you could?"

The witness was cocky. "I certainly did. I wiped the gauge."

"How do you wipe a gauge?"

"That means I put the brakes on in full emergency; that I gave them all the air in the train line."

"Was them good brakes?"

"Yes, sir, the very best—Westinghouse triple-valve air brakes."

"Weren't there something wrong with them?"

"No sirree, they were in perfect condition."

"Did you know how to put them on all right?"

"If I didn't, the company would not allow me on that engine. Young man, I'll have you to know that before I was allowed to go on an engine, I had to pass an examination in the operation of air brakes."

"Did the company give you any book to study for it?"

"Yes, sir, they gave me *Westinghouse's Instruction Book on the Operation of the Triple-Valve Air Brake.*"

"Is that a good book?"

"It certainly is."

"Did the company tell you that what is in that book is true?"

"They certainly did."

"Do you, yourself, know that what that book says is true?"

"Yes sir."

"Every word of it?"

"Yes sir."

I reached in my bag and pulled out the copy I had of the book, and I saw that the witness was startled when he saw it. I immediately threw off my guise of ignoramus and went at him.

"What is this book?"

"It is the book I was talking about."

"Look at the table on page so-and-so, and see within what distance a train on level ground can be stopped if it is running fifty miles per hour and the brakes are applied in full emergency."

"It says ninety feet."

"Look and see how many feet the train would go after the full emergency was applied, if it was running six miles per hour."

"Less than a foot, but it won't always do it."

"Why not?"

He tried to dodge with one or two explanations, but each time I would pin him down with something in the book to the contrary. He soon saw that I knew almost as much about it as he did.

He turned to the judge and asked, "Can I take back everything I have sworn in this case?"

The judge replied, "You are doing the swearing."

He hung his head and said, "I take back all I have said and I am going to tell the truth. I was not expecting to stop at Donaldsonville, which is a flag station. I was running late and was running just as fast as I could. I was not looking down the track at the moment and did not see the boy on it till the fireman called out 'Don't you see that boy on the track?' I saw him just as I hit him. I stopped the train and went back and got some one to take him to the hospital."

The company's attorney next put up a young surgeon and asked him a question. His answer indicated that what he knew was not material. I took him for cross-examination. My client had told me that this doctor had come to him and had urged him to dismiss the case, telling him that he would never get anything out of it, and that I was running up a bill of costs on him just for the experience. I decided to teach him a lesson.

I reached into my bag and pulled out a copy of Langdon Carter Gray's textbook on *Traumatic Injuries and Nervous Diseases*, which I happened to have with me for another purpose, and held it so that the witness could see the title. He had seen me pull the other book out of the bag and ruin the engineer with it.

I first proved his graduation and qualification as a medical expert. I then said, as I turned to a page of the book, "Now, doctor, I wish to ask you about a certain nervous disorder." I looked down as if I were reading. "It is known as 'hebephlebia,' which is ordinarily seen in young male patients, coming on them at about the age of puberty and usually lasting until about the age of twenty-five or thirty, characterized by many of the symptoms of ordinary lunacy; may be attended with either anaemia or hyper-anaemia," and so on through a maze of medical jargon that I had made up.

"I have never had a case of it in my practice," he answered.

"Have you ever had a case of hydrophobia in your practice?" I continued.

"No sir."

"But from your knowledge as a medical expert, you know that there is such a disease, do you not?"

"Oh, yes, I have seen it in the clinics."

"From your knowledge as a medical expert, do you mean to say that there is no such disease as hebephlebia, which I have described to you?"

"I have often seen it in the clinics," he answered.

I left it just there, and never mentioned it again in the trial; but the doctor next day accused me of making him swear to a lie.

"What do you mean?" I asked, as if I did not know.

"Why, you asked me about that disease you made up; and there I was with several of my patients in the audience and if I said that I did not know, they would wonder why I did not know, and if I said there was no such disease, I was afraid that you would prove by the book that there was, as you did about the air brakes with the engineer, so I had to say what I did."

I said to him in reply, "Doctor, I admit that I took an unfair advantage of you, but I felt justified in doing so, because you went out of your way to talk about me to my client. I thought it well to teach you the lesson that it is always dangerous to jump on a lawyer who is going to have the last lick at you. Now you and I are the only ones who know the truth about this matter; I never even mentioned it to the jury. Now if you will never tell it, I will not so long as you live."

Up to the time of his death he was thereafter always appreciative and did me many friendly services.

The verdict in our favor was for ten thousand dollars. The attorneys for the company attempted to get a review of the case by certiorari, made a mistake in their papers, had their proceedings dismissed, and were taxed with damages for delay. They paid us thirteen thousand, six hundred dollars.

Up to this time I had never given Annie either an engagement or a wedding ring. At the time of my proposal, I was so beside myself that I just did not think of it. Later when my oversight came to my attention, I was not able to buy the kind of a ring I wanted her to have. On the morning I left home to go to Bainbridge to try the Stevens case, as I kissed her goodbye, I told her that if I won the case I would buy her a ring. She got the ring. It is that cluster diamond ring she still wears.

An outgrowth of the Stevens case was Miss Mollie King's land case. I relate one incident in connection with it.

When I converted Son Stevens's injuries into a ten-thousand-dollar verdict, my stock as a lawyer went up considerably in and around Donaldsonville. Miss Mollie King, an old maid of that vicinity, consulted Billy Smith, the local constable, about a land case she wanted brought, and he advised her to let him take the papers to me. I looked at her deeds, decided that she was entitled to recover, and filed the suit. A few months later, I was in Donaldsonville on another matter and was sitting on the verandah of a residence which was used as a hotel, when a countryman approached. He hesitated a moment and asked, "Are you Colonel Powell?"

I said that I was. Then after another moment of hesitation he said, "King is my name," and moved toward the middle of the street. I knew the ways of these simple countrymen, and knew that he expected me to walk with him. So we walked together down the "middle of the big road."

After an expected silence, I asked, "Can I do something for you, Mr. King?"

"I just thought I would ask you about my sister's case."

"Who is your sister?" I enquired.

"Miss Mollie King," he said.

I told him that the case had been filed, but would not be for trial until November. About this time we came up behind a buggy, with an elderly lady sitting primly in it and occasionally casting glances backward at us. We continued the conversation, and at a pause in it he looked up at the lady and said, "Sis, this is Colonel Powell."

I bowed. She exclaimed, in surprise, "Is that the lawyer?"

"Yes," her brother said.

"He certainly is a mighty sorry looking one," she calmly remarked.

I am no handsome old man now, but it would be impossible for one who sees me now for the first time to imagine how sorry I looked in those days. Even until I was forty years old, I looked like an immature country boy; and I was constantly getting it rubbed in. However, it did not affect me; it amused me; and I often used my looks as an ambush, when I ran up against a lawyer who had never seen me before.

Cross-examination of a witness is often a very effective weapon in the trial of a case, but it is always attended with the danger of its proving to be a boomerang. Here is an oft-told classic example of this: In a prosecution for mayhem, in which it was charged that in a fight the accused had bitten off the prosecutor's ear, the only eye-witness to the fight was asked by the prosecuting attorney whether he had seen the accused bite the prosecutor's ear off in the fight, had answered that he had not. More than once, in answer to the same question, he persisted that he had not seen the accused bite the prosecutor's ear off. Defendant's counsel, instead of letting good enough alone, decided to cross-examine.

"You state positively that you saw the whole fight, but did not see my client here bite the ear off the prosecutor, sitting there?"

"I do," the witness answered.

"You did not see anything to indicate that any such thing happened in that fight, did you?"

"Well," said the witness, "after the fight was over I did see him spitting pieces of ear out of his mouth."

In line with this is an incident in the trial of a case in which a quaint old fellow employed me to defend his son, but conducted the case himself except for the examination of the witnesses.

The State had only one witness, and we were offering character witnesses to impeach him. "Call Adam Moulton," the old fellow said. Adam took the stand. He was a long, lanky constable from one of the country districts. He talked in a high-pitched voice. During the same term of the court he had had a civil case in which he was very much interested and had won it. In response to my question, he answered that he knew the State's witness, knew his general character and reputation in the community in which he lived, that it was bad and that from that character and reputation he would not believe him on oath.

The solicitor general took him for cross-examination.

"Now, Mr. Moulton, if you had a case in court and he testified on your side of the case, you would believe him, wouldn't you?"

"Well, now," began Adam slowly, but shrilly, "if I had a case like the one I had this week, in which I knew I was right, and he swore in the case and swore just like I did"—he hesitated, and then concluded, "Well, if he did, I would be so sure I was wrong I would give up the case."

In Georgia, the defendant in a criminal case is not allowed to be sworn and be a witness in his own behalf, but our statute permits him to make to the jury just such unsworn statement as he sees fit, and the jury may believe it in preference to the testimony or may disregard it in whole or in part. In many cases this is a very valuable privilege to the accused. Through the use of it, I saw Dan Sasser win his own case, without the aid of his counsel.

Dan was a plain, simple farmer who had in the eastern part of the county a small home and a thirty-acre tract, on which he had lived for the sixty years of his life. He had a wife and twelve children, ranging from a son twenty-five years old down to a year-old baby. He was a quiet, inconspicuous citizen, but he was pretty well known over the county because, for many years, he had been called in to serve at each term of the superior court as jury bailiff—the bailiff who takes the jurors to their room and tends and guards them, by day and night, until the verdict is made.

Then came the news that Dan had killed the tenant of an adjoining small farm in a brawl while the two were returning from a visit to a still in a remote part of the county, where they had bought some moonshine liquor. Dan was indicted for murder. The deceased was a trifling sort of fellow. The only witness to the homicide was not friendly to Dan, but he gave a pretty unbiased account of the killing, under which the jury could have either found Dan guilty of voluntary manslaughter or could have acquitted him.

Dan went to the stand to make his statement. Before him sat his wife, his twenty-five-year-old son, his sixteen-year-old daughter, and his ten other little boys and girls, including the baby. Near her sat the dead man's widow and their ten children, including the babe in her arms. He began:

"Gentlemen of the jury, I believe that if at the last term of this court, or at any of the terms before that when I was here guarding and tending the juries that were trying other men for their lives, anybody had said that at this term of the court a jury would be trying old Dan Sasser for his life, everybody who knows me would have said, 'That can't be so; for Dan has lived in this county for sixty years and he has never said a hard word against anybody and nobody has ever said a hard word against him.' Gentlemen, you may be sure that if it had not been the case of my life or the other man's life, I would not be here now."

He went on to tell how he and the two other men were coming along the path through the woods, when the man he killed, being drunk and taking offense at some inadvertent word or act of Dan's, started toward him with a knife.

"I began to back away," Dan continued, "begging him to stop, but he kept coming and threatening to kill me. I then took out my pistol, which I carried like the other farmers do when we go off into the woods, and fired a shot into the air, thinking that would make him stop; but instead of stopping he began lunging toward me, with me backing backward as fast as I could. My foot caught against a log across the path and I stumbled. He was right on me. I fired one more shot and it killed him."

He then turned to the widow of the man he had killed. "Gentlemen, see that lady sitting there in black, with the baby in her arms, and the other nine little children around her. That's his widow; those are his little children. She is a good woman, though she is poor. She was my neighbor and she can tell you how often I have pitied her and have helped her. I am not a rich man. I have nothing but my little farm and a few head of livestock, but all she had was a little bit of furniture and a cow. Often the cow has broken into my field and damaged my crops, and though we have the stock law, which requires people to keep their stock confined, in our part of the county, I never impounded her cow or charged her for the damage, but I caught it and carried it back to her free."

The air in the courtroom was getting pretty solemn, but Dan talked on calmly.

"Gentlemen, I say to you and to her, that if it were not to save my own life that I did it, I would never have killed her husband who was more to her than all the cows in the world."

A loud sob escaped the lips of his sixteen-year-old daughter. He looked toward her and said "Hush, honey, don't cry. These men are not going to harm your daddy." And with that, he left the stand, and the case closed.

The jurors were weeping in their box, the judge was wiping tears from his eyes, the solicitor was trying to control himself, both families were crying. Dan alone sat calm, and he sat humbly with his head bowed.

The judge said, "You may address the jury, Mr. Solicitor."

The solicitor faced the jury, then turned to the judge and sobbed, "I cannot do it, Your Honor."

The judge then said to the jury, "Gentlemen, will you write your verdict now or do you prefer to be charged and go to your room?"

One of them said "We will write it here," and the others assented.

Some forty years ago, in the superior court, at Americus in an adjoining circuit, a case was tried which created much interest on account of the unusual character of the defendant's statement to the jury and his fantastic conduct in court. While I was not present at the trial, I have seen a copy of the stenographer's report of it and was given an account of it by Frank A. Hooper, Sr., now a prominent Atlanta lawyer, who prosecuted the case as solicitor-general of the Southwestern Circuit. While the account I shall give may not be letter perfect, it is substantially accurate.

Among those who came to Americus to assist in the building of the Savannah, Americus & Montgomery Railroad was a man named Dewees, who hailed from nowhere specially. He lodged in a boarding house near his work, and, in the course of a few weeks, became very much of a gallant in the circle in which he moved. He was slightly beyond middle-aged, Frenchy in type; and the neighbors were greatly surprised when it was announced one morning that on the evening before he had married the matronly woman, some years his senior, at whose home he boarded. Hardly had a week passed before he was arrested, charged with bigamy—he had another wife in Florida. He had no friends or acquaintances of importance in the community, and he was held in jail for two or three months awaiting trial, which occurred in late summer.

Judge Allen Fort, one of our distinguished jurists, presided at the trial; and, as has been said, Frank Hooper represented the State. A local attorney was appointed to defend him. From Florida came the first wife (though not competent as a witness), her daughter about eighteen or twenty years old, and the minister who had performed the ceremony in Florida. In the court were also the second wife and the local minister who had performed the Georgia ceremony.

The State's proof was formal—a certified copy of the license and return of the marriage in Florida and the testimony of the Florida preacher that he had married the accused to the lady who was present in court; a certified copy of the license and return of the marriage in Georgia and the testimony of the Georgia preacher that he had married the accused to the other lady who was present in court.

Defendant's counsel offered no testimony but announced that the defendant would exercise his right of making a statement to the jury in his own behalf.

Dewees jauntily mounted the witness stand, sat down, and, turning his back to the judge, began addressing the jury:

"Gentlemen, here sits before you a stranger in your midst, just a poor jailbird, without friends or money. Dewees is my name, and if you will look into the book of the peerages of France you will find that some hundred years or more ago one Roseland Dewees, for some reason not necessary to state to you, left his proud ancestral home and his native shores of France, and made his way to the wilderness of the United States, the glorious land of freedom and justice. From that illustrious source, I am descended; poor jailbird that I am. I was born in a Southern city, but early in my life my parents died, and I became a wanderer on the face of the earth."

He paused, carefully took from the breast pocket of his coat the fragments of a long-used silk handkerchief, mopped the perspiration from his brow, took off his coat, hung it on the back of the chair in which he was sitting, and blew a long breath, "Whe-ew!" and nonchalantly remarked, "I believe this is the damndest hottest place I ever saw."

The audience tittered. "Order in Court!" said the Judge. "Continue with your statement, Mr. Dewees, but do not use such language again."

Dewees turned toward the Judge. "Who the Hell is talking to you, you damned old baboon? Keep your mouth shut. I am talking to these gentlemen," and he faced the jury again.

Our judges are very careful not to interrupt the statement of a prisoner to the jury, or to say anything to disparage him in their presence, but this was going too far; and Judge Fort said, "Sir, if you do not show more respect for the Court, I shall have to send you to jail for contempt."

"Send me to jail, will you?" Dewees retorted, "Where do you think I have been spending my time during this beautiful spring and early-summer months? My abode for some time has been that dungeon hole of filth and flies, of smells and mosquitoes, that you call 'jail.' To Hell with you and your jail! I am going to talk to these gentlemen, who have some intelligence," and he continued to the jury:

"Gentlemen, as I was saying when this old stinkpot of a judge interrupted"—The judge started to say something but chose that discretion which is the better part of valor, and let him proceed. Dewees went on.

"I wandered from one state to another, from city to city, and from town to town, until one day down in the beautiful Land of Flowers, which some call Florida, there came before my eyes the most beautiful vision it was ever my opportunity to behold—a sweet, lovely young woman leading by the hand a beautiful golden-haired child, a daughter six or seven years old. No angel in Heaven will ever look fairer to me than she did that day. That lovely creature sits in this very room today and her sweet daughter, now grown up, is at her side." And he pointed to the first wife and her daughter in the audience.

"Time has not dealt kindly with her in the years that have passed since then, but her beautiful eyes and sweet face still fill me with a benediction as I look upon them. I decided to make her my wife, if such a thing were possible. For months I worked harder than I ever worked in my life; for months I reformed myself more than I ever thought I could do; for months I wooed her with every plea and prayer I could make, and finally she consented and we were married."

He paused and pointed to the State's witness, the minister from Florida, and addressed him.

"You pious-faced old hypocrite, with a beard on you like a billy goat, they brought you here to testify to the marriage. You damned old fool, you, do you think I would have denied it? I will have you to know that not only do I admit it, but I boast of it, as the most blessed thing that ever happened in my life."

The preacher arose and said, "Your Honor, I demand protection."

Dewees did not wait for the Judge to act, but waved him down. "Sit down, you dirty bastard! Up to your old tricks, are you?—calling on somebody to protect you, instead of protecting yourself."

He turned to the jury. "I lived with that dear woman whom I was proud to call my wife for more than a year—with her and that lovely child of hers, whose amber curls oft nestled against my cheeks and who called me 'Daddy.' In the aching hours of night, often have I looked back upon that year, and it has seemed too good to be true—that it was just a dream, the sweetest dream I ever dreamt. Then my ancient enemy, the Demon Rum, to whom too often have I been a slave, overpowered me and I fell, became a dog and mistreated her, and she did what any decent woman would have done—she ran me off, and I again became a wanderer on the face of the earth."

He paused, jerked loose his necktie, loosed the top of his shirt, drew several deep breaths, and said in somewhat of an aside, "Why in the Hell do men hold court in such damned hot courthouses?" The Judge sat helpless and restrained himself.

He then resumed: "About three years ago I found employment in one of the cities of this State and was there for about a year. Then one day the postman brought me a letter. The envelope has been lost, but always have I kept the letter and have wept over it time and again. Here it is. I will read it to you.

> " 'Dear Mr. Dewees:
>
> " 'I feel it my duty to tell you that my mother, who was once your wife, passed away a week ago today, and was buried last Sunday in the cemetery near our home. I enclose you a clipping from the local paper giving the account of her death and burial. Yours truly,
>
>   " 'Ruth Hanford.' "

He laid the letter on the stenographer's table, and said, "Why she wrote it, I do not know. You may ask her; there she sits. She certainly will not deny that she wrote it, or that it is in her handwriting." He then produced the clipping and read it. It was an account of the death and burial of Mrs. Roseland Dewees; and it gave every appearance of genuineness. He laid that on the stenographer's table.

"I thought she was dead; I mourned her as dead. I gave up my job and became a wanderer again. Time passed, and early this spring just before the peach trees bloomed I came to your lovely little city here, and got me a job working on the new railroad. I thought I was a widower. I thought that the angel who had been my wife had gone back to Heaven whence she came."

He stopped and began shaking his head, muttering "Hot as hell! Hot as hell! And I've got to tell about that damned nightmare here."

He resumed: "I had to have some place to board, and I got in at the boarding house of that hard-faced old hell-cat over there, and in some moment of forgetfulness or folly I married her, and for that they tell me I am a lawbreaker, and a felon, and that I must pay for my crime by serving as a slave for years in the penitentiary. Gentlemen, I want you to be fair with me and I will be fair with you. When I married her I did not think I was committing any crime, but, if it was a crime, I have already paid for it a higher penalty than the law can possibly impose upon me."

He raised his voice. "I slept a week with that tough, tallow-faced, old hell-cat; and, believe me, that's penalty enough for almost any crime.

"Now, gentlemen, I am just a poor, weak failure in life, here at your mercy, in jail, without money and without friends. I would like to have my freedom again. I have not intentionally broken the law. You are Christian gentlemen, and all that I ask of you is that you observe the Golden Rule, and do unto me as you would have others do unto you. It may seem impossible to you, yet it is possible that some day you may be the victim of misfortune and will stand trial before a jury, charged with a crime you had no intention of committing. So all I ask is that you do for me what you would have others do for you in such a case."

He bowed a low bow, put on his coat, slipped from the stand, and sat again with his counsel.

The jury found him not guilty. When the verdict was published he arose, went down the aisle near where his first wife was seated and called to her, "Come, honey, let's go home again." She came to him. "You come, too, Baby," he called to the daughter, and she came. They started to the door, arm in arm. The sheriff said, "Judge, shall I hold him for contempt?"

"NO! No! No!", the judge quickly replied, "Don't stop him, let him get out of here." But Dewees did stop long enough to make a profound obeisance to the judge and to call to him, "Good bye, Judge, you are a wise old baboon." Then he jauntily waved to the second wife and said, "Good bye, Hellcat." And with that, the three walked out.

Frank Hooper told me that a possible explanation was presented when the jailor told him that the first wife and her daughter came to Americus a few days before the trial and had

had several conferences with Dewees at the jail. The clipping was supposed to have been fabricated in a print-shop near by.

There is still a tradition in southwest Georgia that I used to have an old patched pair of breeches which I wore to the courts to curry favor with the country jurors. I will tell how that tradition began.

Newton, the county seat of Baker County, was and still is a number of miles from any railroad. Court met there on the third week in March and in September. I left home to go to Newton on Sunday afternoon before the third Monday in September, expecting to get home the next night. I noticed that the trousers of the summer suit I was wearing were getting pretty threadbare in the seat, but I hoped that they would hold out till I could make the trip.

When I arrived in Newton I was employed in a land case. Before I had finished that, I was employed in another; and this kept up until Friday afternoon, when the court adjourned. I have never had any other such run of luck. I had been employed in every litigated case tried in the court that week and I had won every case. As to the trousers, the seat on the right side began to ravel out on Monday afternoon. The seat on the left side followed suit on Tuesday. As the days passed, the situation got worse. There was no place to buy clothes in Newton and by Friday my underwear on both sides was fully exposed to view.

Old Bob Barnett, a sort of privileged character, even in court, was foreman of the jury in the last case I tried. I was sitting just in front of the clerk's desk, beneath the judge's stand, when the jury came from their room with Bob in the lead. Instead of heading toward the jury box, he came toward me, trying to hand me the case papers and saying, "Here, take your verdict, and if you don't get out of this county with those raggedy breeches of yours, you will steal every foot of land in it."

Judge Spence, pretending not to hear what he said, waved him to the jury box.

Speaking of Judge Spence, I recall that I came very near getting fined for contempt by him one day, when he was organizing the court at Bainbridge. He was very strict about excusing jurors. He would have the clerk call the list, and if a juror failed to respond he would inquire whether anyone present knew why the juror was absent. Unless someone could give him a satisfactory answer, he sent the sheriff with an attachment for the juror. The name of C. L. Boyett (my old friend Lum Boyett) was called and he failed to respond. "Does anyone here know why Mr. Boyett is absent?" asked the Judge.

I arose and very solemnly said, "Since the last term of this court, Mr. Boyett has gone to a better place above."

"Dead?" the Judge asked, a little shocked.

"No, Your Honor," I answered, "he has moved to Blakely."

The Judge cudgeled his mind for a moment to see whether he should fine me for contempt or laugh at my jesting. He compromised by smiling.

One night while I was attending court at Bainbridge, Governor Bob Taylor, of Tennessee, gave one of his famous humorous lectures there. After we came back from the lecture, several of us who were staying at the same hotel as the Governor did, gathered around him, and he regaled us with a number of good stories which the limitations of mixed company had kept him from telling at the opera house. After an hour or so he said:

"Gentlemen, my present situation reminds me of a fellow who fell from the top of a three-story building. People rushed to him; some fanned him; some poured water on him; all wanted to do something. At last he raised his eyes and said, 'How many stories does a man have to drop in this town before somebody offers him a drink?' "

The hint was promptly taken.

We lawyers sometimes overlook the fact that the opposite party to the case does not take our jury arguments and other professional activities against him as impersonally as we do, especially if the opposite party be an ignorant, uncouth back-woodsman. Soon after my admission to the bar, my father and I represented a woman in an action for divorce and alimony against her husband, who was an ignorant but a fairly well-to-do farmer living in a thinly populated section near the corner where Early, Baker, and Miller counties come together. Some ten or twelve years later this man employed me to obtain for his daughter the setting apart for her support, of a portion of her recently deceased husband's estate. I got for her a rather liberal award, and he was bringing me back to Blakely in his buggy. "You know," he said to me casually, "I thought one time I was going to kill you. It was when you were bearing down so hard on me in that alimony case you had for my wife against me. I would see you riding along through the piney woods by your-self in your buggy, and I decided to take my rifle and hide in a gallberry patch and, when you came by, put a rifle ball through you; and your horse would take you home and nobody would know who did it. But I decided that maybe the reason you bore down on me so hard was because you were on the other side of the case, and that if you were on my side you would bear down just as hard for me. Now you have done so good for my daughter in this case, I am glad I didn't kill you."

Up Against the Mob

IN AN EARLIER CONTEXT, I HAVE STATED THAT LYNCHING FOR criminal assault upon a woman is not a phase of the race question—that a white man is in as much danger of being lynched when such a charge is made against him as a Negro is, and I promised to give instances in corroboration of my assertion.

An instance that comes to me is that of a white man I saw hanging to a telephone or light pole just across from the Brown House and in front of the old railway station at Macon, when I was in school there. It seems that on the night of this lynching he came staggering down Fourth Street, which was a thoroughly reputable street, but he had come from Fifth Street, which was not, when a woman began to scream for help and cry out "rape."

Men quickly gathered, seized the man, who in his drunken condition was not able to make any satisfactory defense against the woman's charges, and without stopping to find out what the woman was or to investigate her charges, swung him up to the most convenient pole with a cross-arm on it. If the mob had ever stopped to investigate, the lynching would not have occurred.

In one of our large towns in southeast Georgia about thirty-five years ago, a reputable man from another town was occupying a room in a hotel with another gentleman, who went to bed early and took the room key with him. When, later in the evening he started to bed, not having a key he first tried to open the door by the knob, rattled it a time or two, and then, being unable to open it that way, began calling out, "Let me in," hoping to awaken his roommate. But he had made a mistake in his room number. He was at the door of a reputable woman, and she screamed. A mob gathered, and, but for the man's calmness and respectable appearance, and the woman's good sense, he would have been lynched.

Another incident will illustrate the temper of a mob when it is aroused. Bainbridge is forty miles southeast from Blakely. It is an old town, as ages of towns go in southwest Georgia. Before the middle of the nineteenth century, it was a town of importance, because it had a railroad, and steamboats plied back and forth between there and the Gulf of Mexico, down the Flint and Apalachicola rivers. By the early part of the twentieth century it had grown to be a small city of four or five thousand people. Sawmilling and tobacco-growing gave it wealth and prosperity. It had cultural opportunities not enjoyed by most of the smaller towns in our part of the State. These facts give added point to the incident I am about to relate, which exhibits one of the problems we people of this section had to deal with— extreme emotionalism where assaults upon women or girls were involved.

The largest and most lucrative portion of my practice was then at Bainbridge. When I arrived there one Monday morning to attend court, I found the people in a state of great excitement. A white man named Sutton, who ran a barroom there, had been put in jail charged with kidnapping and assaulting a flaxen-haired girl, supposed to be a mere child.

On the Thursday night before the court met, the hue and cry had rung out through the streets of the little city that this child had been lost or stolen from its foster parents, who had recently come with the child to Bainbridge from Alabama. Every nook and corner of the city, including the swamps of Flint river, had been searched without avail.

Between midnight and day on Friday morning, Sutton, who had hired a team from the livery stable early in the evening before, returned with the team. He was alone, but hanging on the buggy step was a zephyr wrap, which was identified as belonging to the girl. The sheriff was called; Sutton was seized and locked in the dungeon cell where condemned murderers were kept. He protested his innocence, but he was not allowed to communicate with his wife or to see a lawyer.

Wild rumor spread that a man had been seen throwing a child or the body of a child into a creek some miles away. A mob rapidly formed to storm the jail and lynch Sutton. The sheriff took him to a window of the jail, showed him the mob, and told him that he would be lynched in a few minutes unless he could produce the girl. He then told the sheriff that he had taken her to the home of Mrs. Russell, the widow of a deceased lawyer, who lived in Baker County some twenty miles away and conducted a private school for young ladies. The mob agreed to desist until a deputy sheriff could go to Mrs. Russell's and return. In due time the deputy sheriff came back with the girl, and the mob desisted; but when I arrived there on Monday morning excitement was still running high and the local newspaper was keeping it aflame by the issuance of extras every few hours.

That day Mr. Loftin, a highly respected citizen, one of my father's oldest friends, came to me and said that he wanted to employ me to defend Sutton. It was a very unwelcome offer of employment. In the first place, I was trying to confine myself to a civil practice; and other reasons are obvious. But Mr. Loftin was my father's friend, and I could not deny him lightly, especially when he said that Sutton's wife was his daughter, and told me the facts.

The facts as Mrs. Sutton had told them to her father were as follows: The girl and her foster parents boarded near the Sutton home, and Mrs. Sutton had become much attached to the girl. She told Mrs. Sutton that the people she lived with had not adopted her, that when her mother died they had merely taken her away with them, that they treated her very cruelly and were not educating her at all, and that she was very anxious to study music. She pleaded with Mrs. Sutton to hide her till her foster father, who was a member of a bridge-building gang, moved on to another job, and then to adopt her. The Suttons had no children, and Mrs. Sutton was persuaded into consenting to the girl's plans. She herself had taken music from Mrs. Russell; so she finally induced her husband to take the girl by night to Mrs. Russell's home. It was arranged that he would drive by the boarding house soon after nightfall, that the girl would be waiting and would jump into the buggy as he passed. A little later I talked with Mrs. Sutton, a lovely, kind-hearted woman, just the kind of woman to be taken in by the girl's story; and Mrs. Sutton gave me the same account of the affair.

The sheriff at first would not let me talk with the prisoner, but finally did so upon an order from the judge. Sutton's statement to me jibed with what his wife had told me, but he added that the girl had told him she was no mere child of twelve or thirteen years, as she appeared to be, but nearly eighteen, and her greatest complaint was that the people who had her kept her dressed as a young child and would not let her go with the boys.

Judge Spence, who was presiding in the court, was as fair, fearless, and impartial a judge as I ever knew, but he had little girls of his own; and it was quite difficult for him to maintain a judicial poise. He set the case down for trial on the following Monday morning.

Mob psychology is a curious thing. When it became known that I was to defend Sutton, I too became a pariah in the community. My friends, with a few exceptions, shunned me; my best clients avoided me. Women's clubs sent me requests not to defend "the deep-dyed villain." I tried to talk with one of my clients, a banker, a highly intelligent man, a leading and influential citizen, and to tell him that the man was innocent, and to ask him to suspend judgment until the facts came out. He replied, "If the Angel Gabriel were to appear from the skies with flaming sword and bearing a scroll, sealed with the seal of God Almighty Himself, stating that this man is innocent, I would still believe him guilty."

However, throughout it all, I had one friend. I had once done a favor for an old gentleman at Bainbridge, and he had a son who, whatever his faults, had the virtue of gratitude. He came privately to my room, offered me his help, and gave me the in-

formation, which he had secretly acquired, that when the girl
first got home she had denied that Sutton had treated her with
any impropriety, but when her foster mother insisted that the
physician, who had been sent for, make a physical examination
of her, she said that Sutton had tried to harm her, but that she
had prevented him. However, the physician did examine her,
and, while he found no evidence of any recent assault, he did
find evidence of prior unchastity. The young man who told me
this came to my room every night with additional information.

When the morning of the trial came, a mob gathered omi-
nously in and about the courthouse. Judge Spence offered to call
out the militia to protect the prisoner, but I asked him not to do
so, saying, "I would rather see him lynched in the old-fashioned
way than to see him lynched under form of law." To give
prisoner a speedy trial with the mob standing by and the soldiers
guarding him is usually merely a judicial form of lynching.

I realized the difficulty I was under in the selection of a jury.
The county was a very large one, and I knew but a small fraction
of the jurors likely to be put upon the panels. The method of
selecting a jury in a felony case in Georgia is this: The clerk
calls a panel of forty-eight jurors, who are then called one by
one and put upon what is called the *voir dire*, which consists in
some officer, usually the solicitor general, asking each juror (with
a minor exception in capital felonies) only three questions,
couched in general language: first, as to whether from seeing
the crime committed or from having heard sworn testimony he
has formed an opinion as to the prisoner's guilt; second, whether
he has any bias or prejudice against the accused; and third,
whether his mind is perfectly impartial. If the juror answers
these questions categorically yes or no, the prisoner has no right
to ask any other question unless the judge specially permits it.
The State has ten peremptory challenges and the accused twenty.
Before the trial began, I went to the Judge and asked him to
grant me the special privilege of asking additional questions,
stating the handicap I was under, and he refused it. He called
the case and said, "Are you ready?"

I responded, "Ready on the motion to change the venue."
"I did not know there was such a motion," said the Judge.
"I have just filed it," I replied.

I called my first witness. His name was the first on the panel
of forty-eight the clerk had prepared for the trial. I examined
him fully, asking where he lived, what his occupation was,
whether there had been much discussion of the case in his part
of the county, whether he had read the extras in the newspaper,
whether there was much excitement over the case in his part of
the county, whether there was much prejudice against the accused, and so on. The Judge would not let me interrogate the
juror-witness as to his own feelings or prejudices, but usually, if
you ask a man how the people of his community think or feel,
he will reply in terms of himself.

The Judge saw the clerk issuing batches of subpoenas and
handing them to the sheriff for service. He asked the clerk what
he was doing, and the clerk told him that I had directed him to
issue a subpoena for every man in the jury box. I did not know
who would be put on us after the first panel was exhausted. By
the time I had examined ten or twelve of the jurors as witnesses,
the Judge began to squirm and the mob began to grow restless.
I knew that I was taking desperate chances and told my client
that if I kept up the tactics I had adopted he and I might both be
lynched. He said, "Stand your ground; I will take the risk."

After this had gone on for half a day, the Judge called me
to the bench and asked me privately, "Are you really trying to
change the venue or are you merely trying to find out about the
jurors, and how far do you expect to pursue it?"

I replied, "If you are asking me as counsel for the defendant,
my answer is that I am trying to change the venue and I do not
know any higher evidence on the subject than the testimony of
that class of citizens whose names, by reason of their uprightness
and intelligence, have been put into the jury box, but I am willing
to say to you privately and confidentially, as your friend, Arthur
Powell, that if you had allowed me to question the jurors as they
came to the *voir dire*, I would not have filed the motion."

"You seem to have found a way to accomplish your end, and I see no lawful way of stopping you," he said. "On reflection, I think I should have granted your request to question the jurors. Withdraw your motion and you may question them."

I withdrew the motion. Under my questioning many jurors disqualified themselves who probably would never have done so under the three statutory questions. I was able to use my twenty peremptory challenges intelligently, and in the end got a pretty fair jury, better than I had hoped for in the circumstances.

As the jury was being selected my only friend, the grateful son of the father I had once helped, sat across the room from me and communicated with me by a prearranged code. If he put his hand on his right knee, it meant, "Get rid of him." If he put his hand on his left knee, it meant, "I do not know." If he put his hat in his lap, it meant, "Take him."

When the girl came to the witness stand, the mob moved restlessly. She was a petite little thing of the French type, with long curls such as Shirley Temple used to wear, and with a short dress on. Looking closer, one could see evidences of greater maturity than she professed. She was a born actress and was frankly pleased at being the star performer to such a large audience.

Under the questioning of the solicitor general she recited a vivid description of her being kidnapped. She said that at 6:14 o'clock on the evening in question she had gone into the yard at the house where she was boarding, when suddenly a man whom she identified as the defendant on trial, opened the gate, seized her, threw her into his buggy, and drove rapidly with her through the streets of Bainbridge, across the river bridge and on to Mrs. Russell's in Baker County, where he left her; that on the way he had attempted to take certain gross liberties with her, but had desisted when she repelled him. My recollection is that she gave her age as "about twelve."

When it came my time to cross-examine, I realized that I was confronted with a very delicate situation. The girl had manifestly concocted a cock-and-bull story which I could break down by a vigorous cross-examination. If I did so, she would likely break into tears or go into hysterics. If that occurred, there sat the mob ready to seize my client and probably me also.

I led her along very gently. She knew it was 6:14 o'clock when she went into the yard because the city turned on the electric lights that day at 6:13 and the lights had been on just one minute when she went into the yard. Yes, she gave a little scream when the man grabbed her, but maybe they did not hear her in the house. Yes, they came down the main residential street of the city, through the business section, along one side of the public square, by the courthouse and the jail, and on across the river bridge. Yes, she sat on the seat with him but it was entirely against her will that he was carrying her away.

I risked the question, "Why did you not scream as you passed through the business section, with people on the streets?"

She had not thought of that. I was afraid that I had asked the wrong question, when she hesitated and seemed about to cry, so I came to her aid by suggesting, "Perhaps you did call to them, but nobody would pay any attention to you."

She grabbed at the suggestion: "Yes I did keep hollering, but nobody paid any attention to me."

She set the time she passed the railway station at the exact time the evening train arrived there and people were getting off and on the train. She said she screamed to them, but none of them paid any attention to her screaming.

I then asked her about the occurrence which she said had taken place on the road between there and Mrs. Russell's. She recited it off in the same words she had given the solicitor general in reply to his question.

"When you felt him put his hand on your person, what did you do?" I asked.

"I slapped him," she replied with a giggle.

The effect of that giggle upon the spectators in the courtroom was like pouring a dash of cold water into a boiling pot. They began to look askance at one another. The pressure of the mob began to relax.

When the physician who had made the physical examination of her was on the stand, I began to ask him about the other things my friend told me he had found. He refused to reply to my questions till the Judge threatened to send him to jail for contempt of court. I finally corkscrewed it out of him; and he added that these things did not necessarily mean anything wrong to him. But to the practical men of the world on the jury and in the audience, they did mean something; they corroborated that giggle.

Mrs. Sutton, being the wife of the accused, was not permitted to testify. Sutton himself was allowed to make only an unsworn statement. Mrs. Russell, however, was able to supply partly what Mrs. Sutton would have testified, for she testified to what the girl told her while she was at her home.

The jury was out for about twenty-four hours. They finally came in with this remarkable verdict: "We the jury find the defendant guilty, but recommend that he be punished by the lowest punishment known to the law." Manifestly the jury was afraid that there would be a lynching if they found him not guilty.

When the verdict was published and filed, Judge Spence turned to the jury and said, "Gentlemen, if you do not believe the defendant is guilty, you should have acquitted him by your verdict. If he is guilty he deserves the highest, not the lowest punishment known to the law. I shall have to accept your verdict, but I cannot adopt your recommendation." He sentenced the prisoner to fourteen years in the penitentiary. (For sake of brevity, I have told you of this trial as if only one indictment were involved. In fact, there were two: one for abduction and one for felonious assault.)

Having told as much as this, I think I should complete the story.

I appealed to the Supreme Court. Before the case was reached there, a "jail break" occurred at Bainbridge and Sutton was among those who escaped. A few days later I received a letter from him saying that he was safely hidden out, but had been told that if he were not in jail at the time the case was reached in the Supreme Court, his appeal would be dismissed. (His information was correct as to that.) He added that if I were confident of a reversal he wished to surrender himself to the sheriff; but, if I thought otherwise, he wanted to flee the county, and he asked me to advise him.

I wrote him that while no lawyer could safely predict the outcome of any case, I thought the chances of a reversal were favorable, and that if I were he I would surrender myself; that I could not see much choice between serving fourteen years in the penitentiary and being a fugitive from justice for the rest of my life.

On the morning for the argument in the Supreme Court I received a telegram from my client: "I am sitting on the jail steps, and the sheriff will not let me in. Advise me."

I telegraphed him back: "Sit there till the sheriff does let you in."

When the case was called, the solicitor general presented an affidavit from the sheriff that Sutton had escaped and moved a dismissal. In reply I read Sutton's telegram and my answer.

Chief Justice Simmons, who was presiding, asked the solicitor, "What do you know about that?"

The solicitor admitted that he had had a telephone message from the sheriff to that effect.

Judge Simmons's face showed disgust and anger. "I am shocked and surprised that such a thing should happen in this State. Here is a man trying to put himself into custody in order that this Court may determine the legality of his conviction. Here is a sworn officer of the law violating his duty in an attempt to deprive him of his right of appeal. Mr. Solicitor, you telegraph that sheriff that, if he does not let this man into jail immediately, the sheriff of this Court will arrest him and jail him for contempt of this Court. The appeal will not be dismissed."

We won in the Supreme Court. Before another trial could take place, we had opportunity to look up the girl's record in Alabama, where she came from. She was born of low parentage.

I do not care to tell here what her mother was. She was eighteen years old. However, the thing that brought the immediate collapse of the prosecution was that the girl and her foster father were found in a compromising position one evening and fled from the State overnight.

Then came another peculiar phase of mob psychology. Sutton, who before his arrest had been only a small man in the community, immediately became a hero.

The Frank case, which occurred in Atlanta about thirty years ago, bears out my statement as to the white man's danger of being lynched when the accusation against him involves an assault on a female.

A young girl named Mary Phagan, who lived in Marietta and worked in a pencil factory in Atlanta, was brutally murdered. A young Jew named Leo Frank, who was manager of the factory, was charged with the crime. While the official charge was murder, the public believed that the girl was killed in defending her virtue. I need not deal with the general details of the trial, as they are matters of fairly recent history.

Public sentiment against the accused ran high. Judge Leonard S. Roan, who was as fearless a judge as ever lived and who was to try the case, postponed it, from time to time, in the hope that the excitement would abate. It did so far quiet down that he set the case for trial.

At the time of the murder there was little or no prejudice against the Jews in Atlanta, and the aroused feeling against Frank was not originally because of his race, but because he was an employer and the murdered girl was an employee. No girl ever leaves home to go to work in a factory but that her parents feel an inward fear that one of her bosses will take advantage of his position to mistreat her, especially if she repels his advances. This fear is readily converted into passion when a factory manager is accused of having killed a factory girl. The thing that did arouse a most phenomenal racial prejudice against not only Frank but all Jews was that just about the time the trial was to occur, various writers, speakers, civil rights societies, and Jewish organizations began to protest that Frank was being persecuted because he was a Jew. This whipped into flames the passion and prejudice which had been dying down and converted them from a mere feeling of resentment against a factory boss into a spreading racial and religious hatred.

I saw it spread from the Jews to the Roman Catholics, from Atlanta to all Georgia, from Georgia to surrounding States. I saw previously popular and efficient public officers swept from their popularity and their offices by this flood, because of their religious faiths. How far it would have spread it is impossible to say, if it had not been for the vigorous efforts of saner heads to check it and destroy it.

Certain politicians capitalized upon it. Good men and true went down into defeat because they fought back against it. The Ku Klux Klan was organized, and extended the prejudice to the Negroes. Racial and religious prejudices became the guiding force of the times. The solidarity of the Democratic party in the Southern States was split asunder by it. Al Smith almost lost Georgia and did lose Florida by reason of it.

But for the outside interference of the kind of which I have spoken, Frank would probably have been acquitted. As it was, he was convicted, with the mob in the streets around the courthouse grumbling for vengeance and howling for his blood. When the verdict was received the prisoner was not in the court. The judge and his counsel were afraid to have him there lest he be lynched.

A sad feature of the case was Judge Roan himself. I knew him intimately—knew how fair and fearless he was. During the trial, I kept myself away from the courthouse as much as I reasonably could; the spectacle there was utterly disgusting to me. But now and then during the trial, Judge Roan would send for me to get me to look up for him some point of law which had been raised. When he was preparing his charge to the jury, I sat on the bench at his side and he said to me, "This man's innocence is proved to mathematical certainty." The morning he was to pass on the motion for a new trial, I rode into the city on the same streetcar with him. He spoke of the attack made as to the competency of one of the jurors and said, "I shall have to grant the motion, on this, if on no other ground."

As he was about to announce his judgment on the motion, he said the thing that no judge ordinarily would say who was about to refuse a new trial, namely, that despite the verdict he was not convinced of the defendant's guilt, but, he added, "I overrule the motion for a new trial." Not long afterwards he was taken to a sanitarium in another State, where he died. His noble brain had snapped under the strain of the trial.

By a divided bench, the Supreme Court affirmed the conviction, and a petition for executive clemency was filed with Governor John M. Slaton. He was just finishing his second term as governor. Many who did not know him, as some of us knew him and still know him, supposed that he would dodge the issue by granting a reprieve and throwing the matter into the lap of the incoming governor. Those of us who really knew Jack Slaton knew that he would never shirk an unpleasant task that was his.

Jack Slaton is and always has been a man of unflinching physical and moral courage. In this matter he was put to the test. No man in the State had greater personal and political popularity than he had. Any gift in the power of the people was his for the asking. He was ambitious. He had the wealth to gratify his ambitions without suffering financial embarrassments. He knew that unless he let Frank be hanged he would forfeit all his political popularity and ambitions. He commuted the sentence to life imprisonment and told friends privately that he would have granted a full pardon, if he had not believed that in a very short while the truth would come out and the very men who were clamoring for Frank's life would be demanding a pardon for him.

The executive mansion was then in need of repairs, and Governor Slaton and his wife were living in their beautiful country home near Buckhead, some six miles north of Atlanta. The house sits in the middle of a large wooded estate, extending from Peachtree Road on the east to West Andrews Drive on the west. During the evening of the day on which Frank's commutation was announced, a mob of about three thousand was formed, and some went in cars and some on foot and thronged Peachtree Road in front of Governor Slaton's home, but did not enter the grounds because a company of the National Guard had been called out to prevent it. This was a headless, unorganized mob, and the military forces had no great difficulty in turning it back.

The next day the rumor spread that a well-organized and well-armed mob was getting together to lynch the Governor and burn his home. There was fear that the military guardsmen, young and inexperienced as many of them were, would not be able to cope with the situation. Early that evening Logan Bleckley came for me. He had in his car an army rifle and a repeating shotgun, loaded with buckshot shells. He offered me my choice, and I took the shotgun—there is nothing like a shotgun loaded with buckshot to repel a mob. At the gate to the Governor's grounds we identified ourselves and were admitted. When we got inside the house we found a dozen or so of the city's best and most prominent citizens there similarly armed. Jack Slaton and his wife were the calmest of all the party. Colonel Grice and a troop of cavalry scouted the nearby highways; and that night the mob kept away.

The next night, another armed party of the Governor's friends stood guard inside the house, the company of infantry was bivouacked on the grounds with outposts of sentries, and the cavalry kept up its scouting. Just before day the next morning a sentry stationed near the edge of the woods heard a hen fly off a near-by log and give a squawk of alarm. He also saw a man's hand appear momentarily above the log. He fired his rifle. Instantly the guardsmen were on the alert. The company deployed into a swift encircling movement and entrapped some seventy-five men, some armed with firearms, some with blackjacks, some with dynamite. The mob surrendered, and were disarmed and herded by the soldiers into an old carriage house in the rear of the premises.

When the officers came to Governor Slaton and asked him to swear out the warrants for the commitment of the men to prison, he refused to do so. He said, "Let these deluded men, who thought that they were acting in a good cause, go home to their families who need them. Tell them that I did what I knew was right, and I forgive them for any wrong they intended against me."

Jack Slaton is not only a fearless man; he is a Christian gentleman.

Frank was taken to the penitentiary at Milledgeville. A few nights later a mob broke into the penitentiary, overpowered the guards, seized Frank, took him to a point near Marietta, where Mary Phagan had lived, and lynched him.

I am one of the few people who know that Leo Frank was innocent of the crime for which he was convicted and lynched. Subsequent to the trial, and after his conviction had been affirmed by the Supreme Court, I learned who killed Mary Phagan, but the information came to me in such a way that, though I wish I could do so, I can never reveal it so long as certain persons are alive. We lawyers, when we are admitted to the bar, take an oath never to reveal the communications made to us by our clients; and this includes facts revealed in an attempt to employ the lawyer, though he refuses the employment. If the lawyer were to be so forgetful of his oath as to attempt to tell it in court, the judge would be compelled under the law not to receive the evidence. The law on this subject may or may not be a wise law—there are some who think that it is not—but naturally since it is the law, we lawyers and the judges cannot honorably disobey it. Without ever having discussed with Governor Slaton the facts which were revealed to me, I have reason to believe, from a thing contained in the statement he made in connection with the grant of the commutation, that, in some way, these facts came to him and influenced his action. I expect to write out what I know and seal it up; for the day may yet come, after certain deaths occur, when more can be told than I can honorably tell now.

Mrs. Slaton is a queen, if there ever was one. Recently she and Jack and Annie and I were sitting together at the Pancoast Hotel in Miami Beach. She made some request of him and he put his hand over hers and said to Annie and me, "I cannot refuse any request she makes of me. When I had the commutation of Frank's sentence under consideration, I received a thousand, and she no less than a hundred letters, saying that one or both of us would be killed and our home destroyed if I commuted the sentence. I worked downstairs in my library till two o'clock in the morning, preparing a statement and drawing the order. When I went upstairs, Sallie was waiting for me. She asked me, 'Have you reached a decision?' 'Yes,' I said. 'It may mean my death or worse, but I have ordered the sentence commuted.' She kissed me and said, 'I would rather be the widow of a brave and honorable man than the wife of a coward.' "

We Go To Atlanta

ABOUT THE BEGINNING OF THE TWENTIETH CENTURY, THE
Justices of the Supreme Court began to complain seriously
that more cases were coming to the Court than they could possibly handle. The Georgia Bar Association appointed a special
"Committee on the Relief of the Supreme Court," with a member of the committee from each congressional district. I represented the second district. For several years we discussed plan
after plan, each of which was in turn discarded for some practical
reason. Finally, in the spring of 1906, at a meeting of the Committee, with members of the Supreme Court present, we agreed
to ask the General Assembly to create a Court of Appeals, which
would have the same jurisdiction as the Supreme Court and
would take over a part of the docket.

The resolution proposing the necessary constitutional amendment passed the Senate and seemed likely to pass the House. It
contained a provision that the Governor should appoint the
judges. Anticipating the passage and adoption of the amendment, Governor Terrell had consulted the members of the Supreme Court and had agreed with them on H. H. Perry, of
Gainesville, Henry C. Peeples of Atlanta, and me, as the first
three Judges. When the proposal came on for adoption in the
House, Joe Hill Hall, of Macon, one of the most influential
members of that body, offered an amendment requiring that
the Judges be elected by the people. It was adopted; and the
bill passed in that form.

Of course, the agreement between the Governor and the
Justices as to the personnel of the new court had been kept

confidential, but not so secret that I did not catch word of it. I resigned from the committee as soon as I heard that my name had been mentioned.

After the amendment had been proposed by the General Assembly, and before it was submitted to the people for ratification, the bar association committee met and adopted a resolution asking the three of us whom the Governor had agreed to appoint to allow our names to be used in the election and promising their support. Mr. Perry and Mr. Peeples declined, but I asked time to consider the matter. I talked it over with Annie. I had made and collected over ten thousand dollars the year before. I had in process of erection, and so far completed that it was already being occupied in part, a three-story building fronting on the courthouse square which I had rented for enough to retire the mortgage I had put on it and to give me some income besides. I could afford to stay on the bench for a while at least. One consideration that strongly appealed to me was the education in the law I would get from service on the bench. There would be a financial sacrifice involved, as the salary was only four thousand dollars a year, but I could quickly recoup any loss I should incur in that respect, if I resigned after, say, five years, and came back to the practice with the prestige the service on the bench would give. Beyond this, I was not yet thirty-three years old, and the very hope of attaining such an honor at such an age flattered me.

My friends in south Georgia, practically every member of the bar of the Albany and Pataula circuits and many others from near-by circuits, were urging me to run, and promising to give me a clear field in so far as south Georgia was concerned, by keeping all other lawyers from that section out of the race. Annie was willing, and I consented to make the campaign.

Judge John S. Candler had recently retired from the Supreme bench and had organized a large law firm in Atlanta, with offices in the newly opened Candler Building. He was an astute and successful politician of the better sort, and he volunteered to supervise my campaign. He arranged a suite of offices for me next to his own, which was an ideal arrangement for me, since I had decided on a "mail-order" campaign. I knew how I looked; and, while I had had no political experience beyond the limits of Early County, I knew enough to know that it would not do for me to let strangers see me if I expected them to vote for me.

Logan Bleckley would always deny it if anyone charged him with being a politician, and yet in certain types of politics he was the greatest expert I ever knew. He had a genius for organization. He knew men of prominence all over the State, and he was widely beloved and, therefore, widely influential. He was really the power behind the throne in my campaign.

From north and middle Georgia there were twenty-five positively announced or seriously-considering-it candidates. I was the only one from south Georgia.

In the midst of the campaign, Kil, who was then on the faculty at Teachers College in New York, came by my headquarters and volunteered to send out a letter in my behalf to his special friends in Georgia, principally the boys who had been under him when he taught at Mercer. He dictated the form letter to one of the stenographers and gave us the list of names and addresses. We prepared the letters and sent them to New York for signing and mailing.

We caught a stenographic faux pas before much harm was done. Kil had said, "He was my bed fellow in college." The young lady transcribed it, "He was a bad fellow in college."

About two hundred of Kil's letters went out into various parts of the State. His influence over his former pupils was tremendous. No sooner had his letters gone out than I had about two hundred influential young men actively at work for me.

At the October election the amendment was ratified by the people. When the entries for the November election closed, there were sixteen left in the race; but I was still the only one from south Georgia.

I was in my Atlanta headquarters late one afternoon when Gordon Kiser called me and asked me if I knew whose building it was that burned at Blakely the night before. I replied that I knew nothing of the fire. He read me a news item in the afternoon paper. It was my new three-story building that had burned. I went to my hotel, and there were the telegrams telling me of its total destruction.

There was another telegram from Annie telling me she was all right. This was welcome news, because of her condition. It was a few days later that Grace was born.

Also in my box at the hotel was a letter in a long envelope. Any depression caused by the news of the fire was offset by my elation at reading this letter. It was signed "Logan E. Bleckley." It was from the old Chief Justice, whom all Georgia regarded as the greatest jurist of all times and whom the people of north Georgia idolized.

I hesitate to quote this letter because of the apparent immodesty of my doing so; but it was written for publication and was published widely at the time. I use it here not for what it says of me but because it is so characteristic of Judge Bleckley's style that I feel constrained to do so:

"Dear Sir:

"During my service of about twelve years on the bench of the Supreme Court, I studied the minds of lawyers, as well as the cases they argued before me. This experience assured me that, as musicians widely differ in musical touch, so lawyers differ in legal aptitude, or what may be called their legal touch; many of them being moderately gifted, some highly gifted, and a few very highly gifted. The three grades or orders are analogous to the grammatical degrees of positive, comparative and superlative—'good, better, best.'

"The best legal minds are readily distinguished and easily recognized as soon as, with tongue or pen, they touch upon any complex or difficult topic of law, whether in legal argument, their professional documents and writings, or merely in conversation. Whenever the superlative lawyer expresses himself his light is set upon a candlestick; it is hidden under a bushel only when he is silent.

"In view of your candidacy for a seat on the bench of the proposed Court of Appeals, allow me to say that I have seen your light shine with resplendent brightness. I can bear testimony to your being one of the elect few among the members of our profession. You are a genuine lawyer, with a true insight into the nature of law and of its real import, both in letter and spirit. With ample opportunity for judicial service, I am sure you will not fail to prove yourself a great judge.

"Though my letter is addressed to you, it is really intended for other readers, and I request you to publish it.

"My works shall correspond with my faith. In the coming primary I am confidently and cordially for you."

Judge Bleckley need not have signed it, for all readers of the letter who knew him would know that he wrote it.

I wondered what had prompted Judge Bleckley to write the letter. Logan and I had thought of asking him for a simple endorsement of me; but he was usually so chary of endorsing any one that we had thought it best not to ask him. I learned later that Charlie Bass, a young friend of Sam Bennet's and mine, who had first started out to be a lawyer and had changed to the ministry, and who then held a pastorate at Clarkesville, where Judge Bleckley resided, happened to be talking with the Judge about the new court, and my name was mentioned. Charlie expressed the hope that I would be elected. The Judge said he intended to vote for me and added, "If I thought it would do any good, I would write him an endorsement."

Charlie almost shouted, "Do him any good! Why, Judge, if you would let him print an endorsement from you, it would do him good all over Georgia, especially in this section here where everyone knows you and but few know him." The Judge sat down and immediately wrote and mailed the letter; and, of course, I gave it wide circulation.

I think that Annie is indirectly responsible for his willingness to write it. A few years previously the Georgia Bar Association had met at Tallulah Falls, near Judge Bleckley's home. Annie, who was there with me, saw sitting on the rostrum a tall, gaunt, old man, with his locks to his shoulders, and his long white beard streaked with tobacco juice; but his eyes and brow spoke of genius, and he looked like one of the prophets of old. Annie asked me, "Who is that old codger sitting on the rostrum?"

"That," I answered, "is Chief Justice Bleckley."

"*The* Judge Bleckley?" she whispered.

"Yes, *the* Judge Bleckley," I replied, "and the handsome middle-aged woman sitting there near him is his second wife, whom he married a few years ago."

I was on the program that morning with a paper on the taxation of franchises, a subject in which the bar of the State was interested because of the recent passage of a tax act which included franchises for the first time. At the end of the session, Annie and I happened to come to the doorway just as Judge and Mrs. Bleckley did. I spoke to them and introduced Annie. Teasingly, the Judge said to her, "How in the world did a little country girl like you ever catch Arthur Powell, who has just made such a learned talk on a puzzling legal problem?"

I could see Annie's Miller County dander rising, but she managed a smile, as she said, "Well, Judge, I've just been wondering why your wife married you."

"Good! Good!" he exclaimed, and laughed heartily. Her display of spunk had pleased him.

In due time Grace was born. It will be difficult for those who have known her as the handsome girl she became or as the handsome young mother she now is, to imagine what a scrawny, wizen-faced baby she really was. We called her "Tiddledy-winks" and contracted that into "Tildy," but both nicknames she soon outgrew.

The papers first announced the election of Judge Richard B. Russell (who had just run a brilliant, though unsuccessful race for the governorship), Henry Peeples, and me. However, when the final returns came in, it appeared that Benjamin H. Hill, the son of that great statesman, Senator Benjamin Harvey Hill, had nosed Henry Peeples out by a few votes.

My first reaction to my election was a feeling which bore down heavily upon me—that I was tremendously overdrawn at the bank of love and affection; that I owed such an overwhelming debt of gratitude that I could never repay it; that I was bankrupt, but could not take bankruptcy.

In Miller County, Annie's home, only 375 votes were polled. I got 375 votes there.

In my own home county, I lost four votes, three of them being the votes of men who struck my name because, they said, I had once stricken them off a jury.

My card-index at headquarters had indicated that I had no strength in Chattooga County in extreme north Georgia. When the returns came in, I had led the ticket there by about fifteen hundred votes. It was some time later that I learned why.

Just before Christmas of the previous year, I was in the First National Bank at Blakely when a young man came in and presented a check issued by Major Jones, the county school commissioner. I heard the teller say to him, "Mr. Jolly, have you anyone here who can identify you?"

He explained that he knew no one in Blakely except Major Jones, that he had been teaching in one of the county schools, that if he went to get Major Jones to identify him he would miss the train which was due to arrive in a few minutes. I was looking him over. He had a straight-forward, honest appearance, and his explanation seemed reasonable. I stepped forward, introduced myself, and said to the teller, "I will identify Mr. Jolly by endorsing the check."

It turned out that Jesse Jolly was the son of the sheriff of Chattooga County. When he saw from the papers that I was in the race for the judgeship, he had his father send a deputy to every polling place in the county to ask the voters to vote for me. He had made my campaign his campaign.

Various are the reasons that influence men to vote one way or another. I have seen men vote for Judge Fish for the chief-justice-ship because they liked to go fishing. Judge Hill used to say laughingly that the people elected his father, who had been dead several years, instead of him, to the bench. I was once spending the summer in the mountains of north Georgia when the State primary election occurred. My old friend, Luther Brittain, now president of Georgia Tech, was a candidate for the office of State Superintendent of Education, and was opposed by a man named Zettler. I saw one of the voters strike Zettler's name from his ballot. Out of curiosity, I asked him if he knew either of the candidates, and he said that he did not.

"How did you decide to vote for Brittain instead of Zettler?" I asked.

"I would not vote for any damned man whose name begins with a 'Z'," he replied.

The Court of Appeals was to be organized on January 1, 1907. The time intervening between my election and that date, I spent in winding up my affairs and in getting ready to move to Atlanta. My citizenship would remain in Blakely, but the work of the court would keep me in Atlanta the year round, with only an occasional short vacation. Even to this day, when I speak of "going down home," I mean going to Blakely, but I have actually lived in Atlanta ever since the day I moved there.

I arranged for Bob Pottle to take over my law office and to live in my home. I resigned from the vice-presidency of the First National Bank and similar connections. I sold my spirited mare, Ladybuck, and the rubber-tired buggy I had given Annie. Tie after tie was severed. I did not know that I was really giving up an old life and entering upon a new one; but I was.

The bar at Bainbridge gave me a banquet with real champagne and toasts. The felicitations were many. In my heart there was gladness—and sadness.

I made a few trips to Atlanta. With the help of Logan Bleckley, I rented a home on Gordon Street, in West End, a few doors below the Wren's Nest, the home of "Uncle Remus" (Joel Chandler Harris), just a few doors from the home of

Luther Rosser, in the same block with Hugh Culbertson, Judge Bleckley's son-in-law.

Our household goods and personal effects were loaded into a boxcar, and on the morning of December 30, 1906, just seven years from the day my father died, Annie and I, Billy and Frances, and our poor, puny little baby, Grace, who Annie and I both inwardly feared would soon return to sleep with Little Albert, boarded the train for Atlanta. With us came faithful Allen and his newest wife, Jennie (not his first wife, Jennie Bell), and her baby boy, Buster.

Next morning we found that the car with our effects had arrived. The moving vans soon had them in our new home, and we slept there that night.

We were sleeping soundly when we heard a tremendous blast of whistles. In Blakely, that was the fire-alarm—the blowing of the whistles at the waterworks and the light plant. From the way the whistles were shrieking everywhere I thought that all Atlanta must be on fire. I rushed from one window to another, but could see no sign of the conflagration. I turned on the light and looked at the clock. It was midnight, and it dawned on me that Atlanta was saluting the New Year.

* * *

Here ends the story I started out to write—the story of old Blakely and its environs during the thirty-odd years I lived there. Since then I have met many interesting persons and have had many interesting experiences; some day, if time and strength permit, I may write of them. But southwest Georgia and its people will always be my first and greatest love.

I can go home again.